"I met Claude and his family when they moved to here a few years ago. When Claude guest preached, I told my husband I thought we'd just heard the next Tim Keller. Claude is a gifted communicator with a particular flair for speaking to people of different backgrounds and educational levels and carrying a broad audience with him. I'm thrilled that he has applied his skill to this fascinating and timely project. This is his first book, but I'm confident it will not be his last. I see Claude as a rising star, and I look forward to watching God use him in the coming years, both in print and in the pulpit."

—**Rebecca McLaughlin**, author of *Confronting Christianity: 12 Hard Questions for the World's Largest Religion*

"Claude Atcho has artfully crafted a masterpiece of literary and theological reflections. *Reading Black Books* dares us to better see and understand the Black experience and, in doing so, to better see and understand ourselves. Claude is our guide to embracing and embodying a more whole and just faith through the study of Black books."

—**Michelle Ami Reyes**, vice president, Asian American Christian Collaborative; author of *Becoming All Things: How Small Changes Lead to Lasting Connections across Cultures*

"No one knows better or shows better than Atcho how twentieth-century African American literature is equipment for a better, truer orthodoxy. *Reading Black Books* offers brilliant and accessible theological readings of this literature that function—and feel—like the pastoral care we desperately need. Faithful to the works on their own terms, Atcho recognizes both the unflinchingly critical theological challenges and unfailingly constructive theological contributions of these matchless, essential works. His readings bear life-giving theological fruit that nourishes readers toward life together, daring to do so because the literature dares and the gospel declares! For generations, these books have been bread in the wilderness, a table prepared in the presence of enemies. Atcho's work helps readers in these desolate, polarized days to find anew in African American literature the welcome table. This is the book—and its hope *the* hope in Christ—that I have been hungry for as a reader and as a teacher."

—**Tiffany Eberle Kriner**, Wheaton College

"Atcho opens his book with the acknowledgment, 'Right now, Black voices are in.' Thank God for that! But his claim also implies the embarrassing history where Black voices were silenced. For the God who created all people, what a sorrow that churches have been divided and some voices amplified over others. Atcho's book participates in redemption by handing the mic to Ellison, Wright, Hurston, Morrison, and others. Even more than extracting truth from their work or increasing our empathy with their characters, Atcho highlights how this literature discloses eternal verities. We dig into Countee Cullen's portrayal of Christ, Wright's depictions of sin and justice. By attending to Black books, we renew our faith in the God who did not leave us to carve our own path but who revealed himself through his creatures and the stories they tell as they reach for him."

—Jessica Hooten Wilson, author of *The Scandal of Holiness*

"This book is a superb achievement that combines keen theological insight and in-depth literary analysis in a highly accessible format. Under Atcho's masterful guidance, classic works of African American literature become an invitation to Black experience and, thereby, to a deepened Christian imagination. With its focus on the beauty of great stories, *Reading Black Books* has the potential to transcend ideological barriers and to open up new paths of discipleship for all Christians at this cultural moment."

—Rev. Matthew Wilcoxen, rector, St. John's Anglican Church, Sydney, Australia; author of *Divine Humility: God's Morally Perfect Being*

"With literary nuance and careful theological reflection, Claude takes the reader on a potentially transformative journey. The world needs more theologically reflective books on substantive literature, like this one. It deserves wide reading."

—Jonathan Dodson, pastor, City Life Church; author of *Gospel-Centered Discipleship* and *Our Good Crisis*

"This book breathes the Black experience with overtones of strength and hope and Jesus. *Reading Black Books* pays homage to brilliant Black scholarship while demanding we pay attention to the Christ it points to. Well-written and unique."

—Jason Cook, senior pastor, Fellowship Bible Church–Roswell

READING BLACK BOOKS

READING BLACK BOOKS

How African American Literature Can
Make Our Faith More Whole and Just

CLAUDE ATCHO

BrazosPress
a division of Baker Publishing Group
www.BrazosPress.com

Published by Brazos Press
a division of Baker Publishing Group
PO Box 6287, Grand Rapids, MI 49516-6287
www.brazospress.com

Printed in the United States of America

Library of Congress Cataloging-in-Publication Data
Names: Atcho, Claude, 1986– author.
Title: Reading black books : how African American literature can make our faith more whole and just / Claude Atcho.
Description: Grand Rapids, Michigan : Brazos Press, a division of Baker Publishing Group, [2022] | Includes bibliographical references and index.
Identifiers: LCCN 2021050155 | ISBN 9781587435294 (paperback) | ISBN 9781587435645 (casebound) | ISBN 9781493437009 (ebook) | ISBN 9781493437016 (pdf)
Subjects: LCSH: American literature—African American authors—History and criticism. | American literature—20th century—History and criticism. | Christianity in literature. | LCGFT: Literary criticism.
Classification: LCC PS153.B53 A83 2022 | DDC 810.9/896073—dc23/eng/20211208
LC record available at https://lccn.loc.gov/2021050155

Baker Publishing Group publications use paper produced from sustainable forestry practices and post-consumer waste whenever possible.

22   23   24   25   26   27   28   7   6   5   4   3   2   1

For Mom
Thank you for always praying for me.

Contents

Introduction   1

1. Image of God: Ralph Ellison's *Invisible Man*   9
2. Sin: Richard Wright's *Native Son*   27
3. God: James Baldwin's *Go Tell It on the Mountain*   39
4. Jesus: Countee Cullen's "Christ Recrucified" and "The Black Christ"   57
5. Salvation: Zora Neale Hurston's *Moses, Man of the Mountain*   75
6. Racism: Nella Larsen's *Passing*   91
7. Healing and Memory: Toni Morrison's *Beloved*   109
8. Lament: W. E. B. Du Bois's "The Litany of Atlanta"   127
9. Justice: Richard Wright's *The Man Who Lived Underground*   143
10. Hope: Margaret Walker's "For My People"   159

Acknowledgments   173
Discussion Questions   175
Notes   181

Introduction

Right now, Black voices are in. That's why on a recent Target run, as I maneuvered past the grocery section and the LEGO aisles, I was only partly surprised to find myself standing face-to-face with a display of James Baldwin books. In this unique cultural moment where people and corporations are ostensibly committed to listening to Black voices, I want to present this humble offering: one of the best ways to listen to Black voices is to attend to Black stories, specifically the enduring ones captured in classic African American literature.

This book suggests—and performs—listening to Black stories through a particular mode of reading. This way of reading joins the literary and the theological in a dynamic interplay for the spiritual and intellectual enrichment of Christian and spiritually curious readers from all walks of life. In other words, when we read Black literature's twentieth-century classics through a dual lens—the literary *and* the theological—we unearth the ways in which God's truth addresses Black experience and how Black experience, as shown in the literature of our great writers, can prod readers from all backgrounds toward sharper theological thinking and more faithful living. There is a way to read even brutal works like *Native Son* that respects the text and enriches our faith.

The book you are holding in your hands is light on theory and heavy on practice. Each chapter is my reading of a text through this dual lens in reflection on a key Christian truth or reality, like God, hope, and sin. The reading performed in each chapter does not displace a literary reading but stands upon it like on a ladder, elevating our textual engagement from one plane to another, to challenge us and help us gain a more expansive view. To mix analogies, the literary reading—attending to the form, content, themes, and devices of a text—becomes a bridge to theological musings: How does the text in its shape and substance raise important questions or prompt crucial lessons about ourselves, God, and the world as we know it? The answers to these questions, found through these texts being read in this manner, can make our faith more whole and more just.

Reading beyond Empathy

The great film critic Roger Ebert once called movies "empathy machines."[1] The same can be said of literature. To read literature is to incarnate and inhabit the experience of another, as crafted by the author. Literature's empathic power is why abolitionists leveraged slave narratives to warm the cold consciences of northerners indifferent to the suffering of enslaved Black persons. To read literature is to experience what Martha Nussbaum calls "links of possibility," a powerful bond of empathy.[2]

But a theological reading of literature demands we do more than empathize. In fact, a theological approach necessarily demotes empathy from one of the central purposes of our reading to a good product that happens along the way. We are after not less than empathy but more.

A theological reading of literature takes human experience seriously enough to examine it through the grid of divine revelation; it's the sacred, dignifying task of placing our collective story, told through literature, in conversation with God's story. It's listening to the stories of human experience with ears attuned to questions raised, the mind engaged in theological interplay, and the heart sensitive to the concern of human persons and the God whose image we all share.

An example may help. To read Richard Wright's *Native Son* with empathy is to put yourself in Bigger Thomas's traumatized existence, walking hundreds of pages in his protagonist shoes. But to read *Native Son* theologically is to do one better; it's to walk farther in Bigger's shoes, not ending our journey once we reach the road to empathy but seeking to reach the road to Emmaus, finding the intersection between the story of Bigger and the story of Jesus. A theological reading also considers that Wright, the author of *Native Son*, has something interrogative and constructive to say to our faith as we reflect on what that challenging message might be. To read Black literature through a theological lens is to affirm the dignity of these stories, the wisdom of these authors, and the power of God's revelation to speak a word to us amid our collective lived experience.

The Possibility of Reading Black Books Theologically

Literature is ripe for this sort of theological reflection precisely because literature is story. And story preserves and explores our existential longings and our experiential wanderings. Reflecting theologically on literature is not far from reflecting theologically on life in all its piercing pain, profound confusion, and glimpses of joy.

Literature as story not only captures and portrays; it also has explanatory power. It seeks to make sense of life in the world. In *Invisible Man*, Ralph Ellison presents such a question: But what kind of society will make them see me? For just and whole believers, such an inquiry cannot be answered only sociologically. The question begs to be read as a theological ask: How do we see and order human relation so that the God-given dignity of people is seen, not denied? By trying to make theological sense of our stories, we seek to bring the human predicament into the light and sense of God's kingdom.

All of which means that thinking theologically about seminal African American literature to embody a more whole and just faith is especially valuable, though rarely done. Because one's lived experience shapes one's theological inquiry, African American literature is a potent resource for theological reflection. Our literature lays bare the core concerns of modern Black experience, to which our faith has something to say. In a significant way, this book is a broadly Christian *and* a Black Christian project because a key source of reflection is the themes and concerns of Black experience represented in the literature of some of our greatest twentieth-century authors.

The Benefits of Reading Black Books Theologically

I see at least three primary benefits of reading classic Black literature with a theological perspective. First, such a reading provides *edification* and *encouragement* by demonstrating the coherence of Christianity and Black experience and concern. Second, it offers a *constructive challenge* by illuminating the blind spots where our faith and practice have not attended to the concerns of Black experience through a lived biblical ethic, proof of a truncated righteousness and a malnourished theological imagination. Third, it provides *invitation* by showing us new areas where creative and faithful reflection and practice are needed.

Alongside these, there are the literary benefits—empathy, imagination, understanding. It is my profound joy to introduce readers to some of the most riveting texts in our literary tradition and to add a new lens of exploration for those who know these texts intimately. It is my prayer that this dual lens—the literary and the theological—will have a dual impact, making us better readers of the text and better icons of the faith.

So while African American believers will have a profound interest in this work, it is in no way exclusive in its audience or its benefits. I believe those well versed in these literary texts will gain much from these reflections, as will those coming to these works for the very first time. Readers may choose to read the literary text before, alongside, or after the corresponding chapter—each will yield its benefits. (Note that spoilers do abound, but the texts examined here are worthy of multiple readings.) There's much here for Christians of all backgrounds and the spiritually curious to learn concerning both these seminal texts and the Christian faith.

Toward a More Whole and Just Faith

The conviction that a particular reading of African American literature can help make our faith more whole and just is a nod to the famous words of Frederick Douglass, who distinguished between the two forms of Christianity at play in America. Douglass boldly declared:

> What I have said respecting and against religion, I mean strictly to apply to the *slaveholding religion* of this land, and with no possible reference to Christianity proper; for, between the Christianity of this land, and the Christianity of Christ, I recognize the widest possible difference. . . . To be the friend of the one, is of necessity to be the enemy of the other. I love the pure, peaceable, and impartial Christianity of Christ: I therefore hate the corrupt, slaveholding, women-whipping, cradle-plundering, partial and hypocritical Christianity of this land.[3]

According to Douglass, America has been home to two forms of Christianity, one whole and "proper" and one "corrupt" and "partial." Some of the concerns addressed in the literature we'll examine are those that "the

4

Christianity of this land," to borrow Douglass's phrase, has given only cursory or warped attention.

Theological reflection on the experience of Black folks, as told in our seminal literature, therefore encompasses a desire to move from the partial and warped to the whole and holy. This approach shines a multidirectional light, illuminating some of American Christianity's residual blind spots while highlighting the enduring beauty of Black Christian faith particularly and the truth and beauty of "proper" Christianity generally. The separation between doctrine and ethics—between body and soul, between what is believed and what is lived, between orthodoxy and orthopraxy—is the seed of the partial faith Douglass decries. Faithfully integrating body and soul concerns—as a dual-lens reading does—is one critical way to return to a faith that is whole and just.

An Orientation before Reading

What is African American literature? For African descendants in America, our literature was first forged in the same fire that sparked African American Christianity: the harrowing trauma of chattel slavery. Put most simply, African American literature is literary texts concerned with or expressive of Black experience, from the vernacular tradition birthed on cotton fields—our church songs, oral tales, and spirituals—to the literary tradition that includes the poems of Margaret Walker and the novels of Toni Morrison.

Both our literature and our Christian faith were born of our historical experience. Both are like roses that grew from the concrete, beauty emerging from the brutal conditions of our suffering. That slaves—banned from becoming literate—developed both oral and written literary excellence is no small feat. That slaves embraced and purified the very faith held by their slave masters as a proslavery tool of oppression is a wonder and a testimony.

While I caught bits and pieces growing up, I didn't get anything close to a proper introduction to African American literature until my studies as an undergraduate and then in graduate school. Since then, I've wrestled for years with the connection between Black literature and Christianity, first as a student, then briefly as an adjunct English professor, and primarily as a pastor, slowly discovering how our literature can prompt us to think more robustly about our faith and how our faith gives us a grid through which to ponder the experiences described in our literature.

I mention this because, for both the novice and the experienced, African American literature is often difficult to read in form and content. Here Christians should hypothetically be somewhat prepared, since Scripture is often difficult terrain for the same reasons. Like Scripture, African American literature is unflinchingly honest in its depiction of human depravity. As readers engage the literary texts covered in this book, it is important to read prayerfully and communally, remembering that, as with Scripture, description does not mean prescription or endorsement.

In preparing to engage African American literature, readers should recall that the truth is often troubling. The world is a joyful and cold and brutal place—and Christians, of all people, know and reckon with reality in both its glory and its devastation. This means being prepared for the trauma and grime of *Beloved* and the violence of *Native Son*. Readers should respect their conscience, evaluate the work critically in relation to its theme and form, and consider how the truth of the human condition is being unfurled. These are large and difficult tasks to do by oneself. Take up these texts with somebody else and work through the beauty and devastation together. Reading these texts—alongside this book—can help us become incarnate in the stories and wounds of others, as Christ did for us.

Also note that my readings are not a presumption or an argument that any of the authors I engage with possessed an explicit Christian or theological agenda. The theologizing emerges from my reading of their literary forms and themes as a literary-minded pastor-theologian. This means that chapters are a blend of close reading, theological reflection, and Christian proclamation and application. Depending on the literary work in question, chapters vary, with some taking on an apologetic flair—answering the concerns of a text with a particular Christian conception—and others demonstrating how an author's content and craft showcase a positive resonance with or critical approach to the Christian tradition.

To attend to some of the seminal writers of the twentieth century, as I do in this project, is to look at authors who did not necessarily write with an explicit theological purpose the way Phyllis Wheatley or Douglass did. This nonreligious factor makes their concerns, I believe, more pressing and important for Christians to examine. Again, these authors serve as wise guides leading us to grasp afresh the questions and themes of Black experience, which our faith has grappled with—and must continue to do so.

A few others have taken up this important and rich symbiotic connection between Black literature and Christianity. In 1938, Benjamin E. Mays published *The Negro's God as Reflected in His Literature*, turning a keen analytical eye toward the evolution of African Americans' depiction of God and Christianity. I see this present work as a remixed homage to Mays's work, showcasing central questions at the heart of Black experience in America and the contours of Christian faith and responding to such questions biblically, contextually, and prophetically.

I have attempted to come to this book about books as a guide who integrates my affections: my love for these stories, my love for what they say about Black experience in both trials and triumphs, and my love for Jesus and his kingdom. Whether you have just picked up a book by James Baldwin at Target or have a dog-eared copy, it is my prayer that the fruit of this book will reflect something of this motivational origin, that as you generously give of your time to read and engage this work, you will find your own love inflamed and increased both for these texts and for the Word who became flesh to interpret all stories and embrace all peoples. May we lean in together, listening by reading, and in the process may our faith be made more whole and just, to the glory of the Father, Son, and Holy Spirit.

Image of God

Ralph Ellison's *Invisible Man*

> But what kind of society will make him see me . . .
>
> —Ralph Ellison, *Invisible Man*

"I am a man." On February 12, 1968, over two hundred Black sanitation workers in Memphis, Tennessee, bore this revolutionary message written on signs and embodied in their protest against the work conditions that had led to the death of two fellow workers.[1] The strike, which included more than one thousand Black sanitation workers, drew the support of Martin Luther King Jr., who would give the last days of his life to this cause. "You are here," King proclaimed to those on strike, "to demand that Memphis will see the poor." One of the sanitation workers described the motive and message years later: "We felt we would have to let the city know that because we were sanitation workers, we were human beings. The signs we were carrying said 'I Am a Man.'"[2]

Christianity is no stranger to the importance of "I am" statements. God's self-disclosure declared him to be I AM (Exod. 3:14). Through seven "I am" statements, John's Gospel explains who Jesus is, the eternal Word made flesh. There is, then, both theological origin and depth to the "I am a man" declaration of those workers. The declaration is a demand, in the face of the opposite, to be recognized and seen as a person whose being derives from the Creator God himself. It is a call to be seen as fully human and made in the image of God.

The image of God is like a doctrinal diamond, refracting multiple truths about humanity. From its first pages, Scripture sets forth the image of God (*imago Dei*) by declaring God as Creator and humanity as creature-persons: "So God created man in his own image, in the image of God he created him; male and female he created them" (Gen. 1:27).[3] An endless and wondrous catalog of diverse emphases and applications emerges from this doctrine. Two broad categories of this truth—*structure* and *function*—help demonstrate the beauty and, sometimes, the neglect at work in our conception of being image bearers of God.

The image of God answers the existential question, What in the world am I in this world for? In the mandate to worship God, reflect him throughout creation, carry out his rule over the world, exist in flourishing relationship to other image bearers, we encounter the *functional* aspect of being a person, an image bearer. In this truth, we see the wondrous purpose for which each of us was formed and fashioned. We are God's representatives, our image marking his dominion over the earth. We are to be in covenant relationship with him, and we are to reflect his righteousness (Eph. 4:24). The image of God can be understood as "the special status that all human beings have as those made to reflect our Creator's character and commissioned to carry out his purposes in the world."[4]

For such a massive mandate, resources are required. The *structural* aspect of the *imago Dei* means that God has created us with wondrous capacities—rationality, creativity, relationality—that, though marred by sin, still mirror him and help us fulfill our divine function and purpose. The *imago Dei* in us "must therefore be seen as involving both the structure" (our "gifts, capacities, and endowments") and our "functioning" (our "actions," "relationships to God and to others," and the uses of our God-given "gifts").[5]

What's Missing: The Visceral Doctrine

Thinking *structurally* and *functionally* helps us grasp some essential contours of the *imago Dei*, a layered and extensive theological category. Still, when we turn to the realities of image bearers, like those revealed by the sanitation workers in Memphis or expressed in a literary work like *Invisible*

Man (1952), much standard Protestant theological reflection does not account for the doctrinal elephant in the room. What does it mean to live as an image bearer when other image bearers try to limit your existence? While the image of God cannot be extinguished in any person, the freedom to image God can be restricted—not simply by our sin but by the unrighteousness of others. This is a theme not always explored by theologians but vital to African American experience in the face of racism and thus central to Black theologians and novelists and to our very notions of what it means to be human.

What remains overlooked in some conceptions of the *imago Dei* is the necessity of embodied expression. An overemphasis on the structural elements of the *imago Dei* "often emphasizes human capacities in rather disembodied ways."[6] This reductionism in turn leads to what theologian Marc Cortez describes as a temptation "to be satisfied with an account of 'true humanity' as an abstract concept separate from the hard realities of a broken world."[7] Black literature, like *Invisible Man*, will not permit such abstractions. This is its gift, because by situating our understanding of the *imago Dei* alongside the hard realities of a broken world, we escape reductionism and venture into a deeper exploration of what it means to image God. We find that the image of God in us is not solely our relationality, rationality, or creativity: it is those things—and more—strung together, expressed in our actual living, manifested and enacted in our bodies, "extend[ing] to the whole person . . . in soul and body, in all . . . faculties and powers."[8] The agency and power to righteously express one's essence and function as an image bearer—that is, mirroring God, ruling over his creation, exercising autonomy, and being treated with dignity and returning the favor—is part of the image of God in action. *Invisible Man*'s attention to the embodied experience of invisibility pushes us into a deeper recognition that the *imago Dei* is a visceral doctrine concerned with blood and bones, dignity and freedom, bodies and sight.

Ellison's Invisibility and Image

Widely lauded as one of the finest twentieth-century novels, *Invisible Man* is an expansive, landmark text, tracing the painful absurdity of Black life in the Jim Crow South and the thinly veiled racism of the urbane North. Ellison's novel is comedic and tragic, gritty and surreal, mythic and symbolic, layered and accessible. At its center is Ellison's nameless protagonist and his quest to find dignity in an American society devout in its denial of his humanity.

The novel opens with the protagonist mulling over his life's journey—the events readers will soon experience—with an arresting, metaphorical "I am" declaration: "I am an invisible man."[9] Invisibility in *Invisible Man* conveys restricted freedom and selective visibility. Readers quickly find that Invisible, the nameless protagonist, is not seen as a full human complete with autonomy and dignity. He is viewed only as a living pawn to be acted upon or moved in service to any agenda but his own.

Invisible's invisibility demonstrates one manifestation of our fractured, sin-plagued image bearing: image bearers degrading and limiting image bearers. "What makes sin so serious" writes theologian Anthony Hoekema, "is precisely the fact that man is now using God-given and God-imaging powers and gifts to do things that are an affront to his Maker."[10] In *Invisible Man*, the affront to the Maker is the use of God-given imaging powers to inhibit the freedom to image. In a cruel irony that runs against the grain of creation, image bearers strip fellow image bearers of the freedom to image by applying their God-given capacities to restrict the image-bearing capacities of others. To experience such is to be seen not as an image bearer but as a commodity, selectively worthy of humane treatment, one who is in the end expendable and therefore invisible.

The Source of Invisibility

What is the source of Invisible's invisibility? As quickly as we hear Invisible's declaration, "I am an invisible man," we learn the cause of his plight. His invisibility is not the result of a defect in him but is a moral fault found in those who behold him: "My invisibility . . . occurs because of a peculiar disposition of the eyes of those with whom I come in contact. A matter of the construction of their *inner* eyes, those eyes with which they look through their physical eyes upon reality."[11] The problem of Invisible's invisibility—and thus the problem of Black people's disregarded dignity—is firmly in the eyes of the beholder, the eyes of the white individuals who make up the society in which the nameless Invisible navigates as Ellison's proxy for countless Black Americans.

This sort of diagnosis raises the eyebrows of theologically minded readers, drawing us toward the notion of sin—a malfunction of the spirit, a malady that burrows deeper than rational, surface externals. That this "peculiar disposition" is "a matter of . . . their *inner* eyes" suggests that the source of the scourge is not an occasional slipup but more like an error bred in the bones.[12] The problem is more ontological than functional. Though the *inner eyes* of fellow image bearers are the cause of invisibility, the impact upon Invisible is restrictive, and it is felt bodily.

The novel's early battle-royal scene is an appalling example of invisibility and its visceral, bodily consequences. As the high school valedictorian of his southern school, Invisible is invited to deliver a speech on Black humility to an audience of the town's most important white leaders. Upon arrival, Invisible is not called to the podium but forced by the white organizers to partake in the entertainment that precedes his speech. What follows is a traumatizing, degrading debacle: Ten Black students are led into a smoky ballroom under the drunken gaze of "the most important men of the town . . . bankers, lawyers, judges, doctors, fire chiefs, teachers, merchants" and placed before a "magnificent blonde [woman]—stark naked" before being blindfolded, set in a makeshift boxing ring, and commanded to blindly beat each other battle-royal-style while the white townsmen hoot, holler, and hurl racial epithets.[13] Bruised and beaten, Invisible is thankful to close the night with his speech, swallowing his own blood and saliva to expound on the need for Blacks to be humble and socially responsible. He's rewarded with a briefcase and a scholarship to a Negro college. He feels "an importance I had never dreamed."[14]

The battle royal, in the novel's view, is society in miniature: Black people are visible only within the confines of a commodified existence. Representatives of every slice of society gaze upon Invisible as a means to an end, a human prop for fetishized entertainment and a muzzled voice for proclaiming that the absence of equality is due to the absence of Black responsibility. Because Invisible is invisible, he must entertain before he speaks, and even his rhetorical pursuits are confined to the talking points of a segregated society. The crowd hardly listens to a word of Invisible's speech about social responsibility "until, no doubt distracted by having to gulp down my own blood, I made a mistake and yelled a phrase I had often seen denounced in newspaper editorials, heard debated in private"—he yells out "social equality."[15] Then "the laughter hung smokelike in the sudden stillness," and "sounds of displeasure filled the room." Invisible's slip of the tongue puts the crowd at attention and himself under interrogation.

> "You sure that about 'equality' was a mistake?"
> "Oh, yes, sir," I said. "I was swallowing blood."

"Well, you had better speak more slowly so we can understand. We mean to do right by you, but you've got to know your place at all times. All right, now, go on with your speech."[16]

To know his place is to embrace their limits on his freedom, his body, his image bearing. He is restricted in his freedom to image God, his body forced to perform violence and his mind and mouth encouraged to preach a false gospel of dignity through merit.

The Function of Blood

Blood functions in two pivotal ways in this moment in Invisible's journey that illumine the dignity and physicality of the *imago Dei*. Blood, of course, is charged with theological significance. In Scripture, blood makes expiation for sin (Lev. 17:11), and "the life of every creature is its blood" (Lev. 17:14). Hymns like "Nothing but the Blood" and gospel classics that declare "the blood still works" speak to the nature of our salvation: in Jesus, "we have redemption through his blood" (Eph. 1:7). Life, both temporal and eternal, is a matter of blood.

The theological significance of blood reveals deeper insight into Invisible's blood-swallowing denial. To even utter words that blame Black responsibility for the problem of white racism—the message that appeases the white crowd—Invisible must swallow his own blood, the very substance of life within him. To champion social responsibility as the path to human dignity is to deny one's God-given humanity as an image bearer. Dignity by works is a false gospel. Dignity is not earned; it is given, and given by the very hand and heart of God, who fashioned us. Dignity is rooted in the *imago Dei*; it is the inherent freedom of all persons to be; it is the right to live as image bearers. These are the theological realities Invisible must swallow and deny in order to proclaim responsibility as the way out of invisibility, responsibility as the ladder to that basic right of equality. Under the threat of violence upon his body, he must swallow and downplay the life in him.

In Holy Communion, the church partakes in the mystery of the body and the blood of Christ, a sacrament that unites us as one in Christ as we feed on his life and death. To have fellowship with this society that possesses warped inner eyes, Invisible must partake of a disfigured sacrament, one not of union but of denial. He must swallow his own blood, denying his own dignity, to survive and advance. Under the gaze of those who see us as invisible, there can exist no true embodied association befitting an image bearer, only a false peace achieved through an unholy self-denial.

Blood That Cries Out

Invisible's blood speaks another, better word than denial. His blood cries out like Abel's, though not from the ground but from within his own body. Invisible, "distracted by having to gulp down" his own blood, calls out unintentionally for social equality, the very freedom to live as a person imbued with dignity as an image bearer of God. The better word that Invisible speaks, caused by the presence of his blood, is the message of equality and dignity that finds its weightiest anchor in the *imago Dei*: I am a man. What Invisible must deny—his blood—is the very substance that causes him to call out for the dignity befitting all image bearers. It is blood, the source of life and salvation, that causes a divine slip of the tongue: image bearers are made for dignity and freedom.

Invisible Man's focus on the physicality of invisibility can help remind readers that the *imago Dei* is a matter not of abstraction but of embodiment. This does not mean, as disability studies have shown us, that disabled persons are less the image than the able-bodied. Rather, it means that imaging is for all—not simply theoretical but lived. The image of God contains structures like rationality but at the same time supersedes them. What good is it—as in Invisible's case—to reflect on your rational capacities when you can employ them only under the threat of violence or censor? The freedom to be all that God has made a person to be is an indispensable part of what it means to carry the mantle of image bearer.

Theologian Bruce Fields asserts that "the most heinous manifestation of racism is to deny, in various forms, the full humanity of other human beings created in the image of God."[17] This denial is invisibility, a visual rejection of God and his image in all human persons. Just as the *imago Dei* is a bodily doctrine, invisibility is a bodily denial. It leaves persons objectified, dehumanized, forced to choke down, literally or metaphorically, their own blood. This visceral aspect is easily forgotten. As Ta-Nehisi Coates observes, "All our phrasing—*race relations, racial chasm, racial justice, racial profiling, white privilege,* even *white supremacy*—serves to obscure that racism is a visceral experience, that it dislodges brains, blocks airways, rips muscle, extracts organs, cracks bones, breaks teeth."[18] All this, *Invisible Man* reminds us, is connected to the invisibility of human dignity, which is tied to the freedom and flourishing of human persons, not in theory but in flesh.

Living Invisible

Visibility and dignity are at the crux of much of African American history. When Richard Allen and Absalom Jones simply wanted to pray in the front of their church undisturbed, they sought to be seen in body and soul. When Sojourner Truth raised her voice to speak for the rights of Black women, declaring, "Ain't I a woman?" she effectively issued a rhetorical demand to be seen.[19] They sought to be seen as those made and dignified by God, for they knew they were viewed by most as invisible.

Though our stories are not as harrowing as those of centuries past, we each carry our own stories of being rendered invisible. Years later, I'm still shell-shocked that after an innocuous spat, a girl in my seventh-grade class looked at me and did not see me as a whole person but as some*thing* to whom she could declare, "I wish we still had you as slaves." I don't remember if I even uttered a word in response, but I remember what I felt, and invisible is tragically fitting. That moment brings to mind others—friends no longer speaking to me after talking with their parents, and my first assault by the N-word—all producing a strange realization of how I was seen.

Invisible's realization of his invisibility is a traumatic awakening that builds, like a cursed crescendo, through the course of the novel. For most of the novel, Invisible recounts his days prior to recognizing his invisibility. We watch as Invisible lives with pharisaical adherence to the laws of respectability politics and ideals of personal responsibility, only to be boomeranged back and forth between false hope and dehumanizing embarrassment, finding himself used and discarded by each figurehead and institution he encounters. In this way, *Invisible Man* immerses us in the disorienting whirlwind of living as one rendered invisible by fellow persons, structures, and systems.

Living invisible—as one whose dignity is given by God but denied by humanity—produces profound internal tension and can leave an indelible mark of existential confusion. Invisible experiences a dizzying conflict and disorientation at a most fundamental level of personhood: his identity. His existence is marked by a "painful, contradictory voice . . . within me," a pulsating "guilt and puzzlement" as he feels the pull of revenge toward an unjust society and his "obsession with my identity" in the form of questions like, "Who was I, how had I come to be?"[20]

16

These are the grand questions of existence we were made to ask. Danger lurks in the horde of answers that offer definitions of self and dignity in every which way besides the truth of our belonging to God and bearing his image. For those who search for dignity and identity under the harsh gaze of inner eyes that see them as invisible, the challenge takes on another layer of danger. If we are not carefully armed with a countertruth, then how they see us soon becomes how we see ourselves. Like Invisible, we will swallow our own blood and internalize the gaze of their inner eyes. There is then grave danger emotionally, spiritually, and physically of living in a chaotic world that possesses an unholy, demeaning gaze that looks upon image bearers of God and pronounces them invisible.

This danger forms part of the epic conflict pulsating at the heart of *Invisible Man*: Invisible's quest to find himself and assert his dignity against the persons and forces that see him as selectively and partially human. The image of God in man and woman necessitates the freedom to exist and image, but living invisible means, at nearly every turn, having this freedom challenged and constrained, not simply by one's own sin nature but by the unrighteousness of others.

The Search for Visibility

The story line of the novel advances as Invisible experiences the whiplash of his invisibility and responds with new strategies—from personal responsibility to career prospects to political activism—for coping with his invisibility and asserting his personhood as a man.[21] In particular, education, via the scholarship to a Negro college won at the battle royal, becomes Invisible's messianic hope. But he soon suffers a crisis when his college tenure dissolves after he chauffeurs his school's white trustee, Mr. Norton, on a voyeuristic ride to observe the troubling lives of nearby rural Black folks, leaving the trustee deeply traumatized. The Negro college president, Dr. Bledsoe, castigates Invisible for not knowing that he should have lied to Mr. Norton and kept him in the confines of the campus. After rebuking Invisible ("instead of uplifting the race, you've torn it down"[22]), Dr. Bledsoe expels him from the college and sends him into exile: he is to journey to New York City to work and earn tuition for the following year.

Dr. Bledsoe sends Invisible away with seven sealed letters addressed to "several friends of the school" who will do "something" for Invisible upon his arrival in the North. Though the letters are meant to introduce

Invisible and request help to get him a job, Dr. Bledsoe warns that the letters must remain sealed if Invisible wants help, for "white folks are strict about such things."[23] As Invisible's hope shifts from education to employment, Ellison's imagery mirrors John's apocalypse, the book of Revelation, in which the seven seals cannot be opened but by the Lamb, and the seals bring judgment upon the earth (Rev. 6:1–17).

Such biblical allusions foreshadow ominous fortunes for Invisible that he, still unaware of his invisibility, cannot discern. Instead, he sees in the letters the newest path to traverse to arrive at a sense of identity and dignity. Encouraged that the letters "were addressed to some of the most important men in the whole country," Invisible enters his northern exile with a burgeoning sense of dignity on account of the sealed letters, though this confidence is tempered, for the letters are seen by no one:

> I caught myself wishing for someone to show the letters to, someone who could give me a proper reflection of my importance. Finally, I went to the mirror and gave myself an admiring smile as I spread the letters upon the dresser like a hand of high trump cards.[24]

Understood theologically, Invisible's desire for "a proper reflection of my importance" is the longing to be seen by others in such a manner that confirms the image of God in him and ratifies his inherent dignity in deed and in word. This longing is part of Invisible's lifelong search for self: "All my life I had been looking for something and everywhere I turned someone tried to tell me what it was. . . . I was looking for myself."[25] It is the longing of the human heart that is fearfully and wonderfully made: the desire to know ourselves as full of dignity and to have our dignity affirmed, not only in ourselves by ourselves, but by the world at large.

Invisible's longing for a proper reflection of his importance prompts questions about the toil of living invisible and the communal nature of imaging God together. Finding no proper reflection of his importance as an image bearer in a Jim Crow world, Invisible labors to give himself what he has not received from others. He turns to the mirror to gain a proper glimpse of his visibility as it reflects his own image and the sealed letters. But with no one to properly see and affirm his dignity, Invisible's turn toward the mirror falls flat, a demonstration that the image of God in us is most seen and celebrated in community, not in isolation.

It is together, not in isolation, that a proper reflection of our importance as the *imago Dei* is most fully affirmed. "Humanization," Fields notes,

"does not occur autonomously. . . . The capacity to experience full humanity is developed in the context of more than one, that is, in community."[26]
This truth reveals the callous capacity of a Jim Crow society and a broken
humanity. The former's effects linger among us, while the latter is a reality
firmly fixed. Quite naturally, the bent of our land and of our hearts is not
the affirmation of the *imago Dei* but the commodification of the image, the
exaltation of the dollar, and the maintenance of the status quos that thinly
mask racialized realities. In creation, we were made for association—with
God and one another—but in society, we experience alienation. Who, then,
can give us a proper reflection of ourselves in a world that bombards us
with messages that demean and wound us in ways that make us interrogate
our own God-given dignity?

Left to himself, Invisible turns, in part, to himself, lifting his own smile
upon himself, reflecting himself to himself, in a move reminiscent of the
Lord's countenance smiling upon Israel, declared in the Aaronic priestly
blessing (Num. 6:24–26). With no one willing to affirm the reflection of
God in him, Invisible takes that priestly duty upon himself. He does so in
a syncretistic flourish, not solely believing in his dignity as an image bearer
but resting also on the promise of the sealed letters. The scene is tragic,
for the letters in which he hopes are but a flimsy substitute for what he is
himself: one made in God's image.

At this point, Invisible reflects us back to us. There is dignity in our
merits, work, and education. But not the sort of foundational dignity that
can bear the weight of defining us in a world often out to degrade us or to
deify us—both of which distort the image. As those made to mirror God,
we must continually look upward, toward him. We are not those afraid
of the horizontal. We can and must look to the mirror of our existence,
trace the structural gifts of our humanity, feel the spark of dignity in us,
and rehearse, each day, that we are made and seen by a good and gracious
Creator. But we must look to God to know something of the deep dignity
that is within us as those redeemed and covenantally loved by God.

Those rendered invisible by the world must gaze upon the image of
the invisible God (Col. 1:15–20). It is in Jesus of Nazareth, the image of
the invisible God whose image we bear, that we receive a proper reflection of ourselves in the most profound sense. It is this Jesus who came
for and among the invisible of the world: those deemed less than, those
beheld with a gaze of hatred and indifference, those classified by the world
as unworthy, unfit, unlovely. The knowledge and reception of God's love
is transformative for all, but especially for the invisible. Speaking of the

disinherited, a body of people similar to those seen as invisible, Howard Thurman points out that "the awareness of being a child of God tends to stabilize the ego and results in a new courage, fearlessness, and power."[27] To know deep in one's bones that one is made and loved by God is to be filled with reservoirs of resolve to image God in freedom and righteousness, no matter the world's gaze.

The Fault of the Inner Eyes

Because the novel's narrative is foregrounded with the revelation of Invisible's invisibility ("their *inner* eyes") and his opening "I am" declaration ("I had to discover I am an invisible man"), most of the novel sizzles with the tension of anticipation: When and how will Invisible discover he is invisible? Ellison creates a layered sense of dramatic irony. We know, as readers, that Invisible is invisible, and Invisible as the narrator knows the same, but the Invisible we follow in the chapters of the novel is not yet woke from his slumber.

In step with the novel's attention to the embodied nature of visibility and dignity, Invisible's epiphany moment is also visceral. Now a grassroots activist in Harlem for a multiethnic movement called "the Brotherhood," Invisible is a dynamic speaker under the marching orders of Brother Jack, a white man, and the movement's mission to shape "a better world for all people."[28] Here too Ellison's protagonist is soon confronted with the ugly truth of his invisibility. In the eyes of this movement, he is less a person and more a commodity. After leading an unauthorized protest in honor of Brother Tod, Invisible finally understands how he is perceived. As Brother Jack berates Invisible for speaking without the permission of the Brotherhood's committee, he pounds the table and yells his rebuke, and Ellison shows us the root cause of invisibility from Invisible's view:

> Suddenly something seemed to erupt out of his face. You're seeing things, I thought, hearing it strike sharply against the table and roll as his arm shot out and snatched an object the size of a large marble and dropped it, plop! into his glass. . . . And there on the bottom lay an eye. A glass eye.[29]

Ellison conveys the expected in a manner unexpected: Brother Jack has a glass eye, and everyone besides Invisible is firmly in the know. Ellison's protagonist thinks he's been seen in his humanity—after all, he's been a leader, speaker, and influencer in the movement—but the symbolism of the glass eye demonstrates otherwise. Those who possess a glass eye have, in the novel's terms, a "polished and humane facade" of moral sight behind which is a "harsh red rawness."[30] The glass eye enriches the novel's earlier attention to the inner eyes as the cause of invisibility. How we behold others is a projection of one's inner condition on a physical plane of another's flesh. Our inner eyes become flesh in love and association, or glass in facade and exploitation, according to how we view the God-given flesh of others.

Soon, Invisible experiences a deeper revelation: "I looked around a corner of my mind and saw Jack, Norton, and Emerson merge into one single white figure. . . . Now I recognized my invisibility." Each branch of society embodied by these figures—and society as a whole—possesses a glass eye, a defect that renders Black life invisible, not fully worthy of humane treatment but "simply a material, a natural resource to be used."[31]

Invisible's conversion moment—his awakening—is visceral and visionary. He sees things on two planes: the physical—an eye erupting from an angry white face—and the spiritual—his mind prompting a transformative vision. Both revelations affirm that the invisibility of Black people is not the result of a fault in our being or doing. The fault of invisibility resides in the gaze of persons and institutions that blend into "one single white figure."

Though we are not sinless, we are not at fault for the invisibility imposed upon us. Like all persons, we bear God's image. Like all humanity, we share an existence and a nature that is at once broken and beautiful. Like all people, we possess in our very selves a humanity that is worthy of affirmation, that demands an embodied freedom, and that needs gracious redemption.

Imaging rightly demands sight and freedom: true sight of self, God, and others; the freedom of our bodies to image; and, most vitally, Christ's redeeming grace, which gives freedom from sin's power and restores God's image in us (Col. 3:10). Imaging rightly requires not only true self-understanding (theory) but also embodied application (freedom, practice).

Wise readers, then, will recognize that the issue of invisibility is not solved by Invisible's self-discovery alone. No matter how he understands and sees himself, he still lives in a world where others will see him. No matter how we understand ourselves, we must reckon with how others see us—and they must reckon with how we see them. Were Invisible to have recognized his invisibility immediately, he would have stepped out of the waters of racial naivete, but his life and body would still have been, in part, subject to the gaze of others. A proper diagnosis does not automatically produce a remedy. The novel thus continually provokes an urgent question: How can Invisible survive—the very baseline of imaging God—when the problem of his invisibility resides not in his body, his merits, or his actions but in others' inner eyes? Translated into contemporary speak, *Invisible Man* specifically suggests that the problem is not Black lives but white sight.

Black Lives, White Sight

History holds the receipts. Whether literally or metaphorically, in words or in deeds, in aspirations or in actions, when African Americans have asserted, "I am a (wo)man, see and treat me as such," the world by and large has scoffed, alternating between responses as explicit and violent as lynching or as subtle and nefarious as redlining. The dignity of Black persons has far too often been subordinate to the evaluative inner eyes of white sight. Functionally speaking, white sight has often determined whether Black lives matter. Lamenting the seemingly endless killings of unarmed Black people by law enforcement, Michael Eric Dyson has captured it painfully well: "We draw breath. They draw conclusions. Our lives draw to an end."[32] To be invisible is to be a people viewed on a sliding spectrum of dignity dependent on the optics of the situation and our proximity to what is deemed safe and respectable, all on the basis of another's inner eyes.

History tells us that when it comes to the *imago Dei*, one's doctrinal statement can be on point while one's inner eyes are unholy. One prominent pastor-author observes:

> As I reflect on several racial flashpoints over the past few years, I fear I have been too quick to think to myself, *Yes, of course, image of God. Every Christian already knows that and believes that.* But white Christians in this country have *not* always believed that, or at least they have not always acted like they really believe it.[33]

This is where Black literature can push theological reflection closer to biblical wholeness. The image of God, when put in conversation with Black experience through the mode of literature, can never be reduced to theoretical belief. Ellison's work moves us from the theoretical to the lived.

Theologically, this means the test of our belief in the *imago Dei* is not what we believe about the doctrine of the image of God but how we, in real life, view, treat, and relate to our fellow image bearers—particularly those most prone to be rendered invisible. Our doctrine is not tested by its rational precision but by its lived application.

Beyond Binaries

While attuned to the particulars of Black plight on account of white sight, *Invisible Man* also voices concern for the universality of rendering invisibility and being rendered invisible. Ellison's concern for both the specific truth of Black experience and the universal truth of human experience manifests in the novel's structure and bookends. The novel opens with the declaration "I am an invisible man" and ends with a question: "Who knows but that, on the lower frequencies, I speak for you?"[34] *Invisible Man* begins with "I" and concludes with "you," showcasing first the particulars of invisibility manifested in Black experience before asking readers if such an experience of invisibility may also mirror their own.

The first word of the novel is a preached word, an indicative truth—I am an invisible man—and the last word, like the conclusion of a well-crafted sermon, drives the audience toward the ponderous: Does this narrative, in any way, speak for you? In this manner, the novel's framing—epilogue and prologue, opening salvo and final word—reveals part of its urgency and, in our case, its theological wisdom—that is, its pressure to consider our shared human association, how we see each other and live together.

This attention to the particulars and the universality of being invisible reflects Ellison's distinct philosophy of the human predicament, one that distanced him ideologically from the prominent Black writers of his day. Of course, by leaving his protagonist unnamed, Ellison used his character to represent the universality of Black experience in twentieth-century America. But Ellison stubbornly refused to be pigeonholed as a writer of the Black experience alone. True literature, in Ellison's view, is capacious, fingering the jagged grain of the human condition in a way that transcends binaries and division. Unlike Richard Wright, Ellison's friend and early mentor whom we'll examine in later chapters, Ellison did not see Black literature's purpose as the task of protest. Literature, according to Ellison, is a container for the truth, not for protest propaganda. Literature is not indoctrination but revelation, a bright and complex light shining upon the complications of the human condition.[35] For this reason, such literature can deepen our theology, both in theory and in practice, and alert us to the truth of God in places hidden due to our hesitancy to venture into the depths of human experience, Black or otherwise.

For instance, Ellison's I/you dynamic reminds us and reveals in fresh ways that we are made for life together, no matter how polarized our communities might be. We exist in a garment of inescapable mutual destiny that plays out not in the theories we believe about one another but in the dignity and visibility we perceive in and grant to one another in time and space, in embodied flesh, and in enacted freedom. We cannot image God in our fullness apart from the grace of Christ and the practice of association with one another. Thus, to not see others as image bearers is to not properly image ourselves; it is a malfunction of our divine function: life together as image bearers under the rule of the Father, Son, and Holy Spirit. It's also a malfunction of our structure as image bearers, a malfunction of body and soul and a misreading—an immoral seeing—of God's image among us in the embodied flesh of the other.

While our seeing may not be like that of Bledsoe, Norton, or Brother Jack, anytime we see and relate to others as a means to an end, eyeing them and engaging them on the level of personal gain rather than their dignity and need as an image bearer, our seeing is theologically skewed. Honest introspection—if we dare stomach it—may reveal how normalized our rendering others invisible has become. When we view children as a drain and nuisance, coworkers as footstools to our advancement, significant others as receptacles for our frustrations and dispensers of our happiness, we walk in the tragic tradition of fallen humanity, seeing God's visible image bearers not through the true lens of their dignity but selectively, as commodities. We render them invisible.

A New Imagination

Such seeing is a profound moral emergency. It ruptures the association for which we are made and reveals, as its cause, a malfunction of body and soul. Renowned twentieth-century theologian Karl Barth notes, "The human significance of the eye and all seeing" is that through our seeing "the other should be visible to and seen" as human. Tragically, "seeing is inhuman if it does not include this seeing."[36] Barth's wisdom, our acquaintance with sin's pervasive power, and Ellison's I/you dynamic collaborate to keep the theological insights of invisibility and moral sight from remaining comfortably on the dichotomous surface of us vs. them, white vs. Black, minority vs. majority. A confluence of forces and experiences—Scripture, theology, our stories, and the stories of those around us—demands that we take seriously our nature and existence as those who have, in some ways, been rendered invisible and, in other ways, shamefully returned the favor. Invisible's invisibility "exposes severe limitations in the American social imagination."[37] In the face of such a judgment, who among us can claim to be fully clear of the charges?

What, then, is the way forward? If our sight is off, causing us to sin against God and his image bearers, our eyes—that is, our moral and social imagination—must be removed, replaced, redeemed. If our eyes cause us to sin, we must tear them out, Christ declared (Matt. 5:29; 18:9). How is this done with our *inner* eyes? The evaluative gaze must be replaced by our common kinship and human mutuality as those in and of God's creation.

Our sight needs redemption, which requires both repentance and a Redeemer who can give us a fresh vision for human association by drawing us back to the old purpose for which we were made. Christ—the image of God—must be the center of our vision, but not in any one-time, generic sense. He must be the center of our vision continually in the scriptural sense as the image of true humanity and the redeemer of broken humanity. He is the one who seeks the invisible, comforts the outcast, and dissolves the hostilities between those who have seen each other through the lens of hatred, exploitation, and invisibility. It is Christ, the image of the invisible God, who mends and heals broken image bearers—body, soul, eyes, and all—so that we might grow to behold one another rightly, our bodies together in harmony as we image our Creator under the Spirit's powerful, loving sway. For "it is a great and solemn and incomparable moment" when two persons "look themselves in the eye and discover one another." It is this moment of seeing that "is in some sense the root formation of all humanity without which the rest is impossible."[38]

Sin

Richard Wright's *Native Son*

> You have not yet considered the gravity of sin.
>
> —Anselm of Canterbury,
> *Why God Became Man*

Bigger Thomas has just killed a rat. Richard Wright's novel *Native Son* (1940) first plunges readers into the suffocating confines of Bigger's world as a young, Black twenty-year-old in Chicago through a view of his home life. Bigger knows confinement well. Engulfed by racism in society and plagued by poverty at home, Bigger lives a constricted life. He shares a one-bedroom apartment with his mother and two younger siblings, where privacy and personal space are nonexistent. There is no cheery "good morning" to start Bigger's day, only sharp directives from his mother— "turn your heads so I can dress," she demands—that capture their meager existence.[1] Not even at home can Bigger find a refuge from shame. The tiny apartment turns frantic when a "huge black rat" darts across the floor, looking for a means of escape while Bigger's family urges him to kill it. Bigger chases the rat across the room, struggling to kill it before he succeeds by smashing its head with a skillet.

What's hinted at in this first scene becomes unmistakable as Wright's novel progresses. Structured in three parts—Fear, Flight, and Fate—*Native Son* examines how America has confined Bigger, trapped like a rat, searching for an escape, but doomed to a violent fate as a product of his environment. The arc of fear, flight, and fate that Bigger will experience unfolds in parabolic miniature in his rodent encounter.

"Fear," Howard Thurman writes, "is one of the most persistent hounds of hell that dog the footsteps of the poor, the dispossessed, the disinherited."[2] Wright paints his opening scene with focused attention on this problem of fear: "The rat's belly pulsed with fear. Bigger advanced a step and the rat emitted a long thin song of defiance, its black beady eyes glittering, its tiny forefeet pawing the air restlessly."[3] Fear has hounded Bigger his whole life, and as the novel progresses, things turn only more disastrous. Later, after killing twice, Bigger hides in an abandoned apartment, on the run from the police. Confined and hunted, he engages in a defiant standoff as futile and foreordained as his encounter with the rat. In the hindsight of the whole novel, Wright's introductory parallel between Bigger and that fearful, trapped, defiant rat is as clear as it is painful. The fuse of Bigger's inner rage and fear will be lit by the social confines of his impoverished existence. He too will sing a defiant song, and his fate will be violent and crushing.

The Question of Sin

What exactly do the suffocating realities of shame, poverty, and fear have to do with a Christian understanding of Sin? Why insist on capitalizing the word *Sin*? Answers to such questions lead us to more questions: Is Sin personal or systematic? Is Sin a tyrant in the world or simply the product of choices made by sinners? At the risk of overgeneralizing, our lack of dexterity with such questions may be traced to the truncated teaching on Sin that exists in the standard American Sunday sermon. Sin, in these settings, is often presented as a volitional choice of disobedience, a missing of the mark of God's law, and most critically and rightly, an offense against a holy God. This view of Sin is true and incomplete. Present in this understanding of Sin is a reduction that defines Sin as only personally experienced and personally enacted. Sin is solely acts done by individuals and to individuals. But a view of Sin that is exclusively individualized will have insufficient categories through which to fully understand the tragedy of Bigger Thomas and the many similar lives marked by fear, hatred, and oppression. Bigger's story is the type of story African American Christianity seeks to understand, a story of suffocating shame, the deadly folly of Sin, and the complexity of life in an unjust, racialized society. *Native Son* is the type of story that demands our most robust theological reflection, particularly on the question of Sin.

Talk of Sin for those outside, and even inside, the church can be seen as repressive and outdated. Truthfully, notions of Sin escort us into reality and into confrontation with the mangled parts of ourselves and the unnamed powers at work for ill in the world. Sin gives us vocabulary for the things too deep for explanation and too pervasive to ignore. When we come to the Scriptures, we find that Sin is always against God (Ps. 51:4). Sin's first and perpetual orientation is vertical: it is an affront to God's goodness and holiness. Though certainly not less than our transgression against God, Sin is emphatically and tragically more. Even if we confine our grasp of Sin to Romans, often ground zero for such reflection, we find that Sin is a power, strong enough to rule over humanity, Jew and Gentile, until the liberating power of grace comes upon the scene. Only the Holy God whom we've offended under the bondage of Sin is powerful enough to free us from the clutches of Sin.

When the apostle Paul sizes up Sin, he recognizes a formidable, personified foe of cosmic proportions. "Paul's remarks in Romans," New Testament scholar Beverly Gaventa observes, "allow for the construction of a veritable résumé of Sin's achievements."[4] In Romans, Sin reigns (5:21) and kills (7:11), even seizing and perverting God's good law in order to produce more Sin (7:8). In the cosmology of the New Testament, Sin is a verb, which "people perform or engage in," because it is a noun, an enslaving power "under which humanity exists" (3:23; 3:9).[5] Understanding Sin as both a verb and a noun helps us grasp how Sin gives birth to Sin in image bearers, enacting its powers of death wherever humans exist, including in systems and structures.

Wright's Apocalyptic Story

Native Son shares a distinct feature with biblical apocalyptic literature. Apocalyptic literature in the Bible "is not prediction but unmasking—unveiling the realities around us for what they really are." "Apocalyptic literature," James K. A. Smith notes, "is a genre that tries to get us to see the world on a slant and thus see through the spin."[6] *Native Son* presses readers to see through a similar prism.

Wright's novel is crafted with an apocalyptic aim to shock and unmask, to compel readers to see on a slant through the lies of American spin. Wright longed to craft a work of protest and unveiling that would force American readers to reckon with the systemic injustice enmeshed in the fabric of our cities and our nation. Despite a positive reception of his first publication, *Uncle Tom's Children*, Wright was disappointed. He lamented that the collection of stories failed to unveil the plight of Blacks in a way that corresponded with the true severity of their daily reality. To put it in biblical terms, his depiction of systemic sin wasn't stark enough to convict readers of sin, righteousness, and judgment (John 16:8). Wright condemned this shortcoming, regretting that "even bankers' daughters could read [it] . . . and feel good about it."[7]

There's nothing to feel good about when reading *Native Son*. It's a dreadful, at times morbid, case study on the devastating power of Sin. Sin casts a long, daunting shadow, and Bigger has a premonition that his fate is inescapable. "I feel like something awful's going to happen to me," he declares repeatedly.[8] Though he dreams of being a pilot—an image Wright uses to portray freedom from the confines of poverty and racism—Bigger knows that's no option for a Black man. So he and his friends settle for impersonating white folks, running wild on the block, masturbating in theaters, and plotting robberies.

Things look up for Bigger when he's offered a chauffeur job for the Daltons, a wealthy white family. Mr. Dalton interviews Bigger, who almost loses the job when Mary, Mr. Dalton's progressive, communist-leaning daughter, begins talking to Bigger like an equal. Bigger is afraid and confused, for no white person has ever spoken to him in this way. Despite Mary's intrusion, Bigger lands the job. But the situation quickly turns precarious when Mary and her boyfriend get drunk in the city with Bigger in tow, forcing him to bring Mary back into her home by himself at the end of the night.

Bigger sneaks Mary inside, deathly afraid of being caught with a white woman in such a compromising position, aware that such an appearance alone would be grounds for jail or a lynching. Once he gets Mary safely to her room, Bigger lingers, touching Mary's body on the bed. Mrs. Dalton enters the room just as Mary, almost blacked out, murmurs. To stop Mrs.

Dalton from moving closer and discovering him in the dark, Bigger smothers Mary with a pillow, suppressing her drunken babbling. After hearing no sound from Mary, Mrs. Dalton inches closer but stops when she smells the booze. Mrs. Dalton assumes Mary has simply passed out and prays by the bed before leaving the room. Bigger goes undiscovered, only then to discover that he has suffocated and killed Mary Dalton.

There's a cruel irony at play that reveals the pervasive effects of Sin. Deathly afraid to be found with a white woman in her bedroom for fear of violent retribution and accusation, Bigger commits a murder, knowing no one in a racist society would have believed the truth. It's not that *Native Son* excuses Bigger's sin by depicting systemic sin and his societal location. But the systemic and the social give context to the personal. This is the stark unveiling Wright lays bare.

Sin's Emergent Feedback Loop

In *Native Son*, Mr. Dalton can see life only through the lens of individualism. He's unwilling to grasp the mutual connectedness between himself, a wealthy white man, and the poor Blacks like Bigger, whom he charges $8 a month to rent his run-down, one-bedroom, rat-infested apartment. After Mary's death and Bigger's capture, Mr. Dalton surprisingly pronounces his forgiveness. He then purchases ping-pong tables for Blacks in the hood, hoping to deter them from following in Bigger's tragic footsteps. Max, Bigger's lawyer, is outraged at Mr. Dalton's belief in such a minuscule act as a vehicle for change. "What do you want me to do?" responds Mr. Dalton. "Do you want me to die and atone for a suffering I never caused? I'm not responsible for the state of this world."[9] Because Mr. Dalton misdiagnoses Sin as purely individual, he misunderstands both his contribution to the city's plight and the true remedies necessary. Wright makes the grieving Mr. Dalton a misguided benefactor who thinks giving ping-pong tables to the impoverished can mitigate Sin in all its devastating power.

In this way, Mr. Dalton functions like an archetypal character, embodying the tendency to think of Sin as existing in a vacuum with no societal factors, consisting only of personal choices. Mr. Dalton would likely respond to Jesus's words that it's better to drown by a millstone hung around one's neck than to "cause one of these little ones to sin" (Luke 17:2) by folding his arms and muttering under his breath, "I'm not responsible for

31

what other people do." Mr. Dalton's view of Sin is thoroughly American, thoroughly individualist, which means it's likely ours too.

What Mr. Dalton fails to see is what many fail to see. When it comes to Sin, personal responsibility, while primary, does not negate the reality of social responsibility. In fact, our individual sinful actions can be understood as contributing to a "body of Sin," giving rise and agency to systems that perpetuate Sin and tighten its already deadly grip among us. Consider how theologian Matthew Croasmun illustrates this systemic notion of Sin using the example of the London Millennium Bridge:

> When the Millennium Bridge opened on June 10, 2000, the crowds who walked across it were in for quite a surprise. The steel suspension over the River Thames began to sway side to side with an ever-increasing magnitude, to the extent that pedestrian access was first limited and then eventually closed entirely for more than a year while the bridge was repaired. The first question that had to be answered was, what was causing the motion of the bridge?[10]

Video footage of the opening day revealed the cause. "It was discovered that the pedestrians on the bridge, in order to keep themselves from falling over due to the swaying motion of the bridge, had to alter their gait in a way that further drove the swaying of the bridge."[11] The bridge had become a feedback loop. The more the bridge swayed, the more people had to walk in step with it, strengthening the bridge's violent movement. Yet the bridge's initial sway could not have happened without human participation, the action that supplied its collective force. Here's the point: "Human agents sin and from these sins, Sin emerges and Sin as an Agent works back on humans to precipitate more sin and sinning. Sin is ontologically dependent for its existence on human sinning."[12] This is the systemic power of Sin. Our actions serve a lord and produce an effect that reaches beyond the power and orbit of the individual. Though this contradicts Western infatuation with individualism, it's more than possible that "persons who oppose sin on a personal level may be drawn into the corporate nature of sin through the evil acts of government, economic structures, and other forms of group identification."[13] If we grasp Sin in its personal and social levels, as both a verb and a noun, our eyes open to the ways in which we are tied up in a mutual garment of destiny, primarily in service either to the dominion of Sin or to the dominion of Christ.

The Black Christian tradition has seen the ugly truth of Sin's duality in the Scriptures and felt its sting in the lives of our people. We have witnessed the choices of individuals coalesce and emerge into a body of Sin, complete with unrighteous systems of dehumanization, discrimination, and death. Martin Luther King Jr. speaks of this unholy emergence: "The plantation and the ghetto were created by those who had power to confine those who had no power and to perpetuate their powerlessness."[14] In the land of the free and the home of the brave, African Americans have been accosted and redlined, trapped like rodents in government-sanctioned ghettos. In recent years, social media has become home to viral, traumatizing videos of Black deaths at the hands of police and fellow citizens. No longer is it a shock to scroll through a feed and see yet another Black image bearer memorialized as a hashtag. Surely, we have seen our Sin, but we have known the Sin of systems all too well.

The Duality of Sin

Read theologically, *Native Son* is, at its core, a soul-crushing look at how systemic sin exacerbates personal sin. Wright drives home this connection with force as our introduction to Bigger unfolds. After Bigger kills the rat and taunts his sister with the dead body, prompting an argument with his mother, Wright details the inner dialogue in Bigger's mind:

> He hated his family because he knew what they were suffering and that he was powerless to help them. He knew that the moment he allowed himself to feel to its fullness how they lived, the shame and misery of their lives, he would be swept out of himself with fear and despair. So he held toward them an attitude of iron reserve. . . . And toward himself he was even more exacting. He knew that the moment he allowed what his life meant to enter fully into his consciousness, he would either kill himself or someone else.[15]

Part of literature's theological power rests in its capacity to create empathy. Literature preserves "public memory" and places us inside the lived experience of another, from which we can reflect biblically.[16] Can you imagine yourself in Bigger's experience, one in which to keep breathing you must resist the thought of your life's utter misery and shame? Many of us, regardless of our ethnicity, don't need to try hard to imagine such an existence. Specifically, in the wake of slavery and Jim Crow's ungodly legacy among us, Bigger's experience captures all-too-real elements of Black life—an at times dehumanizing experience in a society that has historically flexed its systemic muscles to deny or downplay our God-given dignity. This is Sin in one of its many systematic and satanic manifestations. Through a devastating mixture of poverty and racism, systematic Sin crouches at Bigger's door, seeking to devour him (Gen. 4:7). Sin is the personal choice Bigger makes to enact brutal violence, but Sin is also the cosmic power that enslaves his nature, and the systemic poverty and racism around him that make his vile choices enticing, last-ditch efforts at self-assertion in a world that confines him like a rodent.

Sin's Allure and Our Agency

In 1892, African American preacher and theologian Francis Grimké preached a bold message to a group of African American ministers in Washington, DC, living in the midst of Jim Crow's savage inequalities. Grimké declared that character is "more important to the Negro today than anything else. . . . To make our people strong in morals is to render them invincible in the battle of life" and "against the aggressions of his enemies in this country."[17] Before we dismiss this as uplift suasion, the idea that Blacks could ascend to equality with whites if only we acted morally, consider Grimké's wisdom applied to Bigger. Confronted with a society in which "they got things and we ain't," Bigger can't even contemplate his feelings without a desire to lash out in violence. "Every time I think about it," Bigger confesses, "I feel like somebody's poking a red-hot iron down my throat."[18] Thurman captures Bigger's angst with similar imagery: "There are few things more devastating than to have it burned into you that you do not count."[19] Understood theologically, Bigger does not employ the moral resources to swim against the systems of despair, fear, and racism around him. He denies himself access to his feelings, for considering his inner life would unleash the trauma and anger in him, forces which he can only enact unrighteously. Sin is all around him, and Sin is the disease that has enslaved him, a fallen image bearer, making even righteous anger seem impossible.

Trapped in this burning, existential devastation, Bigger seethes with hate, fear, and shame, until his acts of violence give him a rush of freedom he's never known. Again, Thurman provides insight resonant with Bigger's story. Thurman recounts finding a mouse in his home. Despite the broom in Thurman's hand ready to strike, the mouse stands up to him with "a squeal of defiance, affirming the core of his mouse integrity in the face of descending destruction." Thurman finds a parable in the encounter: in the face of destruction, hatred aids the disinherited by creating "a dimension of self-realization hammered out of the raw materials of injustice."[20] For Bigger, self-realization dawns only through enacted hate. Bigger finds freedom and agency not in any path of righteousness but in the clutches of Sin. Speaking with Max, his inquisitive lawyer, Bigger turns introspective:

> Maybe this sounds crazy . . . but I ain't worried none about them women I killed. For a little while I was free. I was doing something. It was wrong, but I was feeling all right. Maybe God'll get me for it. If He do, all right but I ain't worried. I killed 'em 'cause I was scared and mad. But I been scared and mad all my life and after I killed that first woman, I wasn't scared no more for a little while.[21]

That Bigger retroactively considers his killings a means to being momentarily free is a condemnation of the society that could lead the oppressed to such a hate-filled thought and simultaneously a condemnation of the oppressed for buying such a heinous lie. Bigger's words betray both a belittling of God in his transcendence and a belittling of God's image bearers in their dignity. In his introspection, Bigger can't even utter Mary's name, and he gives no mention to Bessie, his Black girlfriend, whom he murdered to escape the police. Even still, Bigger's sin has not taken place in sheer isolation; it's been drawn out of him through the pressures of life in a society where each day of his twenty-year existence was marked by dehumanizing degradation and discrimination.

Is Bigger to blame, or does the charge of Sin and guilt rest at the feet of society? The answer must be yes. A theological reading of *Native Son* sees both society and Bigger as condemned before the holiness of God in their own tragic, transgressive ways. Whether in the context of burning trauma or the comfort of middle-class posh, the potent allure of Sin is that it convinces humanity that Sin is the way to grasp freedom, agency, and power. For the powerful, blinded by Sin's allure and collaborating with its destructive purposes, a false freedom is achieved through the exploitation of God's image bearers. For the oppressed, Sin deceives as well, making acts of violence against God's image bearers a shallow means of satisfying the hunger for vengeance while winning back a long-lost sense of autonomy and purpose. Sin's false promise of autonomy always appeals to our fallen nature, whether we are powerful or powerless. Even the first humans, in Genesis 3, sought independence by violating God's holy law, seeking to be free from God's gracious rule and to exercise self-rule in his place. If the power of Sin is fierce enough to entice humanity to transgression in the garden of Eden, how much more so is its power in the concrete jungles of our broken society?

Yet there is no true freedom in Sin. As Bigger's tale attests, Sin is a bait and switch, offering only a shadowy illusion of autonomy while hiding its actual substance: bondage, judgment, and death. Martin Luther King Jr., who so often embodied the Black Christian tradition with wisdom and clarity, shows this compounding, cyclical power of Sin in his reflections on violence and evil:

> The ultimate weakness of violence is that it is a descending spiral, begetting the very thing it seeks to destroy. Instead of diminishing evil, it multiplies it. Through violence you may murder the liar but you cannot murder the lie. . . . You may murder the hater but you do not murder hate. Returning violence for violence multiplies violence, adding deeper darkness to a night already devoid of stars.[22]

Through an oppressive, racialized society, the body of Sin is at work, crouching at Bigger's door and seizing an opportunity to draw out and multiply the Sin in him through the Sin around him. Bigger is a personal agent, deeply affected but not exonerated by societal systems participating in Sin. *Native Son*'s attentiveness to the duality of Sin—both personal and systematic, verb and noun—evokes the biblical concept of Sin as a pervasive power that affects systems, structures, and individuals.

The Lone Empirically Verifiable Doctrine

Reinhold Niebuhr famously said, "The doctrine of original Sin is the only empirically verifiable doctrine of the Christian faith."[23] History, both ours and the world's, provides the proof. Human Sin is doubly verified by the lengths we go to in justifying our Sin. Bigger's tale of fear, flight, and fate demonstrates in tragic fashion the duality of Sin and its deceptive power. Bigger himself wrestles with the evil of his acts, at times acknowledging their heinousness: "He would say to himself that it was he who was wrong, that he was no good." At other times, Bigger shifts the moral blame, not able to "convince himself" of his own guilt.[24] Notably, the deceptive power of Sin blinds not only Bigger but also the white and powerful. Mr. Dalton, whose daughter dies at Bigger's hands, simultaneously exploits poor Blacks and props himself up as their generous philanthropist in shining armor. Sin's duality and deceptive power, *Native Son* shows us, are universal.

Reading literature theologically means attending to human experiences in the texts to better understand the intersections of our stories with God's story. *Native Son* is a bleak reminder of the pervasive power of Sin in persons and systems, a power that emerges as a feedback loop and a power that deceives. From Bigger's tragic tale, we learn to ponder: Where are we deluded about our active agency in Sin, even in the face of sins committed against us? From the Daltons and broader societal forces, we learn to see ourselves not simply as individuals or neutral moral agents but as those who contribute to the world in allegiance to either the body of Sin or the body of Christ. In both Bigger and the Daltons, we see pieces of ourselves reflected as both those who are complicit in Sin and those who have been sinned against.

African American Christianity is shaped by stories like *Native Son*. Wright's tragic tale reminds God's people that it is not sufficient to call sinners to repent of their sins and not work to remedy the structures in which Sin is perpetuated and exacerbated. At the same time, *Native Son* is a cautionary tale warning us not to indulge Sin through hate, no matter how much others may sin against us. Our forefathers and mothers in the faith urged that we not find in the face of America's brokenness a permission slip to sin against our oppressors or indulge our sinful nature. In the face of such hostilities, we find no excuse for Sin but a greater need for the Spirit of God to help us resist the Sin crouching at our door and walk in the righteousness of Christ's example while working for righteousness (1 Pet. 2:21).

Where a nontheological reading might see Bigger primarily as a victim or a perpetrator, Christian tradition teaches us to see him with theological clarity as one tragically caught in the web of Sin through the systemic Sin of others, the power of Sin over him, and his immoral assertion of power through sinful violence. We are to understand Bigger in the same categories with which we see ourselves: made in the image of God yet located in a world of Sin, trapped by Sin, and an agent of Sin. *Native Son* leads us to cry out, "Who can deliver us—both persons and systems, both the powerful and the disinherited—from this body of Sin and death?"

The Christian tradition is not fixated on Sin out of any masochistic or pessimistic impulse. To understand Sin is to prepare ourselves to grasp the scope of Christ's redemption. To see Sin clearly in its personal and social forms is to reckon with how much our world needs the saving power of

Christ and to see how Christ calls his people to war against Sin and cultivate righteousness. The more we grasp Sin in its vile nature and effects, as *Native Son* illustrates, the more we must hope in Christ, who brings healing as "far as the curse is found."[25] Jesus Christ is the righteous Redeemer who is concerned with the sins of persons and systems. Nothing will escape his watchful eye, and nothing is beyond his transforming grace. Indeed, a day is coming when the body of Sin in all its sinful machinations will be destroyed because of the death and resurrection of Christ, the one who will reconcile and renew all things (Col. 1:20).

God

James Baldwin's *Go Tell It on the Mountain*

What comes into our minds when we think about God is the most important thing about us.

—A. W. Tozer, *The Knowledge of the Holy*

God's Kingdom of justice and peace is not wrought by the love of power, but by the power of love.

—C. René Padilla

The quickest way to create a caricature is to take something true and blow it out of proportion. The two times I wasted money to get a self-portrait done by a sidewalk artist, I was reminded of the exaggerated nature of caricature, because both times the artist stretched the truth and supersized my nose. But the other path to caricature happens when truth is reduced or, worse, erased altogether. All this is a small wound to the ego when it comes to five-dollar festival portraits, but when it comes to the knowledge

39

of God, caricature creates incalculable damage. Without careful attention, our notion of God can easily become that of a domesticated caricature through exaggeration or evaporation. Faith lived from caricatured thoughts of God produces a witness that broadcasts a lopsided caricature of Christianity as the abundant life with God.

James Baldwin's semi-autobiographical debut novel, *Go Tell It on the Mountain* (1953), helps us reckon with dangerous caricatures and domestications of the divine. On his fourteenth birthday, John Grimes, Baldwin's literary alter ego, is hoping to avoid God. John is searching for an escape from the church and the God of his father. The novel captures one day in John's life as he stands on the brink of a sexual and religious awakening as a member of the Temple of the Fire Baptized, a small Pentecostal storefront church in Harlem. Set during a Saturday night tarry service, the novel tells the generational story of John's family—his aunt Florence, his mother Elizabeth, his father Gabriel—showing the way Christianity became a comforting and corrosive force during their migration north.[1] This familial history stands over John most through the abusive presence of his father, Gabriel, a minister with a callous heart and a toxic faith.

For readers, John's crisis becomes our challenge. *Go Tell It on the Mountain* offers us a searing portrait of Christianity as a complex communal phenomenon by depicting the faith as a means of both sustenance and suffocation for its Black adherents.[2] This portrayal of Christianity presses readers to ask if the toxic faith in the novel is endemic to Christianity or the side effect of a misshaped faith. At root, this question is not simply about the hypocrisy of parishioners or the callousness of ministers. It is a question about God—how God is conceived and represented. In this sense, *Go Tell It on the Mountain*'s sharpest theological dimensions are not primarily about the church in general but about the doctrine of God in particular. Though not devoid of religious hope, *Go Tell It on the Mountain* is a critical generational portrait of the toxic Christian practice that emerges from belief in a loveless God.

The hopeful religious dimension of Baldwin's debut is often obscured by his later writing as well as his personal disavowal of institutional Christianity. Both led readers to retroactively oversimplify the novel as a total critique of both the faith and traditional Christian notions of God.[3] Things are more complicated. Baldwin, it seems, lives in the tension that he describes of John's aunt, Florence: he too seems stuck between a "terrible longing to surrender and a desire to call God to account."[4] In his debut, at least, critique is not synonymous with rejection. There is a case to be made that

Baldwin, in his debut, is like a prophetic voice crying out in the literary wilderness, gesturing toward true religion through critique and negation, holding up Gabriel's shriveled Christianity and pointing the finger to decry, How can this faith and the concept of God animating it possibly be whole or holy? Carefully attending to the paradoxes and problematic nature of such a faith as depicted in Baldwin's debut draws us to contemplate the deep importance of how we conceive of God. The very practice and witness of our faith depend on this conception, for from it flows everything.

Where Is God?

Foundational to thinking theologically about *Go Tell It on the Mountain* is the reality that, to some degree, one's lived performance of Christianity cannot be examined in isolation from one's belief about God. If orthodoxy is (ideally) the road to orthopraxy, then the parallel road for heteropraxy is often paved with hidden troublesome notions of the divine. Other factors matter, like one's affections or desire, but largely speaking, the old dictum is true: show me how you live, and I'll show you what you really believe.[5]

Hovering over and behind the familial and ecclesial chaos in *Go Tell It on the Mountain* is a particular notion of God that characters, like John, must accept, reject, or flee, and that readers, like us, must contemplate and interrogate. While there is a hiddenness to the divine in terms of explicit God-talk, notions of God are laid bare, not in statements but in the actions and motives of those who claim to know and represent him.[6] The way religious characters like Gabriel, the ministerial representative of the church, live and act reflects a particular notion of God—that is, at the heart of the novel's religious frame stands a specific, toxic vision of the divine.

The Church and the World

The conception of God at work in the Christianity of *Go Tell It on the Mountain* is a vision of the Christian God devoid and drained of love. The Christianity that animates the Temple of the Fire Baptized is a streak of Pentecostal holiness built on rigid binaries between the world and the church. These sharp distinctions are not entirely useless. They supply the daily bread of meaning and survival. They sustain souls through experiences of the Spirit and keep congregants from being swallowed whole by the violence of their environment.

At the same time, the binary that sustains and protects also warps souls through toxic cloaks of religious hypocrisy that one must use for cover when salvation is believed to produce uncompromised sanctification. All John expects in the church is this high and hard call of sanctification, a withdrawal into a life of fearful separation. To John, if this is salvation, then salvation may as well be damnation, for it is in the world, not in the church or from his father, where John finds glimpses of love and grace.

Because God is drained of love, tragic theological perversions saturate the novel: truth and grace are housed in the beauty and brokenness of the world, while hypocrisy and toxicity are the property of the church. Because the center of the church—its conception of God—is absent of love, affirmation of John's personhood is found outside the church's walls.[7] Baldwin writes:

> It was when John was five years old and in the first grade that he was first noticed; and since he was noticed by an eye altogether alien and impersonal, he began to perceive, in wild uneasiness, his individual existence.
>
> They were learning the alphabet that day, and six children at a time were sent to the blackboard to write the letters they had memorized. Six had finished and were waiting for the teacher's judgment when the back door opened and the school principal, of whom everyone was terrified, entered the room. No one spoke or moved. In the silence the principal's voice said: "Which child is that?"
>
> She was pointing at the blackboard, at John's letters. The possibility of being distinguished by her notice did not enter John's mind, and so he simply stared at her. Then he realized, by the immobility of the other children and by the way they avoided looking at him, that it was he who was selected for punishment.[8]

Baldwin captures the frightening humiliation through the tenor of Revelation, emphasizing the silence, terror, and stillness that connote a sort of judgment day. Conditioned to expect selection for punishment, John is instead surprised and elected for affirmation.

> "Speak up, John," said the teacher, gently.
>
> On the edge of tears, he mumbled his name and waited. The principal, a woman with white hair and an iron face, looked down at him.
>
> "You're a very bright boy, John Grimes," she said.[9]

42

What John has not received from his father or his church, he receives from the world through his principal. This inversion is a gavel judgment against the church. Something rotten rests at the center of one's Christianity if words of grace and dignity are absent in the church but present in the world.

The Word of Disgrace

The word of dignity John hears from the world is so compelling because, from Christianity, as represented by his father, John hears the proclamation not of being beloved but of being disgraced. Gabriel, who bears the name of the biblical messenger, speaks for God in a word of disgrace to John: "His father [Gabriel] had always said that his [John's] face was the face of Satan—and was there not something—in the lift of the eyebrow, in the way his rough hair formed a V on his brow—that bore witness to his father's words?"[10] The question's tilt shows how this word of disgrace spirals John into self-doubt at the most damaging level, that of his God-given personhood. Gabriel reverses God's truth, calling John "Satan" with such regularity that John considers how the contours of his face affirm his father's false gospel that John is not of God but of the devil.

This is a theological perversion in a novel full of them, for it is Gabriel who smacks of the satanic, a sort of evil father who gives evil gifts (Luke 11:13). Behind the shame and abuse Gabriel heaps upon John is Gabriel's own unresolved disgrace. Every glance at John, born out of wedlock, reminds Gabriel of his own infidelities, and without a vision of God who is filled with love and compassion, Gabriel can only suppress his shame and gaze bitterly at the world—including his family—through the rigid binaries of sinners and saints. Gabriel's words confirm the deadness of his soul, but that deadness snatches another living casualty—John—who, through words of disgrace, is turned away from God.[11]

The Heart of the Matter

Through characters like Gabriel, Baldwin's debut mirrors the Bible's serious concern with the dissonance between appearance and substance. Jesus warns of "false prophets, who come to you in sheep's clothing but inwardly are ravenous wolves" (Matt. 7:15). At a pivotal point in redemptive history, the Lord speaks to the prophet Samuel, revealing what matters most in divine assessment: "The LORD sees not as man sees: man looks on the outward appearance, but the LORD looks on the heart" (1 Sam. 16:7). In a way, this verse might best capture the themes at the heart of the novel's pivotal section, "The Prayers of the Saints," which recounts the prayers of John's family—Florence, Gabriel, and Elizabeth—over the course of the night tarry service. Through narrative flashbacks, Baldwin transforms these moments of prayer into vehicles that transport readers past appearances into the hearts and histories of the Grimes family with a penetrating, divine-like perspective.

Through this entrance into time—*chronos*—readers are led to a true sight of *kardia*—the heart. This structural device ultimately exposes the vast and tragic chasm between religious appearance and substance, as especially embodied by Gabriel. Gabriel's true nature is shown during Florence's wailing prayer, as she is aware "that Gabriel rejoiced, not that her humility might lead to grace" but that her prayers "revealed that she was suffering, and this her brother was glad to see."[12]

A Conversion to What?

The reason Gabriel embodies a loveless faith is largely because of his religious origins: he was converted not by or to the love of God but by the love of power supplied him in God's name. Gabriel's pharisaical nature, evident from the novel's earliest moments, is cemented through the heart-level view into his conversion. The silence that follows Florence's prayer during the tarry service, "like a corridor, carried Gabriel back to the silence that had preceded his birth in Christ."[13] Like John after him, Gabriel bears the weight of familial religious expectation. A promiscuous binge drinker, Gabriel rejected the pleas of his pious mother, who until her last breath prayed for his conversion, refusing to "go to her rest until her son . . . should have entered the communion of the saints." Because the context of Gabriel's conversion, as we will see below, is his mother's expectations at the expense of his experience with God, his conversion is detached from the divine. Though Gabriel grasps the "desperate wickedness of his heart," he cannot even personalize and vocalize repentance in his own words ("[he] prayed without words to be forgiven"). The deep guilt and impersonal repentance that mark his conversion will go forth to mark his life. Ultimately, his conversion is driven less by the hope of forgiveness and more by the promise of power:

> He desired in his soul, with fear and trembling, all the glories that his mother prayed he should find. Yes, he wanted power—he wanted to know himself to be the Lord's anointed, His well-beloved, and worthy, nearly, of that snow-white dove which had been sent down from Heaven to testify that Jesus was the Son of God. He wanted to be master, to speak with that authority which could only come from God.[14]

Converted after a one-night stand, Gabriel, in effect, has moved from one lust to another.[15] Without discounting some semblance of genuine guilt in Gabriel, it is a lust for power and a singular drive for validation that form and fuel his conversion. He "wanted power," the sort that comes from a new religious identity ("he wanted to know himself to be the Lord's anointed"). And Gabriel yearns to enact this religious authority upon others as a "master" who "speaks" with the seal of divine endorsement. A man who cannot even vocalize his own repentance wants to become God's mouthpiece to the world.[16] Such are the seeds of the worst forms of Christianity, those that are centered on power rather than love, self rather than Christ. The root of Gabriel's faith is religious power, and the fruit is lovelessness.

Fear and Trembling in Every Direction

Baldwin's portrayal of Gabriel should fill readers with a strong measure of righteous anger. Gabriel's parental abuse, his power-based conversion, his callous hypocrisy, his extreme self-righteousness fueled by deep-seated guilt rightly make him the target of our animosity. But alongside our anger there must live a sense of fear and a sense of trembling. Gabriel is the target of our righteous indignation, but he is also a caution and a measurement for readers' morality, especially for readers of faith. The passion with which we detest Gabriel is the same passion with which we must interrogate where the seeds of his toxic faith and power lust might be found in our own moral and spiritual soil. More generally, Gabriel alerts us to one of humanity's tragic skills: inverting seeking and serving God into seeking God for self-serving ends. If it is in our nature—and it is—to be as audacious as to turn the notion of God into a tool for idolatrous self-gain, then the warning is for the religious and the irreligious: humanity under sin has nearly no restraint; trapped in our self-serving ways and haunted by guilt and shame, we can fashion anything and everything in our broken hands into a means to our ends above all else. Gabriel is one extreme manifestation of the sort of power lust and lovelessness of which we are fully and tragically capable.

Measured against Jesus's teaching, Gabriel stands exposed as one who claims the mantle of prophet but upon examination is "the diseased tree [that] bears bad fruit" (Matt. 7:17). This much seems obvious, but Gabriel's bad fruit is grounded particularly in his attempts to domesticate God. The irony here is that the African American Christian tradition has at its center what is sometimes referred to as a "Big God theology," the sort of faith that would seem to guard against such domestication.[17] As a people who have faced unspeakable pain and endured with unshakable faith, we have believed that God is sovereign and compassionate, powerful and holy, merciful and just, undefeated and good—even as we have walked four centuries in the valley of the shadow of slavery, racism, and evil.

This Big God tradition has largely held that God is both bigger than our suffering and with us in the midst of our fiery furnace. No matter what trials we face, this tradition proclaims that God is still on the throne. Spoken flippantly, those words read like proof of an opiate faith. Spoken in faith, from a person and a people who have limped through serious suffering, those words express trust in the God who sets captives free, who makes a way out of no way, the very God who raises us from the pit of despair, precisely because this very God raised Jesus of Nazareth from the dead. Against the backdrop of this tradition, Gabriel's perversions in the name of the Lord come into more alarming focus: there is a way to live and think that domesticates and shrinks the incomprehensible into the self-serving, to turn, in one's conception, the expansive God of our faith into a small god of our making.

Domesticating the Divine

What does it mean to domesticate God? Domestication implies submission, taking something that one did not control and subduing it into a state of compliance, like an animal that has learned to relinquish its autonomy to heed the call of its owner. Already, then, to put "God" and "domesticate" in the same sentence is to deal with a categorical absurdity: How can a creature domesticate the Creator who is blessed forever? God in his *essence* can never be domesticated. But we can domesticate God in our own diluted understanding, which we then broadcast before others, performing, proclaiming, and prescribing a dysfunctional notion of God either in malice or in blindness.

This sort of domestication is operative in Gabriel's notion of God, and the toxic effects scar everyone in his unholy orbit. Gabriel's vision of God is a strange shape-shifting God, ratcheting up in violence and judgment, enacted by Gabriel, when and where Gabriel's domineering ways are crossed, and decreasing in holiness when and where it serves Gabriel's self-understanding as the Lord's anointed. This is most apparent when Gabriel, as a young, married preacher, meets the irreligious Esther, who quickly becomes an object of his sensual lust, though this is cloaked in his desire to see her repent.[18] As he fixates on Esther, he grows in disgust for his devout wife Deborah, seeing "as though for the first time, how black and how bony was this wife of his" and lamenting "the joyless groaning of their marriage bed."[19] When Esther is not converted by Gabriel's passionate preaching, he acts on his sensual desires. Gabriel then hides his philandering, resulting in death and tragedy. Gabriel's condemnation is compounded when he blames his adultery and its tragic outcomes on Esther because "her mind weren't on the Lord."[20]

Gabriel's domesticated god always bows to Gabriel's self-protecting whims. Gabriel's god gives "cheap grace," as Dietrich Bonhoeffer calls it, "the cheap grace that we bestow on ourselves" in an attempt to skirt having to deal with our guilt and sin before God.[21] Hard legalism gives Gabriel authority over his family as he attempts to maintain a sense of holiness and power despite his hidden shame. Cheap grace permits Gabriel to still envision himself as the Lord's anointed with minimal need to seek repentance and restitution.

What might this mean for us? Possibly the clearest sign of our willful or subconscious domestication of God is when the norms of who God is shift to accommodate, elevate, or validate us at the expense of others. As Timothy Keller often remarks, "If your god never disagrees with you, you might just be worshiping an idealized version of yourself."[22] In other words, if we are already always on the right side with God—never needing to repent, never embarrassingly wrong—then we are likely not fully dealing with God as he is; we are dealing with a dispenser of "cheap grace," a self-styled projection of the divine. The concept known as God then becomes a mental container for a peculiar mix of Christian categories filled with self-indulgence, self-justification, and self-aggrandizement but mentally branded as the one true, undomesticated God.

An Image of the Slave Master's God

The Gospel of John's magisterial prologue declares Jesus as the Word become flesh, full of grace and truth, God incarnate revealed. *Go Tell It on the Mountain* has its own sense of incarnation, but one that is purposefully bent toward a toxic perversion. Gabriel is, as one critic puts it, "the personification of the vengeful God of Baldwin's fundamentalist Christian imagination."[23] Personification, however, does not fully convey the stakes of Gabriel's faith and practice. Gabriel is better understood as a sort of incarnation of a loveless vision of God. In his person and work, Gabriel's toxic beliefs of the divine become enfleshed as a "Christian" life that terrorizes, full of bitterness and lovelessness. As one who "wanted to be master," as one who beats his children in God's name, Gabriel represents the essence of slaveholding religion: the denial of the fullness of God's character and revelation in exchange for a domesticated god who ensures that power remains firmly in one's own hands.[24]

Under the light of Baldwin's later work, Gabriel as a representative of a slaveholding God becomes more pronounced, as does the reflection needed to learn from such a perversion of Christian faith. In *A Rap on Race*, Baldwin decries "the white Christian world" as "being nothing but a tissue of lies, nothing but an excuse for power," and "as removed as anything can possibly be . . . from any sense of love."[25] Baldwin sees the white Christian world of his day as those practicing the Christianity of Gabriel, operating from a power lust that prevents them from "even deal[ing] with God," since "God for them seems to be a metaphor . . . for safety."[26] Rather than seeing Blacks and whites as "bound together forever" as neighbors, Baldwin finds the white American Christendom of his time choosing a life of self-love marked by the rabid paranoia that such a life together, a demonstration of Christ's call to neighbor love, would not be an enriching gain but a perilous loss—a loss of status and power.[27] Christian love, it seems, was too much a cross for many to carry.

When our notion of God becomes a tool to avoid what God actually desires, unrighteousness of the starkest form is upon us. History reminds us that in the name of fear and safety, the white American Christendom of Baldwin's era marshaled the violence of racial mobs, constructed prison-like ghettos, and violently advocated for segregation, all in an attempt to not love Black people. Many altered institutions, shed blood, and obstructed justice, all in an effort to stand against a life of love with Black Americans. Much of this evil was sanctioned in the name of the Christian

God.[28] Thus Baldwin lays his critique of hate and racism against Black people at one of their central sources, a broken concept of the divine:

> I suggest that the role of the Negro in American life has something to do with what our concept of God is, and from my point of view, this concept is not big enough. It has got to be made much bigger than it is because God is, after all, not anybody's toy. To be with God is really to be involved with some enormous, overwhelming desire, and joy, and power which you cannot control, which controls you.[29]

Baldwin's words reveal Gabriel and his controlling faith as an early analogue in Baldwin's corpus of white Christianity and its "dwarfed, self-serving image of God."[30]

Mercy for the Loveless

Unlike Wright's *Native Son*, which attempts to make its protest clear by turning Bigger into a flattened character, Baldwin's debut, like most of his novels, maintains a thread of mercy and compassion seen in his exploration of why people are as they are. This compassion and curiosity extends even to Gabriel, a curiosity no doubt inspired by Baldwin's attempts to understand the harshness of his own father, after whom Gabriel is modeled.

Go Tell It on the Mountain gazes upon Gabriel critically—as we have discussed—but also mercifully, believing that to do one necessarily entails doing the other. This gaze, in which mercy and critique are not isolated, is why the novel attends to not simply *what* Gabriel is and does but *why*. There is a reason Gabriel holds to a slave master's religion and its subsequent view of God: this is the view of God that has saturated and formed his consciousness, not just in his conversion, as we've discussed, but in the daily reality of his formative years.

Through Baldwin's attention to backstory—showing *kardia* through *chronos*—he reveals why Gabriel's faith is toxic. Not only was his conversion under power, but his existence was also under the slaveholder's power. In a critical flashback, Gabriel hears his mother's prayers for his sister's safety after a crew of white men gang-raped Deborah (whom Gabriel will later marry). This, alongside his conversion, shows that in Baldwin's hands, backstory is less a method of judgment and more a means for understanding. A brother powerless to protect himself would gravitate toward a view of God that gave him power—power like that of the white men who could snuff out his life at a moment's notice or violate his sister or mother with no recompense.

In this sense, Baldwin portrays Gabriel with the very thing his character lacks—love—by showing how Gabriel became what he is: a loveless man in an environment devoid of love. This in a real sense is an act of mercy. Baldwin does not gloss over the toxicity of Gabriel. The novel seeks both understanding and accountability. Is this not a twofold movement of love?

A Democratic Domestication

Part of Baldwin's prophetic contribution is his insistence that the concept of the divine can be and has been reduced to a self-serving, loveless toy by more than one demographic. This domesticated notion of God is not in any way exclusive to white churches. Growing up and ministering in Black Pentecostal churches, Baldwin discovered that those congregations, and their white counterparts, were shaped by the same tragic principles of "Blindness, Loneliness, and Terror."[31] This religious domestication is therefore a mistake devout people can easily and unknowingly repeat in new but no less destructive ways.

How do we avoid these same mistakes in our knowledge of God and in our living and loving in his world? We must begin reflectively with the imminent threat of possibility: the Christianity of Gabriel—centered on power and glory rather than on Christ and love—is not a relic of the past but a threat of the present. We must then "beware of attitudes," as Michael Ramsey once said to a group of soon-to-be-ordained priests, "which try to make God smaller than the God who has revealed himself to us in Jesus."[32] Out of this watchfulness, Baldwin's suggestion that our "concept of God . . . is not big enough"[33] should not be dismissed quickly, especially on the grounds that this suggestive word comes from a voice outside the walls of the church. Though Baldwin's concept of liberation has places of marked discontinuity, his suggestion placed inside the apostolic sources of the faith is a gift to Christians, a painful rebuke that calls us to divine realignment. How have we, in our living and loving, revealed our concept of God to be smaller than the God of holy love revealed to us in Jesus, the Word become flesh?

The domestication of the divine in Baldwin's debut and the challenge in his words about our notions of God are resolved not in revision but in radical retrieval. We must return to our first love and determine to deal

50

with God, not caricatures of our own crafting.[34] Baldwin's critique of Gabriel's faith and, by extension, American Christianity reminds us of and announces our need for a continuous return to the sources of God's revealing love in Jesus, a love that liberates all recipients into the freedom and fullness of God's good purposes, a love that reconciles creation to Creator, a love that loves the world—sinners and saints—at great cost, just as the Son loved the world to the point of death, even death on a cross. Apart from a continual return to God's revelation of the living and loving Word, about whom the scriptural word testifies, our vision of God will shrink and shift to take on the shape of ourselves and the substance and spirit of our age. Tragically, this means our living and loving will shrink too—scaling down to the size of personal capacities for kindness and forbearance, limited by the self-seeking flesh that resides in us all.

The Primacy of Love

Our ability to obscure the primacy of love is proof that we have kept closer company with self-interest and power than with Christ and Scripture. But power is not Lord; Jesus is. And there is nothing more urgent and central for the people of God than a life of love. This means that love, not in a sentimental sense but in a serious, radical, Christian sense—that is, a *Christ*like sense—must be recentered as the shape and substance of both our faith and our living. A return to a faith marked by love is a return to a faith centered on Jesus. Did not Jesus say that the world would know we are his disciples not by our power but by our love (John 13:35)? Did not Jesus sum up the Father's will for us in the inseparable call to love both God and neighbor (Matt. 22:37–40)? Indeed, if we are to believe the apostle Paul, love, not knowledge, is proof of our abiding knowledge of the triune God (1 Cor. 13:2).

Even with this scriptural witness, there is often an unspoken thought that to affirm love as central to the faith is in some way to discard holiness. This is not only false thinking but also a fast track toward the Christianity of Gabriel, the very opposite of the Christianity of Christ. The apostle John shatters such false binaries, declaring that "God is love"—certainly this is part of what makes him holy—transcendent, a one of one, with whom there is no possible rival or potential comparison. And this love of God is not vacuous but patterned in the self-giving of God in his Son, as 1 John 4:10–11 states: "In this is love, not that we have loved God but that he loved us and sent his Son to be the propitiation for our sins. Beloved, if God so loved us, we also ought to love one another." This love, God's love, then animates us to love in the most staggering way possible: as God loves, giving ourselves for the good of even those who do not love us. We give ourselves for sinners *and* saints, for we know that the line between good and evil runs down the middle of every human heart.

One way we have failed as God's people is that the presence of sound doctrine has made us overlook the absence of Christian love. The apostle Paul tells us that love rejoices with the truth; it has a doctrinal, ethical edge. But we also know that love has an edge of indiscriminate action. Jesus himself "was an extremist for love," to borrow Martin Luther King Jr.'s words.[35] Christians are those who, from faith, strive in the power of the Spirit to become, in miniature, living icons of Jesus, extremists for love.

Though much more can be said about God's love, without a vision of God's love as revealed in the living Word and the scriptural Word, the beliefs about God as displayed in our actions will not expand out to showcase God's expansive love in Jesus but will collapse under the power of our flesh and our allegiance to our comforts. In other words, we will live and love in a way that testifies more to Gabriel's god than to the God and Father of our Lord Jesus Christ. Baldwin's incisive portrait and prophetic words, limited as even brilliant human words are, remind us of an apostolic truth that sets right our theological reversals: we do not control Christ, but "the love of Christ controls us" (2 Cor. 5:14).

Failure to Love

That American Christianity over the centuries has categorically failed to be controlled by love toward those of African descent is partially why some Black Americans continue to wonder if Christianity is the white man's religion. For many Black people, questions of theodicy are heightened. Our psyches do not simply weather the universal pain of life in a broken world. We deal with a particular suffering upon our collective conscience, the disorienting historical trauma that comes from knowing that over the centuries the people who claimed to know God best have terrorized our lineage most. A multigenerational apologetic crisis has at its root the people of God domesticating God—all in an effort to avoid loving like God.

Baldwin's debut speaks an important word to this apologetic crisis though John and Gabriel, a father-son relationship that symbolizes Black

Americans and the Christian God. In John's inquiry, "Is Daddy a good man?" and in his wondering "how to make his father love him," we find questions of divine estrangement inside the fatherly estrangement experienced by John, Baldwin's literary alter ego. What John wonders of Gabriel is what Baldwin wondered of his father and what people have asked of the God Gabriel in part represents.[36] Even Gabriel's words to John—"you're the devil's son"—mirror the words white Christians have claimed that God spoke to Black people, as pitiful heathens trapped under Ham's curse. If Gabriel embodies the spirit of a white, slaveholding vision of god, there is an important symbolic element at work, one that asks, alongside Black people through the centuries with trembling heartache bordering on rage, Is the Christian God like Gabriel, loving his pure "white" sons but hating his illegitimate "Black" children?

Just as Baldwin personally longed for a loving father, Black people collectively have wondered—amid the claims that we are the face of Satan, cursed of Ham—who our true Father is: To whom do we belong? Under whose care do we live? Baldwin's and John's estrangement from their cruel ministerial fathers becomes a symbol of God cursing "the African to a base position of sonship."[37] The failure to love, the selection of power over people, as embodied in Gabriel and the Christianity he represents, have seared the faith of many.

These themes show that while Baldwin left the pulpit, his sermonic edge and religious concern remained and were sharpened to hold the faith accountable to the high call of love. Deep skepticism about the love and goodness of God for Black Americans often exists because of the failure of Christians, over the centuries, to spiritually and politically express Christian love for the other. The absence of embodied Christian love is at the root of the difference between what Frederick Douglass called "the Christianity of Christ" and "the Christianity of this land."[38]

This difference between the Christianity of Christ and that which resembles the faith and god of Gabriel must then be measured not simply by statements of doctrine but by lives of righteousness. The Christian life is not a matter of power but of the reception and practice of love, first the divine love that overflows from the triune God to us, and then this love that is embodied in us and shown to God's world in God's name by God's Spirit.

In his own words and in his own way, Baldwin sensed something of this primacy of love. Baldwin believed, according to one scholar, that Christianity was to be verified "by how it has affected the colored peoples of the world."[39] In other words, the validity of Christianity is tested by loving paternity: Does the practice of the faith demonstrate in action that the "colored peoples of the world" are not the children of the devil but loved and embraced by God the Father?

Whose Words, Whose Witness

Through figures like Gabriel and those whom he represents, this question must be answered in the negative. But this is precisely the novel's critique through negation: the reality, even if overwhelming, of a toxic Christianity does not mean its toxicity is innate; it may mean there is a profound failure of witness. One common refrain in the African American Christian tradition is the rhetorical call, "Can I get a witness?" The task of a witness is to affirm or unfold testimony of who God is, what God has done, what God will do. The theme of witness is paramount in Baldwin's debut. Gabriel believes he is the Lord's witness, but his witness is perverted, driving people away from the God for whom he claims to speak.[40]

Baldwin suggests through Gabriel's conversion, divine domestication, and loveless incarnation that those who most powerfully claim to know and represent God are often the most hazardous, for they do not even know God in any transformative, loving way. They do not deal with the Father, Son, and Holy Spirit but instead commune with fear, power, and control. What they know is not so much God but the control and power that derive from speaking in his name. Taken together, this means that Baldwin's critique, at least in his debut, may not center as much on God in proper theological terms as on the process of how God is understood and co-opted by people for power and control and how churches, both white and Black, go along for this theatrical ride, offering naive "amens!" at every turn.

This failed witness is both an epistemic emergency and a representational tragedy. Those like Gabriel fail to know God in any substantive way and then lead others astray through their venomous representational witness. Baldwin highlights this epistemic emergency when characters repeatedly say to others, "You mark my words." Baldwin charges this common phrase with epistemic significance by using it to illustrate the confusion about who really speaks with "divine authority." As Florence, Elizabeth, Gabriel, and others call people to "mark" their words—often in ways that contradict the assertions of others and the heart-level view granted readers through flashbacks—an epistemic whirlwind comes upon us. Everyone asserts they speak for God. Who, if anyone, is bearing true and loving witness?

A Threefold Witness

Despite those who misconceive and misrepresent God, *Go Tell It on the Mountain* presents a world where God is not left without a witness. Again, it is a voice beyond the church that speaks the truth of God. Roy, Gabriel's rebellious son, speaks against Gabriel's false representation of God the Father, declaring, "I know the Lord ain't as hard as Daddy."[41] It is the words of the knife-toting preacher's son that are to be marked as a declaration of apophatic theology—declaring what God is by declaring what God is *not*. This is a microcosm of the novel's witness, a quiet gesture toward a whole faith through a stark portrayal of its toxic inverse.

The most vivid witness arises when John, despite his desires to escape the faith, is caught up by the Spirit at the conclusion of the night tarry service. John is given a divine vision, difficult to untangle. How one reads this vision plays a significant part in whether the novel represents "an ironic indictment of Christianity" or "a stirring vindication [of the faith]."[42] As expected, faith as both substance and suffocation wars within John's vision. Viewed through the lens of witness, the fact that the Spirit falls upon John and gives him a vision of his father as a demonic figure cements the novel's critique of Christianity. At the same time, John's subversive vision suggests a spiritual hope because something—or Someone—outside of John unveils the truth through his vision: the toxic faith of his father, which John rightly desires to avoid, leads only to despair. Though Gabriel has divine hope for his son, Roy, and only disdain for his stepson, John, it is John who catches the Spirit *and* the truth about Gabriel's false faith. And it is John who "saw the Lord—for a moment only."[43] The unanswered question is whether John can remain in the faith without succumbing to its poisonous manifestation.

This witness of the Spirit is accompanied by the witness of the Word for the sake of truth and mercy. In this way, the narrative suggests that the faith is not toxic by nature, though it readily becomes toxic in the hands of the powerful and fearful. Where Roy speaks as an apophatic witness, Florence bears witness against Gabriel's toxic faith, confronting him with the religious text Gabriel has muzzled in the name of self-protection. "I done read the Bible, too," Florence tells him, "and it tells me you going to know the tree by its fruit. What fruit I seen from you if it ain't been just sin and sorrow and shame?"[44]

In this final confrontation between Florence and Gabriel, Florence is the voice of prophetic witness, a Nathan-like figure speaking the truth about

Gabriel's hidden, scandalous sin—his adultery and "bastard" child—of which Deborah, another witness, wrote in a letter sent to Florence decades earlier. Florence refuses "to go in silence"—her witness will be told from the mountain so that Elizabeth will know "she ain't the only sinner . . . in your holy house" and John will "know he ain't the only bastard."[45] Gabriel can only stammer religious platitudes—"[the Lord] sees the heart" and "be careful how you talk to the Lord's anointed"—as the truth comes to light. In the end, Gabriel, who "done caused souls right and left to stumble and fall, and lose their happiness, and their souls," is being called to account—itself a merciful act that may save his own soul.[46] Because of the love of God, no one is ever too far gone. And, somehow, the novel suggests, God, despite the toxicity of those who most vocally bear his name, will not be left without a voice of truth bearing witness.

Jesus

Countee Cullen's "Christ Recrucified" and "The Black Christ"

The South is crucifying Christ again
By all the laws of ancient rote and rule:
The ribald cries of "Save yourself" and "fool"
Din in his ear, the thorns grope for his brain,
And where they bite, swift springing rivers stain. . . .

Christ's awful wrong is that he's dark of hue,
The sin for which no blamelessness atones;
But lest the sameness of the cross should tire,
They kill him now with famished tongues of fire,
And while he burns, good men, and women too,
Shout, battling for black and brittle bones.

> —Countee Cullen, "Christ Recrucified"

How Calvary in Palestine,
Extending down to me and mine,
Was but the first leaf in a line

Of trees on which a Man should swing
World without end, in suffering
For all men's healing, let me sing.
—Countee Cullen, "The Black Christ"

For a time, I grew up with White Jesus watching over me. Though my mother is a dark-skinned, brown-eyed African from Côte d'Ivoire, what adorned our wall was a photo of a white-skinned Jesus. Each day I passed in and out of our small apartment under his blue-eyed gaze. Recently, I had the chance to ask my mother about that photo of White Jesus. Was this the Jesus she knew back home in her village? Why did we embrace it? What did she think of it now?

The Jesus we receive is of course something we ought to spend a great deal of time considering. This chapter isn't primarily about the literal color of Jesus. That topic has spawned plenty of important writing and reflection, and even a few comical memes. The stakes, however, are inordinately high, for the way we conceive of Jesus's color reveals how we conceive of Jesus's concern. Incalculable damage has been wrought because of the valorization of white and the demonization of Black that White Jesus demands. This is why images of White Jesus, like the one that hung in my home, are so off-putting—they signify that Jesus does not understand or identify with any of us of non-Anglo descent. Yet there is no religious figure who can so empathize with the pain and grit of human experience, including the story of Black Americans over the centuries. White Jesus, de-historicized from his Jewishness and detached from the everyday concerns of the weak and suffering, tells a different story, one in which European values, people, and agendas are supreme:

By wrapping itself with the alleged form of Jesus, whiteness gave itself a holy face. But he was a shape-shifting totem of white supremacy. The differing and evolving physical renderings of white Jesus figures not only bore witness to the flexibility of racial constructions but also helped create the perception that whiteness was sacred and everlasting. With Jesus as white, Americans could feel that sacred whiteness stretched back in time thousands of years and forward in sacred space to heaven and the second coming.[1]

One of the richest sources for combating distortions of Jesus is literary works like Countee Cullen's poems, which sought to course-correct idolatrous notions of White Jesus in real time. Cullen, a son of an African Methodist Episcopal (AME) minister and star of the Harlem Renaissance, was not the first nor the last to contemplate Christ's concern with Black people through an interlocking of Black suffering with Christ's suffering. Still, there is poignancy to Cullen's work, which uses traditional form to offer an untraditional thought: to see Christ as one with suffering Blacks. "Christ Recrucified" (1922) and "The Black Christ" (1929) do what good poems do. They unleash an imaginative confrontation through a startling association of powerful images: Jesus hanging not from a Roman cross but from a southern poplar tree.

Inside the unspeakable trauma of American lynching, Cullen's poems find one of the pillars of the Black Christian tradition. This pillar is the unwavering belief that there is a deep, mysterious connection between Jesus's suffering and Black pain. In the symbolic identification of lynched Black persons with the crucified Christ, we receive constructive shock to our religious imagination and the opportunity to embrace the testimony of Scripture and Black religious thought that Jesus suffered not only *for* us as our representative but also *with* us, in solidarity with the world's despised and forsaken. In this way, Cullen's two poems help us contemplate the paradoxical mystery of the cross by looking at the cross from the poetic, historic, and personal angles that the African American Christian experience offers—thereby deepening the magnitude of Jesus and his sacrifice and inspiring us toward greater faith and love in the process.

The Cross and the Lynching Tree

The depth and religious imagination of "Christ Recrucified" and "The Black Christ" remain locked and inaccessible unless we confront the racial terror of lynching. For Black Americans, the close of the plantation was not followed by comprehensive freedom but by the rise of the lynching tree. Lynching was the primary tool of terror, purposefully designed and widely employed to halt the nascent freedom and agency of Black persons. From the end of the Civil War in 1865 to the civil rights era in the 1960s, roughly five thousand Black Americans were lynched, mainly in the South but all across the face of America.

Numbers are a strange thing. In this case, they disclose the magnitude of a heinous evil and also obscure it. Behind each number stands a man like "Parks Banks, lynched in Mississippi in 1922 for carrying a photograph of a white woman," or an entire family—woman, man, and child—as in the case of "Mary Turner, who after denouncing her husband's lynching by a rampaging white mob, was hung upside down, burned and then sliced open so that her unborn child fell to the ground."[2] These are horrors unspeakable. These are horrors that our natural instincts urge us to suppress, forget, or obscure through the anonymity of the numbers. We must remember rightly if we are to heal and grow. Indeed, we must remember that lynchings were not isolated acts of evil. They were "public spectacles, often announced in advance in newspapers and over radios, attracting crowds of up to twenty thousand people."[3] These numbers too reveal and obscure the staggering depth of evil and sin.

Any reflection on the connection between the cross of Jesus and the lynching of Black persons is indebted, as is this chapter, to the late theologian James Cone and his seminal work *The Cross and the Lynching Tree*. Though separated by two thousand years, the cross and the lynching tree, Cone argues, are the two most emotionally resonant symbols in African American life. While "both are symbols of death, one represents a message of hope and salvation, while the other signifies the negation of that message by white supremacy." Cone details how, "despite the obvious similarities between Jesus' death on a cross and the death of thousands of black men and women strung up to die on a lamppost or tree, relatively few people, apart from black poets, novelists, and other reality-seeing artists, have explored the symbolic connections." This missed connection, Cone argues, is a glaring failure of white theologians. But to confront the pain and connection between both trees is to rescue the cross from being "a harmless, non-offensive ornament" and to remember and thus deal with past and present racial evils.[4] It is also a step toward a fuller grasp of the biblical and historical Jesus for all peoples.

The Cross of Condemnation and Identification

"The South is crucifying Christ again" opens Cullen's 1922 poem, "Christ Recrucified." This first line guides us into the principal crux of Cullen's poem, that the connection between the lynching tree and the cross of Jesus is incontestably a word of moral condemnation and symbolic identification. In the vile lynching of Black persons, the American South, for all its religious fervor and worship, is condemned, and Black persons, for all their perceived worthlessness, are identified in their suffering with Christ.

The subject of this racial terror—"the South"—is condemned as a perpetrator of callous, anti-Christian evil. Identified as a corporate agent—not unlike the notion of Sin discussed earlier in reference to *Native Son*—"the South," through the direct and indirect action of people, churches, and systems, performs and permits a staggering act of sin that proves a staggering moral blindness. In hanging Black people from trees, the Christian South is reenacting on a mass scale the very sort of death that befell the Lord they profess. Like Jesus, who was crucified under the corruption and evil collusion of Israel's religious leaders and Roman power, lynched Black people of the South are similarly innocent sufferers under a collection of persons and forces that claim higher moral ground.

"Christ Recrucified" is framed by moral disgust with and condemnation of the constellation of persons and systems that comprise "the South," those who crucify people "dark of hue." The closing image shows the depths of evil and white supremacy. Ostensibly good, religious white men and women shout, not in resistance or lament but in a perverse religious fervor, for the bones of the lynched. Cullen's moral rebuke is mirrored in the words of AME bishop Reverdy Ransom:

> A Negro may be beaten . . . for an alleged crime against a white person and in many instances no crime at all. He may be tortured and put to death with all the shocking horror of savage ferocity. These things are done within the borders of this nation and have become so common that if the public conscience is not dead, it is at least asleep for the time. The perpetrators of mob violence have ceased to mask themselves, not even shielding themselves with the veil of darkness. They stalk abroad in the open light of day, quite frequently that Day, the holy Sabbath. It is made a gala day, the railroads run excursions to the scene of burning at the stake, children, reared in our [American] Sunday schools and Christian homes are witnesses to these scenes, while men contend with each other for ghastly trophies of the incinerated bodies of the victims. Against all these there is no united voice of protest from the American pulpit.[5]

Cullen's poem intensifies this historical rebuke. The pulpits are quiet and consciences are dormant because the South is enacting a figural killing of their Lord. Connecting those lynched with Christ crucified and the religious South with the "ancient rote and rule" of those who shouted "Crucify!" the poem collapses the two thousand years between Christ and the lynched in an attempt to wake up America to the unfathomable perversion and condemnation we have both wrought and endured.

Really, then, "Christ Recrucified" is an incontestable word of moral condemnation *through* symbolic identification. This word of condemnation convicts through the poem's identification of the lynched with Christ and of Christ with the lynched, both being those who suffer innocently. Though this connection is implicit from its opening, the poem holds its identification of Christ with lynched Black persons until the middle movement ("Christ's awful wrong is that he's dark of hue, / The sin for which no blamelessness atones"). By layering the overlapping images of the crucifixion and lynching, the poem asks the reader a sensory question: How can you not see that what they did to Christ *then*, they who claim Christ are doing to us *now*? Though the Christian South and, by extension, America sang, "I was blind but now I see," many white Christians failed to see the condemning irony between the two trees.

Contrasting the Close

What might Cullen's work mean for our understanding of Jesus? The poem's identification of lynched Black persons with the crucified Christ condemns the South, as we have seen. But on a quieter, secondary note, it offers a hint of solace to the suffering. Through its shock to our imagination, the poem demands readers consider Jesus with and among the wounded and forsaken. Cullen's symbolic link between Christ and the lynched serves our understanding of Jesus through the poetic reminder that Jesus is not aloof from the suffering of the lynched. On the contrary, Jesus is symbolically found among the despised.

While this note of solace through identification is implied and secondary to the poem's stringent condemnation of the American South, Cullen's "The Black Christ" explores the link between Christ and the lynched more overtly and typologically. In this poem, Cullen's church roots are shown more prominently as the poem marvels over God's saving activity:

> How God, who needs no man's applause,
> For love of my stark soul, of flaws
> Composed, seeing it slip, did stoop
> Down to the mire and pick me up.[6]

Yet this grace is also tied to a burden ("until I die my burthen be"). The death of Christ on the cross of Calvary was the first in a cycle of men dying on trees:

How Calvary in Palestine,
Extending down to me and mine,
Was but the first leaf in a line
Of trees on which a Man should swing
World without end, in suffering
For all men's healing, let me sing.[7]

The poem as a whole connects Christ to Black suffering but also explores the tensions and struggles of theodicy therein. Though the ending suggests an intercessory petition, Cone nonetheless writes that in this poem, Cullen, like many before and after him, still "saw the liberating power of 'The Black Christ' for suffering black people."[8] Most notable is the typological connection between Jesus and lynched Blacks ("Calvary . . . / Was but the first leaf in a line / Of trees on which a Man should swing"). To look at the lynched is to be drawn to the preeminent lynchee, whose own unjust suffering controls how we see the lynched, as ones who suffered unjustly like Christ himself.

Thus the close of each poem represents one aspect of the double message that emerges from seeing the connection between the cross and the lynching tree. "Christ Recrucified" closes with its gaze upon the cruelty of the perpetrators, who have a lust for novel wickedness and who clamor for a souvenir from the body they have burned. "The Black Christ" shows a typological thread that ties the suffering of Jesus to the suffering of the lynched. Together, the poems indict white Christianity's moral blindness and gesture toward the liberating power of Christ's cross for the brutalized and suffering.

Considering the Cross Theologically

"No theology is genuinely Christian," writes theologian John Stott, "which does not arise from and focus on the cross."[9] Christ's atoning sacrifice stands, as it must, at the center of Christian faith, practice, and worship. The cross looms large in the minds and hearts of all God's people and in the works of theologians across the centuries. And it will loom large into the ages as we sing praises to "the Lamb who was slain" (Rev. 5:12).

This much is clear and glorious. But how we are to grasp the depths of the atonement is a bit more complicated. The Scriptures speak of Christ's death, its nature and its achievements, through an interconnected set of metaphors or images—substitution, justification, propitiation, redemption, recapitulation, reconciliation—that, at their essence, describe and declare the wondrous achievement that God in Christ has won for us.[10] But there are also theories of the atonement that try to sort and relate the thrilling assortment of atonement images and motifs in order to answer the following:

1. Which image of the cross is primary? (matters of priority)
2. How do the various biblical images of the cross relate to one another? (integration and relationship)
3. How exactly does the death of Jesus accomplish all this? (the mystery of mechanism)

Peering into the wondrous cross brings comfort and salvation to the human heart, but even for the faithful, it is an exercise that can stretch and confound the human mind. Such are the unsearchable mysteries of the crucified God, whose thoughts and ways transcend what our minds and hearts can fully grasp.

While not a substitute for biblical or theological sources, Cullen's two poems help us wade a bit deeper into the wondrous mystery of the cross by contemplating the cross from the poetic, historic, and personal angles that the African American Christian experience offers. From this angle, we can sidestep the two popular errors that befall even the brightest theologians' minds and devoted believers: reductionism (reducing the multifaceted wonder of the atonement to a single image/theory) and relativism (flattening all the images in the atonement).

Both are errors of extremity. One error is like spreading the pieces of a puzzle on a table, finding the biggest piece, and saying, "The puzzle is complete! This piece is all we need." The other error looks at all the pieces and says, "Don't mind their edges, colors, and sizes—put them together however you want." The point of avoiding these errors is not to intellectualize the cross for logical mastery but to create an integrated "faith seeking understanding" that produces devotion, freedom, and praise. For "the proper response to the atonement is not a confident attempt to figure it out; the proper response is *worship*."[11]

Instead of leading to reductionism or relativism, Cullen's poems quietly gesture toward what the Black Christian tradition proclaims in a full-throated shout: that Christ has suffered *for* us and that he has suffered *with* us. In the person and work of Jesus, God accomplished on that old rugged cross the definitive act of atonement and solidarity, which is the ultimate call and cause for worship.

In Our Place: Instead of Us and with Us

This brings us to the heart of the atonement—substitution—what God in Christ did "in our place, instead of us."[12] That Christ's death is substitutionary in nature, that it is for our benefit and on our behalf, means solidarity should be a prominent aspect of our understanding of Jesus and the atonement.[13] Substitution implies solidarity. Karl Barth recognizes such, repeatedly highlighting solidarity as part of the work of Jesus: "He who knew no sin took our place and status, caused our situation to be His, accepted solidarity with us sinners."[14] Indeed, from the start of Christ's ministry, when he, though sinless, steps into the river with sinners for a baptism of repentance, all the way to his death in our place, Jesus joyfully gives his whole self to share in the common lot of the ungodly of the world.

This leads us to representation, a reality inextricable from substitution, one that in fact subsumes the category. In taking our place as our substitute, Jesus represented us. Representation brings us into another aspect of what Christ has done for us: he has acted in our place with us. This idea of incorporation, related to union with Christ, is seen in the stirring testimony of the apostle Paul: "I have been crucified *with* Christ" (Gal. 2:20). The whole of Jesus's incarnation, birth, life, death, and resurrection *for* us is why through his name one is redeemed (Gal. 1:4; Eph. 1:7), justified (Rom. 5:1), reconciled (5:10), and saved from sin, Satan, death, and judgment.

The One Who Suffers for Us and like Us

This limited exploration of the cross sets the table for us to appreciate the unique flavor of the cross as seen in Cullen's interlocking of the cross and the lynching tree. The atonement is a *sensory substitution*; because of his unfathomable love for the world, God in Christ experienced what we should have—tasting the sting of death, the curse of sin, the weight of divine forsakenness, and judgment for us. The Judge was judged in our place. Praise be to God! But the Black lynched and enslaved experienced the news of Christ crucified with an added element of wonder and appreciation.

When they surveyed the wondrous and gruesome cross "on which the Prince of glory died," they saw a *sensory solidarity* of a particular kind.[15] They saw Jesus, Son of God and Son of Man, experience and embrace a manner of death and shame not unlike their own. He died for them, and he died like them.

The cross of our Lord is seen in these two interconnected respects when we ask, as theologian Fleming Rutledge suggests, not only why Jesus died but also why he died by *crucifixion*. Cullen's work subtly stimulates this type of reflection on the manner of Christ's death through its poetic proxy of Black lynched persons with the person of Christ. The poems bring Christ down from theological abstractions into the gritty, vile, shameful public deaths of Black persons hanging from poplar trees. This draws us to consider the "first leaf in a line"—the historical parallels of Jesus crucified on Roman wood. To be crucified, as Jesus was, was to endure the "death of a nobody," a manner of death reserved for those branded the refuse of the world. Refuse needed to die in a manner that told the tale of their worthlessness—with public shame, brutality, humiliation, and suffering. Rutledge describes this as the very nature of crucifixion:

> Bodily functions uncontrolled, insects feasting on wounds and orifices, unspeakable thirst, muscle cramps, bolts of pain from the severed median nerves in their wrists, scourged back scraping against the wooden stripes. It is more than any of us are capable of fully imagining. The verbal abuse and other actions such as spitting and throwing refuse by the spectators, Roman soldiers, and passersby added the final touch.[16]

Here the parallels between our crucified Lord and lynched Black Americans are stark and clear. In such reflection, we must sit again in worshipful trembling over the fact that "Christianity is the only major religion to have as its central focus the suffering and degradation of its God."[17] The public brutality of the lynching tree lifts our eyes and hearts to the one who suffered *for* us (sensory substitution), *like* us (sensory solidarity), and *with* us (incorporation) at Calvary—when we were opposed to him.

This reception and grasp of the atonement opens our eyes and hearts to hold the wondrous doctrinal realities of the atonement—with all their transformative power—alongside the intimate bond that comes from knowing that Jesus understands by bodily experience the traumatic contours of our suffering. Though Cone seems to downplay and, sadly at times, discard some central doctrines of the atonement, he summarizes well the impact of knowing that Jesus has a sensory solidarity with the despised and lynched through his physical suffering:

> In the mystery of God's revelation, black Christians believed that just knowing that Jesus went through an experience of suffering in a manner similar to theirs gave them faith that God was with them, even in suffering on lynching trees, just as God was present with Jesus in suffering on the cross.[18]

The cross is thus the towering monument of God's revelation, displaying and demonstrating the love of God (Rom. 5:8), a love that redeems and saves and broadcasts God in Christ's solidarity and presence with the suffering. What Cone suggests here is reminiscent of Peter Abelard's (1079–1142) moral influence theory of the atonement. A French philosopher and theologian, Abelard is known as the first in a long line of theologians who believe the cross is preeminently a revelation that inspires transformation. This theory holds that the cross reveals God's love, inspiring a moral change in our living for God more than an objective change in our status before God. Against his contemporary Anselm, Abelard saw the cross not primarily as an objective satisfaction for sin but as a subjective inspiration of love returned to God, who in the cross revealed his love for us.[19] The sight of his love transforms us to love God and others in return.

The point of this very limited attention to medieval theology is that it helps us see the long thread of thought in Cone's assessment of how Black people received and understood Jesus's death. The lynched and enslaved saw something subjective in the cross that influenced and inspired them. They saw a revelation of Christ's experiential solidarity with the despised and suffering of the world: themselves. In Jesus, fellowship is found with the one who has tasted, like the lynched, an unearned suffering unto death. Indeed, the whips that lashed him were like the whips that lashed us. The tree on which he died resembled those on which we hung. The two thousand years in between do not matter because Jesus lives and nobody knows the trouble we've seen except he who was unjustly "killed by the hands of lawless men" (Acts 2:23).

This view of the cross is not a rival to the other classic atonement realities but an interrelated companion, another piece of the glorious life-altering and cosmos-altering realities that flow down into the lives of the undeserving from the crucified—and resurrected—flesh of Jesus. Christ's cross is certified solidarity all the way down from each and every angle for all who trust in him. From the Reformational angle of the courtroom, Christ has performed an earth-shattering forensic solidarity, the double imputation of our sin upon him and his righteousness credited unto us. From the two narrative angles of every human story—the sin we commit and the sin committed against us—Jesus stands in saving and compassionate solidarity with the suffering. Restricted from theological education, early African American believers saw their suffering and heard of Jesus's and said, "This God *knows* our pain." The paradox of the cross is that in Jesus's unearned suffering, God in Christ achieved for us salvation and victory over evil, thus transforming every instance of pain and suffering that might lay its heavy hand upon us.[20] Grasping this paradox of the cross inspires hope and faith in the God who makes a way out of no way.

Something about the Name Jesus

This Jesus—the one who suffers for, like, with—is decidedly not the Jesus preached to enslaved and lynched African Americans by white Christian America. White Christians lynched our bodies in the name of the Lord. Before and alongside this assault, they tried to lynch our spirits by giving us a Lord who sanctioned our suffering. This "White Christ" was neither just nor compassionate, allowing and supporting "the justification of slavery" and "the compatibility of Christianity with the extreme cruelty of slavery."[21] This Jesus, white in color and in concern, was a strictly transcendent Jesus, selectively concerned with the things above, heaven and eternity, so that white Christians might powerfully control the things below: profits, bodies, nations.

Like a diamond against a black matte backdrop, this historical background of the slave master's Jesus makes Cullen's poetic claims of intimacy between the suffering of Jesus and the suffering of Black people instructive and inspiring. These poems gaze upon Jesus from a different vantage point, looking at Jesus from below, from the perspective of the Black lynched and the Black enslaved. From this angle, the view of Jesus can become more biblical, not less. When we gaze from below—that is, when we see who and what the suffering see when they gaze upon the crucified Jesus—our view of Jesus becomes more whole. We find that Jesus is not simply transcendent but immanent, concerned not simply with heaven but with earth. Jesus is not a heavenly bystander to our suffering; he stands by us in the fiery furnace then and now. He is the one who is "near to the brokenhearted and [who] saves the crushed in spirit" (Ps. 34:18).

By claiming a poetic intimacy between the assaulted flesh of Black people and the detested flesh of Jesus, we exchange the lies of White Jesus for the scriptural witness: "He was despised and rejected by men, a man of sorrows and acquainted with grief; and as one from whom men hide their faces he was despised, and we esteemed him not" (Isa. 53:3). These poems demonstrate shades of the identification our Black American forebears found in the crucified Jesus. Jesus, for Black Christian imagination, is in the very best sense of the phrase our personal Lord and Savior.[22] Thabiti Anyabwile summarizes this profound reality:

> If the slave had resigned himself to the Savior of European sermons, he would not have found a Friend in such preaching. But in the vacuum created by the intentional intellectual suppression foisted upon bondservants arose a Savior whose affinity for the faithful surpassed anything imagined by Western orthodoxy.[23]

This affinity comes from seeing the echo of our suffering in his own. The despised flesh of the enslaved was drawn to "the one whose despised flesh is the salvation of the world."[24] Moral influence gives way to cruciform attraction. This is why Black Christian faith speaks about, sings of, and worships Jesus so passionately. His sympathy for sinners and sufferers breeds a warm friendship and intimacy that can at times feel a bit cold and detached in other rooms of the great house that is the Christian church. In contemplating Jesus, those despised by the world set their weary eyes on the consummate sufferer whose unjust suffering was transformed into victory and who will do the same for all who look to him. Thus, "the slave found in the person of Jesus, a savior, a friend, and fellow sufferer at the hands of unjust oppressors, who would do anything but fail."[25] Cruciform attraction leads to hope resurrected.

These insights show how these poems reflect the imaginative pathway that gave rise to African American Christianity in the fire of chattel slavery and the backwoods of the master's plantation. In Jesus of Nazareth, the despised of the world find not an enemy who endorses their subjugation but a friend who stands for their spiritual and physical deliverance. This is why there is for Black believers something about the name Jesus. It is the sweetest name we know.

Which Jesus?

There is something about the name Jesus, something so mesmerizing and so powerful that groups and figures try to claim him as their own with exclusive branding rights to the color of his skin, the concern of his heart, and the content of his message. Francis Schaeffer writes this about the challenge of *which* Jesus:

> When I hear the word "Jesus"—which means so much to me because of the historic Jesus and His work—I listen carefully because I have with sorrow become more afraid of the word "Jesus" than almost any other word in the modern world. The word is used as contentless banner. . . . There is no rational scriptural content by which to test it. . . .
>
> Increasingly over the past few years the word "Jesus," separated from the content of the Scriptures, has been the enemy of the Jesus of history, the Jesus who died and rose and is coming again and who is the eternal Son of God.[26]

Schaeffer is right, and the contested and customizable treatment of Jesus has only increased with time. But I'd also offer that the deepest sorrow is not that Jesus is used as a "contentless banner" that has "no rational scriptural content." The separation of Jesus from Scripture, and the story line therein, is a nonsensical and flawed project. Is it possible that the deeper sorrow is when the historic Jesus is constructed of selective and warped "scriptural content," as in the case of the Jesus who kept Black slaves in chains and the plantations humming? It is imperative that we help the world understand Jesus rightly. But the damage wrought by a White Jesus who anointed the slave ship, the plantation, and the lynching tree plagues minority communities and all just-minded folks to this day—an apologetic crisis that may be with us until the last day.

This White Jesus lives on in new, upgraded forms that are deceptively selective, warping the Jesus of Scripture and history into a Jesus of agendas. At times it feels as though the ideological shelves are stocked full and everyone wants you to leave your questions at the door and run to the register and pick *their* Jesus to be *your* Jesus. The choices are plentiful: Compassionate Jesus, Conservative Jesus, BLM Jesus, Blue Lives Matter Jesus, Black Jesus, Warrior–White Supremacist Jesus, as seen in the prison drawings of domestic terrorist Dylann Roof, and even Progressive Protestant Jesus sent by "a God without wrath to bring folks without sin into a Kingdom without judgment through the ministry of a Christ without a Cross."[27] When we warp Jesus's name like the withered hand of the man in Mark's Gospel, I imagine Jesus's response to our conceptual distortion is like his response to the Pharisees' displeasure at his healing of the wound—angry and grieved at our hardness of heart (Mark 3:5). And even as we seek to divide him, he continues to mercifully mend what we have warped, even our conceptions of him.

Who Do You Say That I Am?

African American literature like Cullen's provocative work is then one more gift that forces confrontation with the seismic question that each of us must answer. It is the question Jesus posed to his original disciples: Who do you say that I am? Christian creeds and councils have wrestled with this question, and a new bestseller emerges every few years with a "new" answer to this inquiry. Each of us must attend to this question as well. The obvious danger is to answer apart from the biblical story and thus Jesus's own self-conception. But a more insidious danger comes in selectively dividing the biblical testimony against itself.

False Jesuses are usually not unbiblical in totality; more alarmingly, they are selectively incomplete. False Jesuses are molded and fashioned in subservience to the image of our desire but often with just enough textures of the scriptural data to be convincing. Returning to White Jesus as the prime American historical christological error, let us take caution not to obstruct Jesus's identity by restricting the people with whom he is concerned.

The polarized nature of contemporary American thought and discourse exacerbates our fleshly desire to use favorable selectivity. Hindered by our bent toward self-seeking and self-justification, we all too easily settle for a divided Christ, and thus a divided faith. But we cannot conceive of Jesus rightly without the balance and mystery that come from understanding Jesus through attention to Scripture as authoritative—with history, reason, and experience informing, at another level, our understanding of Jesus and discipleship to him.

Something is gained, something more holistic, as we have seen, when we contemplate the biblical data and story about Jesus from above and from below. To see Jesus from only one perspective—only his loftiness or his lowliness—is to divide Christ.

May it never be. Jesus is true God *and* true man, born of a woman *and* eternally begotten of the Father, the King of the cosmos *and* the peasant who roamed the streets of Nazareth. He died *and* was raised, he is victor *and* exemplar, he forgives *and* he judges. His sacrifice atones for oppressed *and* oppressor, powerful *and* weak, the haves *and* the have-nots. Any impulse to divide Christ is a fast track to christological caricature and the compromised faith that always follows on its heels. Jesus is not the property of the left or the right or an indecisive middle. Jesus meets all peoples and causes and concerns with particular threads of connection and, above all, the confrontation and comfort and transformation that are inextricable from the gospel message. As one great African American preacher often says, Jesus did not come to take sides; he came to take over.[28]

In fact, the surest way to lose the presence of Jesus is to attempt to co-opt him and subordinate his person and agenda to our own. Jesus, as James Baldwin expressed, is "nobody's toy."[29] In John's Gospel, when the crowds tried to prop up Jesus for their agenda, he withdrew from them (6:15). In nearly every other case, Jesus drew near to sinners. Only when people try to usurp his agenda with their own does Jesus pull back from those who, in reality, need him desperately.

The logical question at this point is, Aren't Cullen's poems a case of using Jesus? In his poem "Heritage," Cullen is sensitive to this very charge, writing, "Lord, forgive me if my need / Sometimes shapes a human creed."[30] I would offer that in the case of the poems we have explored, there is a difference between symbolic connection and a subjected conception of Jesus. The historical context of Cullen's work demonstrates how the poems sought to contest the totality of Jesus and unshackle it from entrapments of racial violence and whiteness.

Theologian J. Deotis Roberts valued the "Black Christ"—one who identified with and spoke to the plights of Blacks—but even so, Roberts argues the Black Christ is penultimate. It is ultimately the colorless Christ, who in his person and work reconciles humanity to God and establishes a kingdom not of this earth, which is the very means by which his kingdom transforms this earth.[31]

To see the cross in symbolic connection with the lynching tree is to see the connection Christ's atonement has with the plight of Black Americans while at the same time embracing the global scope of Christ's suffering and solidarity with sinners and sufferers. Galatians 3:13–14, one of the texts that leads to the symbolic proxy between the cross and the lynching tree, emphasizes the global outcome of Christ's suffering:

Christ redeemed us from the curse of the law by becoming a curse for us—for it is written, "Cursed is everyone who is hanged on a tree"—so that in

Christ Jesus the blessing of Abraham might come to the Gentiles, so that we might receive the promised Spirit through faith.

On American soil, this text found a particular fulfillment as Black people saw the connection between the two trees and received the Savior who identified with their wounds and redeemed them into the multiethnic family of God. One tree was a tool of vicious hate and division, while the other bore the fruit of healing and life for the world.

Our Eyes Have Seen the Lord

The recent conversation with my mother about White Jesus did not produce the groundbreaking insights for which I had hoped. I spent most of our conversation trying to convince her that White Jesus really did hang from the wall of our house. "White Jesus?" she said with her face tilted sideways in disbelief. "Jesus isn't white!" I agreed but reminded her that in the photo on our wall, he was. Eventually, the truth came out. White Jesus was a gift from a friend that hung on our wall for a time until we moved to a new city. Why did we hang White Jesus on our wall? "I don't know. I guess, for a little bit, I just didn't think about it much."

Again, we ought to consider carefully the Jesus we receive. Cullen's poems are powerful because they stir up all sorts of historical and imaginative reflection, some of which we have sketched out. But more broadly, these poems press us to consider what image of Jesus hangs not simply on the walls of apartments and homes and churches but on the walls of our imaginations. Which Jesus is figuratively enfleshed through the practice of our lives, our love, our faith?

In taking to heart the elements of substitution and solidarity in Jesus's crucifixion, we avoid dividing Jesus and we gain a deeper wonder of Christ's concern for all people as the one mediator between humanity and God (1 Tim. 2:5–6). I find that these words from Hannah King bring much of what we have covered in this chapter into focus:

> Jesus's death was not only the purchase of our redemption. It was also the greatest and most intimate act of solidarity with those who have been violated. He entered into the nightmare of suffering, not abstractly but concretely. He became a victim of violence with all the physical and psychological terror that entails.[32]

Those inflicting violence upon others would find every reason to trap Jesus in transcendent categories and not attend to this aspect of Jesus's suffering. Both our view of Jesus and our faith practice are enriched as we meditate on Christ, whose cross achieves our salvation and demonstrates his solidarity with the weak, the ungodly, the despised, the forsaken. The cross then calls us to follow his cruciform pattern as his disciples who are by no means above our teacher (Matt. 10:24). This cruciform pattern means putting our sin to death (Col. 3:5–10) and suffering with and for his name's sake (Rom. 8:17). But it also demands our own Christlike solidarity, not with favored religious folks or those who are in vogue among the cultural elite but with the forlorn and the suffering of our neighborhoods. This is not where influence and reputation are found. But it is where we serve Christ, doing for the least of these in his name (Matt. 25:34–40).

This sort of christological understanding does not encourage us to pontificate about liberation and justice only in theoretical terms. This view of Jesus's person and work—suffering for, suffering like, and suffering with—cannot give birth to arrogance or apathy but only to the flames of Spirit-filled love. By seeing the cross as the paradoxical revelation of God's love, his rescue of sinners, and his solidarity with the suffering and the forsaken, we are transformed and enflamed by the Spirit to receive and imitate Christ's love and purged of idolatrous desires that prize only ourselves and our tribe. By his blood, we receive as divine gift a transformation and inspiration in the richest sense: no suffering can extinguish our hope, for our eyes have seen the solidarity and victory of the crucified Lord.

Salvation

Zora Neale Hurston's *Moses, Man of the Mountain*

The theological energy of the Bible is toward *liberation*.
—Esau McCaulley, *Reading While Black*

The Christian life is conducted in story conditions. . . . Story is the primary verbal means of bringing God's word to us. . . . Story doesn't just tell us something and leave it there, it invites our participation.
—Eugene Peterson, *Eat This Book*

"So Hollywood really made a movie about Africans like me," my mother whispered with proud surprise. Together we were watching the film *Black Panther*, and it was the first time she, an immigrant from Côte d'Ivoire, witnessed herself in a Hollywood mirror. Educators are fond of pointing out how books and art can function like mirrors, helping us see ourselves in new and empowering ways, or like windows, giving us fresh perspectives through which to see the world.

For African American Christians, the book of Exodus has been both a mirror and a window with a creative force that is nearly unparalleled.

The story of God's miraculous deliverance of the Hebrew slaves through the mediation of Moses gave Black slaves both a hope of liberation and a place of identification with the God of the Scriptures who sets captives free. Stories, biblical or otherwise, can be mirrors or windows but "also sliding glass doors," which "readers have only to walk through in imagination to become part of whatever world has been created."[1] Without the sliding door of the exodus, there would likely be no African American Christianity as we know it. "No other story in the Bible," observes Eddie Glaude Jr., "has quite captured the imagination of African Americans like that of Exodus."[2]

Zora Neale Hurston's *Moses, Man of the Mountain* (1939) is such an example. Hurston stands tall in a long line of Black bards casting their gourds down the well of the exodus narrative to draw up creative visions of inspiration applied to Black experience. In *Moses*, Hurston combines the biblical story of the exodus with Black folklore to reconfigure the person of Moses as a blend of Old Testament narrative and Black folk legend. For biblically literate readers, *Moses*'s narrative is a mix of the familiar with doses of substantial innovation. By reimagining the exodus, the foundational text of African American faith and cultural history, *Moses* brings us afresh to the sliding door of the exodus narrative. Hurston's reimagining invites theologically curious readers to reimagine and contemplate their participation in both Scripture and the central themes of the exodus—liberation and salvation—by shaking up their cognitive familiarity with the biblical story.

This disruption—Hurston's emphasis on hoodoo and magic and her creative alterations of the biblical exodus story—may make some faithful readers squeamish. But ultimately, *Moses* is a text that drives us back to the biblical text. Hurston, herself a daughter of a Baptist preacher, by no means embraced Christianity, and yet *Moses*, over which she labored for half a decade, can nonetheless instruct believers on the participatory dynamics of the Christian faith. For those who embrace a closed canon but not a closed imagination, Hurston's alternative foray into the world of the exodus and her method of folkloric engagement yields unique lessons for the life of faith about salvation, participation, and liberation.

Understanding Folklore

To grasp the disruptive significance of Hurston's reimagining, we need to understand its genre elements. Black folklore, alongside the slave narrative, is one of the foundational pillars of African American literature. Primarily an oral genre, Black folklore served as a sacred vessel for preserving communal stories and customs and protecting them from being washed away by the onslaught of chattel slavery. Forbidden from gaining literacy, inhabiting native practices, or speaking in their mother tongues, African slaves in the New World spoke folkloric tales to retain a sense of their past and to retell the story of their present with a rebellious slant toward freedom. Black folklore was birthed and designed not for the page but for performance, seen and heard outside the watchful eyes of unjust authorities.

Partially a result of Black folklore's orality and performative nature, its quality and power "has seldom been achieved in the novel, short story, or poetry," observes Ralph Ellison.[3] Hurston, a traveling ethnographer and skillful anthropologist, is the rare Black writer who, throughout her work, encased the shining achievement of Black folklore in novelistic form, broadcasting it to the public and preserving it for generations.

The Exodus in Folklore

In *Moses*, Hurston blends the exodus story with the folkloric tradition in two notable ways, each recasting the biblical story with direct lines of imaginative application to Black lives.

First, there's the figure of Moses, whom Hurston paints as a bona fide African folk figure. This is Hurston's attempt to redeem Moses from being portrayed as white in color and in concern, as depicted in Cecil B. De-Mille's 1923 *Ten Commandments*, the second biggest film of that year. Thus Hurston eagerly draws from the folkloric tradition of Asian and African legend that envisions Moses as "the fountain of mystic powers" who could speak face-to-face with God and is even worshiped as such.[4] Hurston reimagines Moses not as an Israelite but as a grandson of Pharaoh, a child of Egypt, in order to grant him a critical moment of conversion to the side of the suffering slaves. Moses's power is tied not primarily to the Lord but to Moses's mythic journey as a hero, the study of magic, and the power of his right hand. In the biblical text, Moses is a man in the hands of God. In *Moses*, God plays a limited supporting role, as Hurston seeks to make Moses uniquely liberative.

There is also the novel's oral nature. *Moses*'s orality, the way the novel crackles with a lively sense of speech and sound, recasts the exodus as a Black story in Black words. More specifically, Hurston tells her exodus story through the ancestral voice of Negro spirituals, creating a version of the exodus that is deeply African American in both theme—liberation—and sound. The orality of Black folklore, which is meant to be more heard than read, is a difficult feature to capture in written prose. Hurston overcomes this challenge by crafting her exodus retelling with a spiritually tinged Black idiom that registers in the reader's ears even when only consumed with the reader's eyes. A prime example is the arrival of freedom. This moment of liberation sends the enslaved people of Goshen into somber, tearful emotion as they cry out:

> Free at last! Free at last! Thank God Almighty I'm free at last! No more toting sand and mixing mortar! No more taking rocks and building things for Pharaoh! No more whipping and bloody backs! No more slaving from can't see in the morning to can't see at night! Free! Free! So free till I'm foolish![5]

Hurston employs the cadence of a preacher, each anaphoric repetition of "no more" gaining steam, lending her prose the pace and flavor of a riveting sermonic close. This feels like Ralph Ellison's rare achievement: the emotive sights and sounds of folklore captured and preserved in novelistic ink. For most contemporary readers, the refrain "free at last" evokes Martin Luther King Jr.'s rousing close to his 1963 "I Have a Dream" speech. But the certain allusion for Hurston—and what King decades later drew from himself—is in fact the language of the Negro spiritual tradition. Through this rich referent, Hurston places Black slaves' folkloric songs of deliverance inside the narrative of the exodus. Hurston effectively puts the story of the exodus in the mouths of Black people. In situating African Americans inside her mythic exodus narrative, Hurston captures and reinforces in her novel the sort of participatory identification scores of African Americans have carried in their imaginations and hearts.

Moses helps the Black diaspora continue to see themselves inside the biblical story in other ways, such as through the common textures of daily speech known as vernacular. In one of many rhetorical showdowns with his uncle and eventual Pharaoh, Ta-Phar, Moses insults his cowardice in Black vernacular terms: "I'd have to run you down and hem you up before I could get a fight out of you. You don't want no parts of me and I know it; and you know it, and you know that I know you know it."[6] This sort of dissing or playing the dozens invites Black diasporic readers to find themselves linked to Hurston's folkloric retelling of the exodus story through the signification and witticism indicative of Black idiom. Both pivotal moments of liberation and petty moments of conflict are captured in the sounds and cadences of Black experience.

The particularly bold and participatory way Hurston engages with the biblical text—melding it with mythology and enfolding Black experience within it—presses us to evaluate our own posture toward the Word and our own place in God's story, even as we set aside Hurston's theological miscues. On both a metalevel, through Hurston's formation of a folkloric novel that blends biblical narrative with Black experience, and a granular level, through Hurston's use of the vernacular, *Moses* evokes the performative power of folktales by giving Black folks a place in the exodus story. We must then ask, "What is our posture toward the sliding door of Scripture that brings us into the true, strange, and wondrous world of the Bible?"

Participation in Scripture and Story

Hurston's folkloric reappropriation of the exodus helps us inhabit rather than merely assent to—or ignore—the story of God told in Scripture. In this way, *Moses* can be seen as inching us closer to the participatory interpretative patterns of Black Christian slaves. In *Eat This Book*, Eugene Peterson provides a corrective caution to our usual postures toward Scripture, asserting, "It is entirely possible to come to the Bible in total sincerity, responding to the intellectual challenge it gives, or for the moral guidance it offers, or for the spiritual uplift it provides, and not in any way have to deal with a personally revealing God who has personal designs on you."[7] If we would be willing to briefly dismiss our inner lawyers, most of us would confess that the sort of reading Peterson describes is not just possible but commonplace.

In contrast, the Black tradition of drawing from the exodus, in which *Moses* stands and points toward, opens us up to engaging Scripture from a posture of personal participation. A posture of participation unfolds possibilities for creative obedience and deep immersion in God's story. Like our enslaved ancestors in the faith, we read Scripture not as an enclosed tale of redemptive history that happened long ago in cultural moments far away with residual nuggets of inspiration to be mined for modern life. We read Scripture as the living story of the redemptive movement of God forming and molding reality from the very beginning, the metanarrative and true reality crashing upon us even now like a tidal wave. A posture of detachment might identify Scripture as an object to be studied and dissected, its information cataloged and assented to, whereas a posture of participation causes us to seek to study and dissect so as to live shaped by and inside the story revealed. The posture of detachment is natural to those who come to Scripture rich in spirit, feeling no pull of need or urgency for the living God. Those who hunger and thirst for the rectifying power and presence of God cannot afford detachment. Instead they hunger and thirst for a sustaining word from God.

For African American slaves, the exodus was precisely this sort of life-giving word. They grasped its plotlines clearly: It is God who owns reality, not the slave master—whether Pharaoh or the white man. It is God who makes a way out of no way. It is God who graciously saves, frees, and claims those whom the world despises. Because our ancestors read and heard the exodus under the force of chain and whip, it could not be an abstract tale. In the exodus, they entered a story with a pulse, a living story that sustained them as well as the generations to come. In entering and believing this story, and the God whom it revealed, Black Christian slaves preserved a gift even for the nation that held them in bondage. By finding themselves in the story of the exodus, Black slaves rescued Christianity in America from existing solely in the compromised iteration of a slaveholding faith. As Howard Thurman observes, "By some amazing but vastly creative spiritual insight the slave undertook the redemption of a religion that the master had profaned in his midst."[8] They preserved a more faithful witness of the faith.

Their reception of Scripture, both in hearing and, for those able, in reading, was part of this creative spiritual insight that preserved a faithful Christian witness in our land. The line in the sand between the Christianity of the slaves and that of the slaveholders was their posture toward the exodus: "There is widespread agreement among interpreters of black religion that central to the difference between slave Christianity and slaveholding Christianity was their respective appropriation of the Exodus motif of the Old Testament."[9]

By attending to Scripture and Black experience, Hurston's *Moses* can be seen as a member of this interpretive lineage. Most importantly, that Hurston sees the exodus as narrative to partake of is reminiscent of the slave tradition and can help us retrieve the best of its instincts, instructing us to stretch beyond assenting to God's story to inhabiting it.

There's a participatory overlap between Black folklore, the posture of Black Christian slaves toward the exodus, and Scripture itself. What our folklore encourages and how our ancestors read the exodus—that is, appropriation of and participation in the tale told—Scripture, in essence, requires. Scripture "calls for appropriation on the part of the believing community—in a word, performance."[10] The gospel is a "theo-drama," the dramatic act of what God has done and will do in Jesus Christ, and our response "should be equally dramatic." Faith, then, "seeks nothing less than a performance understanding." The performance of faith is shaped by Scripture as "the script in and through which the Spirit guides God's people into the truth, which is to say truthful ways of living."[11] The participation and performance that are part and parcel of the Black folkloric tradition point toward Scripture's greater demand of the same participatory posture.

If the people are, as Hurston describes it, "free at last!" then this freedom must be lived into and seized. Spirituals, a genre within the Black folkloric tradition from which Hurston draws, have long embodied this performative scriptural instinct. Consider the words of a well-known spiritual: "Didn't my Lord deliver Daniel, an' why not-a every man?" Here Scripture is appropriated and applied to the plight of the slave in accord with a vibrant belief in God's power to accomplish one's deliverance—that is, salvation. A sophisticated foundation underlies the simple words. To place "every man" in the lineage of the Lord's deliverance of Daniel is to believe that Daniel's Lord is not limited to the acts of old but is *still* active, *still* unfolding his drama of redemption, even in our time. It is to believe that the Lord is not for some people but for *every* person. It's divinely sourced encouragement to the slave and divine rebuke to the slaveholder. Alongside all this, the spiritual holds forth an implicit call through a participatory posture to perform—that is, to live fully into the freedom God gives. *Moses*, and the tradition in which it partly stands, prods us toward seeing the power and activity of God and our place in his theo-drama, a story in which knowing God and being free are not competing ideals but bound up together by divine design.

Reading the Story Right

That Hurston takes up the exodus narrative for reinvention suggests a sense of dissatisfaction with the ways in which the exodus narrative had been read. If her retelling is illustrative of Africa having "its mouth on Moses," it may be that others have improperly had their mouths on this story as well, breathing into it participatory readings less than ideal.[12] Hurston's *Moses* prompts reflection not only on our posture toward the Word and our participation in the story but also on the caution and wisdom necessary for such a task.

The history of interpretation of the exodus warns us that inhabiting the story of Scripture is a discipline that must be done with the utmost care. Albert Raboteau, scholar of African American religion, notes that "from the earliest days of colonization, white Christians had represented their journey across the Atlantic to America as the exodus of a New Israel," while "slaves identified themselves as the Old Israel, suffering bondage under a new Pharaoh."[13] While African Americans saw their experience as parallel to that of Israel, British and Spanish colonizers partook of the scriptural story by replacing Israel. In their reading, they entered into the Scripture story not through the sliding door of humble human identification but upon the red carpet of exceptionalism as the self-identified divinely favored nation. This latter reading effectively displaced Israel from redemptive history through the belief that Israel's role had now been conferred upon the "new" Israel of European Christians. Under this manner of reading Scripture and redemptive history, called supersessionism, colonizers found and fashioned biblical and theological rationale for their conquest of the New World and the enslavement of Blacks and indigenous natives.[14] Thus, when colonialists set their gaze upon the New World, they did so in scriptural terms. When Black people enslaved in the New World caught wind of the exodus, they spoke of their freedom in scriptural terms. When every party places itself at the center of the scriptural narrative, the question becomes, Whose reading—or entering—of the story is right?

Reading Scripture as the story of God in which we partake requires a set of hermeneutical controls and a community that expands beyond tribal lines.[15] This means, as New Testament scholar Esau McCaulley suggests, Scripture is to be read theologically, canonically, and patiently and with attention to social location.[16] Pressing further, the chief protagonist in our reading must be God—the Father, Son, and Holy Spirit. Our place in the story must accord with the metanarrative of the whole Bible and submit to God's standard of righteousness and justice as revealed in Scripture, in step with Christian tradition, and worked out in Christian community. Our relation to other human actors must be rooted in God's body-and-soul concern for all peoples. We must see others—even our enemies—with love and through the lens of the *imago Dei*, a lens we tragically distort when we consider God to be the special servant of our nation or program to the exclusion of others.

The Shape of Salvation

One of the more dramatic narrative alterations *Moses* makes to its biblical source material is portraying the Hebrews as a godless people. "They're down there in Egypt without no god of their own and no more protection than a bareheaded mule," Jethro says to Moses, his son-in-law and protégé, before urging him to evangelize the Hebrews. "How come you can't go down there and lead them out?"[17] By making Moses both deliverer and missionary to the people, *Moses* centers its titular character as an all-encompassing mythic mediator. In *Moses*, the Lord delivers the people not on account of his promise to Abraham and their forefathers (Gen. 12:1–3) but on account of Moses's advocacy and powerful signs.[18] This alteration abandons the centrality of God, which is why Moses will fall short. Liberation is not fundamentally sourced from myths or persons but from the movement of God.

Though Hurston likely makes this alteration to elevate her mythic-heroic view of Moses, making the Hebrews godless underscores the biblical truth that salvation is both revelation and liberation. Despite excising the fulfillment motif of the exodus, *Moses* emphasizes the shape of salvation in the exodus as both revelation ("they're down there with no god of their own") and liberation ("go down there and lead them out").[19]

In describing salvation, the New Testament writers "embraced the Exodus paradigm of salvation to explain the life, death, resurrection and ascension of Jesus Christ."[20] Just as no other biblical story so captured the minds of African Americans, no other biblical narrative so molded the minds of New Testament writers concerning the saving act of God in Jesus:

> The apostle Paul encapsulates this when he writes, "For Christ, our Passover, has been sacrificed" (1 Cor. 5:7; ESV). Describing Jesus Christ as "a lamb without blemish or defect" (1 Pet. 1:19), the apostle Peter states that those who are ransomed by Christ's blood (1 Pet. 1:18) become "a royal priesthood, a holy nation, God's special possession" (1 Pet. 2:9), echoing Exodus 19:6. All the Gospel writers place the death of Jesus at Passover, with John observing that Jesus' bones were not broken, like those of the Passover sacrifice (John 19:31–37; cf. Exod. 12:46; Num. 9:12). Reflecting the consecration dimension of Passover, the author of Hebrews states that Jesus is "the one who makes people holy" (Heb. 2:11).[21]

By gravitating toward the exodus narrative as a controlling paradigm for salvation, African American believers, by instinct, providence, and circumstance, approached the terrain of New Testament writers, finding in the exodus the structure of salvation fulfilled in Jesus, concerned with both knowing God and being free.

This both/and dynamic has been and is debated not on its truthfulness but in its practice. What can the church actually do with its finite energies? Put in the language of Black Christianity in America, is the shape of salvation—and thus the attention of our heart, head, and hands—to be the sin of slavery or our slavery to sin? Is it piety or activism, revelation or liberation?

This tension—the sin of slavery or our slavery to sin—flows through the lifeblood of African American Christianity today and has from its very birth. Raphael Warnock identifies this tension between "personal and social salvation, revivalistic piety and radical protest," as the very center of what he calls "the divided mind of the black church."[22]

It's no profound insight to note that we avoid complexity in the name of simplicity. What it means to be a faithful Christian or church is more straightforward, less strenuous, and less challenging if we buy into a reductionistic mold, if salvation is either all *piety*—being saved by grace and growing in grace—or all *liberation*—working to combat sin's effect in social spheres.

Sometimes we spiritualize things not in the name of simplicity but, ironically, in the name of sin. Returning again to "the divided mind," remember how white Christian denominations failed to the point of not even being divided. By a complex set of sinful factors—including animus, greed, and a supersessionist reading of the exodus narrative—they possessed not a divided mind but a compromised one: they preached against slavery to sin while propagating the sin of slavery in Jesus's name.[23]

The impact of this compromised mind is still among us and, in some cases, in us, firmly lodged between our temples. One common manifestation is a truncated view of salvation that decries Christian social concern as tertiary at best or pejoratively Marxist at worst. Yet when we turn down the volume on our preconceived conclusions, we allow Scripture to clearly speak to the essential need for humanity and creation to be restored to the triune God, and we recognize the dark powers of sin and death that collaborate with our disordered hearts to unleash social and systemic unrighteousness.

This means that a defamiliarized return to the biblical exodus narrative precipitated by Hurston's work can help mend the divided mind. Indeed, the exodus looms large in African American religious imagination precisely because the deliverance of the exodus elides the false dichotomy of a truncated salvation. Hurston's *Moses* points in the same direction—toward imagining a fully orbed salvation, as did our enslaved ancestors: revelation and liberation.

Is our attention, then, to be fixed on the sin of slavery or our slavery to sin? Personal piety in the power of the Spirit or social change in Jesus's name? Liberation or revelation? In the exodus, the Lord frees his people so that they might exist in freedom for him. It is liberation through revelation and atonement. God's revelation (Exod. 9:4, 16, 29; 10:1–2; 11:7; 14:4), the necessity of atonement (13:13, 15), the urgency of liberation (2:23–25), and the subsequent call to holiness (31:13; Lev. 20:8) cannot be isolated. In the exodus, each motif exists in relation, forming the full melody of salvation. The song of salvation is not played in only one key. The contextual pressures of human experience can force us, understandably at times, to prize piety or liberation when truly salvation expands and contains both—and more.

Salvation and Liberation

If *liberation* feels like a term that is both bloated and nebulous, it's partly because the word has been pumped full of competing meanings and concomitant ideologies, from political coups to antinomian manifestos to wholesale theological programs. Nonetheless, we must, as best we can, let the Scriptures set the terms. In *Reading While Black*, McCaulley observes that "the theological energy of the Bible is toward *liberation*."[24] This is liberation as defined and trademarked by the triune God. The exodus reminds us that this liberation in its fullest sense belongs to the realm of God's saving activity, where God attends to both the physical and the spiritual plight of humanity under sin, suffering, and evil. Physical liberation, in many contexts of African American Christianity, has been closely linked to God's order through the *imago Dei* and understood as "the innate desire of all human beings to enjoy freedom of movement and association and the rights of self-determination."[25] Self-determination is liberating only to the degree that God sets the terms—if one's self-determination lives inside the holy orbit of what is determined by God. Self-determination apart from God's revelation leads to the idolatry of the golden calf.

Many of contemporary culture's notions of liberation and freedom co-opt the language and pulse of the exodus and the civil rights movement, only to offer us permission for self-defined, often slickly marketed self-actualization, which turns out to be a set of chains by another name. Upon this tragic path, we become our own golden calves, while corporations collect the profits.

The impulse to link self-expression with liberation is not entirely misguided. At its core, physical liberation biblically conceived is about the embodied expression of our deepest, truest self—it is about the basic freedom to image God, the ability to live and be as God intended humanity to be. At bottom, this means the physical freedom to live and thrive, as we examined earlier. At its climax, the cutting edge of human living, it is both physical and spiritual liberation: restoration with God, cultivating his creation, flourishing in our giftedness, and pursuing harmony with God and neighbor. Under the power of sin and under the thumb of Egypt, the freedom to image God is restricted from within and without. From within, we are blocked from the highest of imaging—worship of God and his healing, saving grace. From without, we are restricted from the basic rights to image—freedom to live, move, and have our being. As the exodus demonstrates, God in Christ is then concerned with a saving program that is multidimensional in its gracious liberating power.

The Movement of Salvation

In Hurston's novel, when Moses details his mission to Pharaoh, he declares, "I am commanded to lead them out of their suffering to something better."[26] Under Egypt's vicious rule, the enslaved could not image or worship God or be guaranteed survival through the day. Hurston's Moses speaks of the movement of salvation: we are liberated *from* something in order to be freed *for* something, something and someone better than Pharaoh.

Salvation does not liberate us unto ourselves but unto God. At the same time, the shape of salvation leaves an indelible mark upon the self. "The story of the Exodus," Raboteau asserts, "contradicted the claim made by white Christians that God intended Africans to be slaves. Exodus proved that slavery was against God's will and that slavery inevitably would end, even though the when and the how remained hidden in the providence of God."[27] The story of salvation—being rescued by God—counters the claims of the world and places upon us a dignity that the world cannot bestow or rescind: the beloved of God.

Subsequently, "by appropriating the story of Exodus as their own story, black Christians articulated their own sense of peoplehood," for the exodus gave and "symbolized their common history and common destiny."[28] This dignity is born of God's saving act in Christ for us but also rooted in how God's saving act counters and reconstitutes our notions of God, the world, and the story of our existence. By God's saving power, we become those who have a new history and destiny, a purpose and direction, a revelation and liberation that is present and forthcoming.

Participation in Salvation

Both Hurston's *Moses* and the Bible's exodus narrative push against a myopic view of salvation that gazes and rests on conversion alone. Salvation is much larger. When the apostle Paul reminds the Corinthian church of the gospel message, he traffics in the tenses of salvation: they received the gospel, they stand in the gospel, and they are being saved by virtue of Christ's gospel work (1 Cor. 15:1–2). The exodus emphasizes the same but narratively, in story form. First, Israel—and many from Egypt (Exod. 12:38)—are saved by the Lord's powerful acts of judgment and deliverance (Exod. 7–14). Then they stand and walk in their redemption as the newly constituted people of God (Exod. 20–34).

Tragically, Israel's refusal to be faithful after the saving acts of God results in decades of wilderness wanderings. Their refusal to faithfully play their part in the story of God's saving program leads to the gradual dissolution of their divine destiny as a light to the nations.

Hurston dramatizes this rebellious spirit in a way that adds imaginative color, through Black vernacular, to the biblical narrative. This rhetorical move enriches the readers' sense of human folly by capturing it in a more recognizable form: their own idiom. She translates the Hebrews' fear and unbelief as Pharaoh's army seeks to hunt them down (Exod. 14:10–12) into Black parlance:

> Voices broke out everywhere and all were sprung with fear. The war chariots of Pharaoh were in plain view now though distant on the plain. Moses could hear many things as he shoved through the camp.
>
> "Couldn't that man find graves enough in Egypt to bury us all without dragging us out here in the wilderness to die?"
>
> "Didn't I say all along that this Moses was some fake prophet? That god he made up out of his own head—"
>
> "Didn't I always tell you all that them Egyptians was nice people to work for? You couldn't find no better bossmen nowhere."[29]

Hurston is regularly interested in dynamics of human weakness that, according to the biblical text, kept Israel from submitting their allegiance and obedience to their God and Redeemer and thereby refusing to partake in the gift of their salvation. Hurston's vernacular rendering is a mirror to readers: under which story and script are we formed—the old empire or the coming kingdom? Of course, what Hurston might simply consider the weak idiosyncrasies of the human spirit, Christianity calls sin, but her dramatization of this proclivity, named rightly or not at all, still points to the fact that getting the slave out of Egypt is not the same as getting Egypt out of the slave. If folklore is the "boiled-down juice of human living," as Hurston once remarked, then Hurston's attention to the people's weakness of spirit teaches an essential lesson about humanity.[30] Under the cross pressures of life's trials, the people, in a heart-level reflex reminiscent of our own, revert to the old scripts—their past conceptions of self and the world—which prize ease over freedom, or in biblical terms, the familiarity of Egypt over the redemption of God. They partake of the old story in which God's mediator is "fake" and the brutal enslaving empire is "nice."

Such conclusions defy rationality and therefore unmask the true culprit: the powerful hold of sin, unbelief, and human fear. The people must be saved not only from Pharaoh's viciousness and idolatry but also from sin and its false scripts that reside inside them. Salvation is both deliverance and formation. Raboteau notes how the exodus story entered the hearts and bones of Black Christian slaves through worship: "Sermons, prayers, and sons recreated in the imagination . . . the travail and triumph of Israel. . . . In the ecstasy of worship, time and distance collapsed, and the slaves became the children of Israel."[31] Made God's beloved through his Son, and by inhabiting his story in the Spirit's power, we are formed further into his image and his ways through faithful participation.

Reaching the Promised Land

Recently, I overheard my mother and aunt—two Black women—lamenting life's endless stream of difficulties and trials. They recounted long tales, recent and past, of pain and disappointment, the loneliness of widowhood, the stress of faltering health, and the sharp sense that while for some the last decades of life are filled with travel and rest, theirs would be a different sort of episode, a rerun of decades previous: hard work for low pay, twilight years of barely getting by. To borrow from Langston Hughes's poem, I was listening to my mother detail how, for her, "life ain't been no crystal stair."[32] Still, at the end of the conversation, I heard my mom utter these words: "This life is hard, isn't it? But somehow, with God, we're going to make it to the end." That hope—making it to the end by the mercy of God—is the hope of reaching the promised land.

If the exodus looms large in African American Christian imagination, so too does reaching the finish line of the promised land. The promised land is a multidimensional motif that speaks to God's saving deliverance partially realized in the present and gloriously complete in the future of eternity. In Black cultural history, it is the day when we possess basic freedom to image God unbothered. Dr. King spoke of this land at the close of his final sermon: "I may not get there with you. But I want you to know tonight that we as a people will get to the Promised Land."[33] Decades later, with racial injustice among us in new and familiar forms, the march to the promised land and the fight for justice in our land, though not without significant progress, still urgently continues.

In redemptive history, the promised land is akin to that great day when, in the words of the Apostles' Creed, "Christ will return to judge the living and the dead." On that great day, all of redeemed humanity will again dwell with God and God with us in the world renewed (Rev. 21:3). It's the day when our wilderness wanderings cease, trials end, and faith is made sight. In the in-between time, faith, faithfulness, wisdom, and endurance are required in abundance. As the old gospel classic puts it, we must "hold on to God's unchanging hand."

In Hurston's *Moses*, liberation is stifled, in part because everything rests in the wrong hands. As the redeemed slaves approach the brink of the promised land, Hurston's Moses departs from his people, then reflects on his journey as liberator and leader and whether one single agent can truly and fully free a people:

> He had meant to make a perfect people, free and just, noble and strong, that should be a light for all the world and for time and eternity. And he wasn't sure he had succeeded. He had found out that no man may make another free. . . . All you could do was to give the opportunity for freedom and the man himself must make his own emancipation.[34]

That these critical reflections on failed liberation come in Moses's introspection through a loosely omniscient narrative voice is suggestive. The mythic Moses falls short, for his power is of his own mighty hand, not of the Lord's. And yet there is a thread of instruction in the failure of Hurston's Moses: liberation is to be seized. Moses's mighty hand cannot set the inner or outer person free—only the Spirit of God can, and joyfully does, for all willing to lay hold of this gospel gift through participation. For whom the Son sets free is free indeed (John 8:36). There is freeing and transformative grace that transcends circumstance—a freedom that chains cannot stifle and death cannot hold. This is the Christian story. And to reach the end of the story, we are called into the movements of the story, loving and living not out of our self-published narratives but together in the theo-drama of the Father, Son, and Holy Spirit.

Racism

Nella Larsen's *Passing*

Race in America is a form of religious faith, and we will never be able to understand or address it with the necessary knowledge, energy or commitment until we comprehend its true architecture.

—Willie James Jennings, "Overcoming Racial Faith"

The Spirit loves women and men, poor and rich, young and old, and every shade of black and white and brown.

—Beth Felker Jones, *Practicing Christian Doctrine*

Film critic Roger Ebert once quipped that what matters with movies is not so much *what* they are about but *how* they are about it.[1] The same is true of literature.

Though the Harlem Renaissance (1918–30s) produced many great works exploring the era of the New Negro, racial prejudice, and new racially liberating ideas, no work quite examined race like Nella Larsen's *Passing* (1929). "Out of all the fiction published during the Harlem Renaissance,"

Passing offers "arguably the most sophisticated attempt to question the very idea of race."[2] *Passing* questions race and racism by demonstrating that racism is a performative pull that draws all manner of peoples into its orbit and scripts, forcing us to consider the nature of race, the narrative of racial hierarchy, and the stories by which we live.

Passing is the ability to publicly present as a different racialized group from one's own. *Passing*'s two central characters—Irene Redfield and Clare Kendry—are both affluent Black women who can pass, when needed or desired, through societal spaces as white—or Black. Larsen's novel centers on this ability and the tense relationship between these two Black women. The novel examines each woman's distinct circumstances and the tragic manner in which their lives and actions collide.

Clare and Irene are a study in contrast. Irene is conservative, risk-averse, focused on her children, and loyal to her race, while Clare is a thrill-seeker, a disinterested mother, and a self-professed betrayer of her people. Only Clare passes fully, immersing her whole life into the realm of white people and marrying a wealthy, racist white man who says of Black people, "I don't dislike them. I hate them."[3] How and why each woman chooses to perform racially demonstrates the nature and danger of our racialized scripts.

Race/Racism's Nature and Challenge

How *Passing* questions the idea of race is more important than the fact that it questions race. A quick glance at its contemporaries shows *Passing*'s unique importance. *Nigger Heaven* (1926), written by Carl Van Vechten, a white patron of the Harlem Renaissance and mentor to Larsen, tries to explore race but paints an exotic picture of Black life in Harlem. George Schuyler's *Black No More* (1931) questions race by showing its absurdity in a satirical manner that would remind contemporary readers of a Dave Chappelle skit. *Passing* addresses race differently.

Neither satirical nor male-centric, *Passing* illustrates both the nature and the challenge of race and racism through its attention to racial performance. By dealing with race through the theatrics of passing, Larsen's novel exposes racism's real nature: less a sentiment and more a script. Racism is a pervasive narrative force that shoves Black people into ways of living that are contradictory, dehumanizing, bold, and fraught. This is the challenge of racism. It sits unseen in the director's chair, arranging persons, particularly Black women, on society's stage to perform—that is, to live—according to its narrative script of racial hierarchy, the belief that white is supreme. On this stage, the outcome is rarely applause but instead bruised psyches, wounded bodies, dead persons.

Passing presents racism as both director and script through race. Together, race and racism form a ubiquitous but quiet director of Black bodies, operating through deception, confusion, and contradiction. The amorphous notion of race is part of racism's nature and challenge. Irene's husband, Brian, implies that he, himself a Black physician living through racism, does not quite "know what race is."[4] A century later, not much has changed. In America, large swaths of Christians remain confused and divided about both the definitions (What is race? What is racism?) and the problem (Is racism real, personal, or systemic?), not to mention any attempted solutions. The sort of sophisticated reflection on race presented in *Passing* is something Christians should welcome, the way one might welcome an invasive surgery: painful yet essential for walking rightly again.

Passing centers on racial performance, the theatrics that accompany one's existence in a world where race and color can bless, curse, or kill. The act of passing is inherently performative, as illustrated in the novel's opening, when Irene flashes back to her first encounter with Clare in years. On the rooftop of the Drayton Hotel, Irene is passing. Unknown to Irene, Clare is giving the same performance. In a chance encounter after twelve years of lost contact, the women reunite as they each perform the racial actions that permit them to luxuriate on a hot summer day. That Irene recounts this rooftop encounter in one of the novel's many cinema-style flashbacks only solidifies the novel's theatrical, performative feel. This element of performance is present even in the novel's structure—Encounter, Re-encounter, Finale—evoking the theatrics of a stage play.

Race Assembled

Passing reveals the nature of race as a construct assembled and reinforced by the tools and hands of Christians. The definitive example comes when, reunited on the Drayton rooftop, Irene learns of Clare's impetus to pass. Irene wonders why Clare risks passing, just as Clare, assertive and knowing, places the social taboo front and center: "I've often wondered why more colored girls, girls like you . . . never 'passed' over. It's such a frightfully easy thing to do. If one's the type, all that's needed is a little nerve."[5] Clare then reveals the initial impetus for her passing. Upon the death of her alcoholic father, Clare, at age sixteen, had no family for refuge besides her father's religious, white aunts.

> "Being good Christians," she continued, "when dad came to his tipsy end, they did their duty and gave me a home of sorts. I was, it was true, expected to earn my keep by doing all the housework and most of the washing. But do you realize, 'Rene, that if it hadn't been for them, I shouldn't have had a home in the world? . . . Besides, to their notion, hard labour was good for me. I had Negro blood and they belonged to the generation that had written and read long articles headed: 'Will the Blacks Work?' Too, they weren't quite sure that the good God hadn't intended the sons and daughters of Ham to sweat because he had poked fun at old man Noah once when he had taken a drop too much. I remember the aunts telling me that that old drunkard had cursed Ham and his sons for all time."[6]

What Clare divulges and the ensuing exchange with Irene form a significant moment of revelation and mutuality. That this is the only place of mutual understanding between Clare and Irene in the entire novel demonstrates just how strongly the script of racial hierarchy has been historically underwritten by Christians. Irene comprehends and asks, "Have you ever stopped to think, Clare, . . . how much unhappiness and downright cruelty are laid to the loving-kindness of the Lord? And always by His most ardent followers, it seems."[7]

To Clare, this observation is not simply a thought but the very story of her origin: "Have I? . . . It, they, made me what I am today. For, of course, I was determined to get away, to be a person and not a charity or a problem, or even a daughter of the indiscreet Ham."[8] Clare passes in order to escape artificial inhuman roles—"charity," "problem," or "daughter of Ham"— that society and often white Christians place upon Black people. Clare is perceived and defined in every way except by her God-given personhood. Thus, passing, for Clare, is not occasional but essential and defensive. It is a way up and a way out, a means of escape from anticreational definitions. In performing life as a white woman, instead of a Black woman, Clare has vistas of agency and social mobility open before her. Because passing makes her the beloved race, Clare is no longer branded a daughter of Ham or a cause for charity but a white woman who can freely live, move, and be in the world.

If Black womanhood seals Clare's denigration but white womanhood secures, briefly, her liberation, what does this reveal about how our world has codified and valued dark and light women? To secure her agency and dignity, Clare becomes, despite the trauma it induces, that which is supreme in the racial hierarchy: white. What is God-given and thus very good—her ancestry and color—must be denied and hidden. In its place, a lie must be performed.

Race as Biological Difference

Clare's words—"I had Negro blood"—demonstrate the fallout of racism and race sanctioned under the banner of Christianity. Her words reveal three essential elements by which race is conceptualized and constructed, chief among them the notion of race as biological difference. We earlier noted the rich manner in which blood functions in *Invisible Man*, and here, in *Passing*, we encounter blood again having a symbolic thickness.

"Negro blood" represents and illustrates the racial ideology "that the races are meaningfully different in their biology and that these differences create a hierarchy of value."[9] "Negro blood" is the building block of race through the myth of biological difference, which is inseparable from the narrative of racial hierarchy. No matter the age or place, this construction of race always preaches this narrative: some are fundamentally different, and if some are fundamentally different, then some groups are fundamentally superior. This narrative of racial hierarchy produces and reinforces a "value gap" in which white lives and standards are supreme and other persons are expendable.[10]

Racism is built on the notion of Clare's "different" blood—her race— which then demands that both she and the aunts live out a particular racial performance. Even familial charity is circumscribed by the construct of race. The charity that Clare receives from the aunts is not far removed from the labor of a house slave: Clare's blood demands that she keep the house in order to earn her keep. Notions of race infuse blood with life-defining power, and the myth of biological difference makes blood the harbinger of race and racism. *Passing* presents the nature of race and racism as that which is crafted through a conceptual narrative of racial hierarchy and enforces a racial performance that doubles back and reinforces both the hierarchy and the performance.

Taken as a whole, Clare's words show that race is constructed to denigrate and direct the lives of image bearers by multiple unholy forces. These are three essential ways that race is conceptualized and constructed. First, the rationale for her familial subjugation is pseudoscientific biological difference (she has "Negro blood" distinct from "white blood"). Second, sociological racism emerges from the notion of biological difference (Blacks need to learn to work). Last, there is the belief in divine sanction for racial subjugation and difference (Clare is among the cursed sons of Ham). In this racial script, biology breeds behavior, and the Bible, so it is claimed, backs it up.

Faith in the Blood

Blood can only transform into a mark of racial and biological difference through the unnatural machinations of persons and systems. Normally, blood does not function in this way. As Karen E. Fields and Barbara J. Fields observe, natural blood "only sustains biological functioning." Thus, if blood "is to perform metaphorical tasks," such as "define a community and police the borders thereof" or "profane and pollute," then "human beings must carry out those tasks on its behalf."[11]

How does this happen? Through a perversion of faith. This is faith not in Christ's blood but in racial blood, the narrative difference of race. Racism, as George Kelsey claims, "is a declaration of faith that is neither supported nor weakened by any objective fact." For Kelsey, "racism is an expression of the will to believe" and consequently an unmistakable form of faith turned idolatrous.[12] Through belief and action, one reinforcing the other in an insidious spiral, faith in the blood of racial difference shapes race and supports racism.

And yet—and this is a central point—this faith is imbibed even by those who have not explicitly assented to the creed of racial difference and the narrative of racial hierarchy. Since the narrative of racial hierarchy is so historic, so atmospheric, mental assent is not always required. Our imaginations have already imbibed it; it is already, to some extent, in us. Through particular social and theological beliefs, the narrative of racial hierarchy and racist action is "imagined, acted upon, and re-imagined, the action and imagining inextricably intertwined." This results in a "mental terrain" and a "pervasive belief" that "Americans navigate regularly."[13]

Family History as American Christians

Passing captures the distinct challenge Christians face when it comes to race and the incalculable damage wrought by Christianity's past insistence on race as a difference in biology. American Christianity has too often been an evangelist for and enforcer of racial hierarchy, promoting the erroneous reading of the curse of Ham (Gen. 9:18–27) and the notion of race as biological difference despite the creation of one humanity in Adam (1:27–28). In theory, Christianity is most equipped to wage war on the myth of racial difference and racism. The *imago Dei* strikes at the jugular of racist ideology. But, as we examined in our discussion of Ralph Ellison and the *imago Dei*, theory is different from practice. To heal, grow, and do better, we cannot play dumb about our family history. We must embrace the full range of our ancestral family tree, affirming the many Christians who fought racism because of their faith while reckoning with the hordes of believers and denominations who were aligned not with God's truth but with the narrative of racial superiority and white supremacy.

A shallow grasp of race and history leads Christians to fight racism as if it were a single skirmish on the individual battlefield of personal emotion and nicety without realizing the battle is part of a complex war fought on fronts beyond what we can see: our imaginations, our assumptions, our notions of difference, our systems, and among principalities and powers. Christianity's ethic of repentance demands the interrogation of self and system in ways few find comfortable. Comforting the comfortable may be why so many contemporary churches are quiet and confused on these matters of life and death, failing to drive the stake of the *imago Dei* into the heart of racial hierarchy by declaring with equal force the dignity of all persons *and* the myth of racial difference/hierarchy *and* the reality of racism. Attacking only one is nearly as impotent as addressing none.

Despite the historic use of science and Christianity to sanction race and racism, both are designed to drive us off the well-trodden path of racism and into a new and open world of equity and dignity. Christian theology and science are, as one should expect, aligned: "In addition to this theological grounding [of the image of God], science has shown us that what we call 'race' is merely an indication of the amount of melanin in one's skin; 99.9 percent of our DNA is identical from one person to the next."[14] There is more biological difference between members of the same ancestry than between persons we would classify as Black or white.

This makes the historic errors of both our faith and our society all the more tragic, demonstrating our need to contemplate our notions of race and racism with our minds and hearts attuned in theological and cultural reflection, the very sort of work *Passing* presents to us.

The Spirit of the Aunts

The sharp critical gaze contemporary readers levy at the aunts for believing in a form of God-sanctioned biological difference and racism is right, but it is only righteous if the response turns reflective. Reading well, after all, means we question characters to question ourselves. Clare notes that the aunts belonged to a particular "generation" that wrote, read, and imbibed biological racism. Wise readers will ask, What of this racist residue can be found in and around me? It is a form of chronological snobbery to think the residual beliefs and effects of biological difference have evaporated from both the world and the church, that our culture could drink so deep and so long from this poisoned well and yet no trace remains in our personal and collective bloodstream. Where these questions go unasked, where the topic goes untouched, a contradictory and volatile view of race lives unquestioned and undisturbed.

In other words, a lack of critical reflection on the notion of race has produced in our churches and society a sort of dissonant racial understanding. Ibram X. Kendi, a highly polarizing writer on race, explains this well:

> I grew up believing the first idea of biological racial difference. I grew up disbelieving the second idea of biological racial hierarchy, which conflicted with the biblical creation story I'd learned through religious study, in which all humans descend from Adam and Eve. . . . My acceptance of biological racial distinction and rejection of biological racial hierarchy was like accepting water and rejecting its wetness.[15]

Many of us have quietly imbibed this dueling racial consciousness, having been taught equity as the ideal but difference as the reality, and thus hierarchy is our quiet, latent, unchecked assumption.

Racial Performance

In *Passing*, the dangers of a dueling racial consciousness become pronounced after Irene learns the extent of Clare's passing. Irene resolves to be "through with Clare Kendry."[16] Why let Clare's passing presence entangle her in a public scandal, tainting her reputation and disrupting her upper-class life? Ever the masterful manipulator, Clare manages to coax Irene to join her again for tea, along with Gertrude, a Black friend from their childhood. Irene's inability to escape Clare, try as she might, represents her inability to find full cover from the shadows of race and racism.

The tea scene demonstrates how racism forces inhumane ways of being in the world upon Black women, often through a dueling racial consciousness. In a just world, Black women speaking of their children ought to be an unremarkable conversation. Under the specter of racism, both the act and the talk of motherhood become a spiraling performance in contradiction, featuring self-affirmation and self-denigration. Gertrude, unlike Clare, has married a white man without passing. Among two Black women married to white men, Irene feels "annoyance," which she later admits "arose from a feeling of being outnumbered, a sense of aloneness, in her adherence to her own class and kind; not merely in the great thing of marriage, but in the whole pattern of her life as well."[17] But Gertrude, like Irene, is mother to two boys, the news of which leads to Clare's declaration:

> I have no boys and I don't think I'll ever have any. I'm afraid. I nearly died of terror the whole nine months before Margery was born for fear that she might be dark. Thank goodness, she turned out all right. But I'll never risk it again. Never! The strain is simply too—too hellish.[18]

This time Clare's words are met with mutuality, not from Irene but from Gertrude.

> Gertrude Martin nodded in complete comprehension.
> This time it was Irene who said nothing.
> "You don't have to tell me!" Gertrude said fervently. "I know what it is all right. . . . No more [children] for me either. . . . It's awful the way it skips generations and then pops out. . . . Nobody wants a dark child."[19]

Racism transforms Black mothers' ordinary talk of their children into the rejection and fear of their own God-given flesh and seed. "The strain" that is "too hellish"—note the religious imagery—and "the way *it* skips generations and then pops out" reflects the lived application of the doctrine of racial hierarchy. These words align Gertrude and Clare with the aunts' belief in "Negro blood." The difference is, while the aunts might represent the powerful whites who craft and drive the narrative, Clare and Gertrude are "de mule[s] uh de world" who experience and internalize it.[20] One constructs and assembles the crossbeams, the others carry them, suffering under the weight and internalizing the shame.

This distinction demonstrates why these Black women might utter such words against their own flesh, not simply out of racial self-loathing but out of self-preservation. If color is the stigma of race inextricably knotted together with racism, then there is a tragic and illuminating calculation behind these statements. In a world that despises Blackness, these women are at once playing by the rules of racism and trying to save their seed from ever having to enter the fray.[21]

The nature of racism poisons human life in a manner so antithetical to God's design that self-loathing becomes a means of self-preservation. Under the specter of racism, mothers do not admire their children's appearance but fear and despise it because of how it will be feared and despised by the world. They are performing within the confines of the script of racial hierarchy that they—and we—have inherited.

Colorism and Class

The tea scene showcases the problem of colorism. Coined by Alice Walker, colorism describes the "prejudicial or preferential treatment of same-race people based solely on their color."[22]

Passing explores colorism at work in the continuation of the tea scene through Irene, who breaks from the racial script and shatters the momentary solidarity between Clare and Gertrude. Irene's emotional range, alongside Clare's and Gertrude's denigration of dark complexion, points to the problem of colorism:

> Irene, whose head had gone up with a quick little jerk, now said in a voice of whose even tones she was proud: "One of my boys is dark."
>
> Gertrude jumped as if she had been shot at. . . . She tried to speak, but could not immediately get the words out. Finally, she managed to stammer: "Oh! And your husband, is he—is he—er—dark, too?"
>
> Irene, who was struggling with a flood of feelings, resentment, anger, contempt, was, however, still able to answer as coolly as if she had not that sense of not belonging to and of despising the company in which she found herself drinking iced teas from tall amber glasses on that hot August afternoon. Her husband, she informed them quietly, couldn't exactly "pass."[23]

Irene's emotions are most noteworthy—internally she is boiling, but externally she is cool and collected—because she is so deeply class conscious. For this reason, Irene, in "even tones" of which "she was proud," affirms her son's dark complexion. The pride here is the pride of class composure above and against her "company." Irene is the unflappable, composed, middle-class Black woman—and proudly so.

In reality, some semblance of anger at this racial hierarchy would be righteous and warranted. But Irene's character is revealed as content to accept colorism if it maintains her class status.[24] Thus, she speaks of colorism "coolly" and "quietly." She plays by the script that preserves her class rank and identity, even as her emotional and moral integrity is compromised.

Colorism and Wounds

Colorism thus has a strong class dynamic, which exacerbates its capacity to wound as an offspring of racism and its powerful reinforcer. Colorism is often manifested as we have seen in *Passing*: the dignifying of light and the denigration of dark. In a racialized society that elevates notions of white, people of color grapple not just with racism in general but with colorism in particular.

Colorism often encourages assimilation into looking white. It is why Clare and Gertrude bemoan the possibility of bearing dark-skinned children. The preference for light skin has a long and foul history in the Black community, from the paper-bag test administered at Black churches to ensure light complexion for membership to the well-known Black children's playground rhyme: If you're white, you're right. If you're yellow, you're mellow. If you're brown, stick around. If you're black, get back.[25] A global export of racism, colorism turns skin-bleaching products into million-dollar money makers for companies around the globe.[26] Colorism explains why "employers of any race prefer light-skinned black men to dark-skinned men regardless of their qualifications."[27] Colorism plagues "millions of dark-skinned black women" with "stunted" romantic prospects; they are either fetishized or cast aside.[28]

Just as sin curves us inward on ourselves, Clare's and Gertrude's embrace of colorism shows how racism bends and wounds in the same direction. Racism and colorism wound one's soul interior. All ethnicities face a profound psychological challenge to not equate dark with inferiority or light with superiority. This challenge is external and internal.

Usually in a well-intentioned way, colorism is combated with colorblindness. But this too has shortcomings. Even those of us who see the fault of colorblindness often stay on the surface of rejecting colorism and do not take the whole and holy plunge into loving Blackness.

Colorism is solved not by colorblindness but by a rich affirmation of God's creative design manifested in our complexion. Affirmation inherently necessitates denial. The affirmation of God's good design is to be flanked by interrogation and repudiation of the spirit of the world—and the spirit of the aunts—which deifies white in order to demonize Black. Dark skin is wondrous, dignified by God in creation. As those made in the image of God, our Black color and ancestry is a heavenly gift, even if the world treats it as a hellish curse. In Jesus's name, this must be made known and made loud. The "Black is beautiful" mantra of the Black Power era was speaking an irrefutable though ignored fact of creation. "To declare, 'Black is beautiful!'" M. Shawn Copeland writes, "states a disregarded theological truth, nourishes and restores bruised interiority."[29] In the sight of God, our lives, our color, our bodies are a gift, not a curse.

Colorism must also be combated through the flesh of Christ. Contra docetism, Jesus was not passing among us in the appearance of man while actually being solely divine (Phil. 2:4–8). Jesus himself descended to embrace brown Hebrew flesh, embodying it as his own, dwelling among us as a dark man, and ascending to the Father's right hand as such. It is a brown-fleshed man who reigns and rules over all things. There are then both creational and christological grounds against colorism. As a true and tangible human being, Christ chose to become brown flesh in order to redeem all flesh. When God revealed himself in the flesh, that flesh was dark. Let that linger. Dark skin is dignified by God in creation, honored in the incarnation, and enthroned right now in Christ's heavenly session. Our labor is to honor God and his image bearers by bringing our imaginations, narratives, and lives under these truths and to condemn any lie that claims otherwise.

The Erasure of Race

As Clare passes with more boldness, entering Irene's social life and family, she becomes more a threat. Irene, in return, begins to believe herself free of the burden of race while using the scripts of racism to endorse violence against Clare, who threatens Irene's stability and status. This is the outcome of racial scripts: escalating danger and calculating self-preserving violence.

Because *Passing* is relayed to us from Irene's vantage point, we as readers are told how different the two women are. There's truth here. Clare herself says to Irene, "Can't you realize that I'm not like you a bit? Why, to get the things I want badly enough, I'd do anything, hurt anybody, throw anything away. . . . I'm not safe."[30] These stark differences are important because they begin to dissolve as Irene's life of stability starts to topple. Racial scripts can be used by the respectable to justify profound hurt and harm.

The novel moves precisely in this direction as Clare, eager to be among Black people, more regularly frequents the Redfields' Harlem social circle. Irene suspects Clare has begun an affair with her husband, Brian. Devastated, Irene plots how to secure her life and marriage:

> Strange, she had not before realized how easily she could put Clare out of her life! She had only to tell John Bellew that his wife—No. Not that! But if he should somehow learn of these Harlem visits—Why should she hesitate? Why spare Clare?[31]

Clare's self-description as a woman willing to hurt anyone to secure her desires is being revealed as true of Irene. What stops Irene, for the moment, is her dueling racial consciousness.

> She caught herself between two allegiances, different, yet the same. Herself. Her race. Race! The thing that bound and suffocated her. Whatever steps she took, or if she took none at all, something would be crushed. A person or the race. Clare, herself, or the race. Or, it might be, all three.[32]

This precarious allegiance to Clare and race is poised to crumble. After Irene, with a Black friend, encounters John Bellew, Irene realizes Clare's jig is up. Bellew can now deduce that his wife associates with Negroes—and is passing, as Irene was at tea.

Irene realizes that Clare is more dangerous as an outed Black woman than she was passing: she is now "free" from Bellew and free to turn her affair with Brian into something more permanent, completely upending the life Irene has constructed. The threat of Clare drives Irene to sever her allegiances to everything but herself and to ponder Clare's total demise:

> Then came a thought which she tried to drive away. If Clare should die! Then—Oh, it was vile! To think, yes, to wish that! She felt faint and sick. But the thought stayed with her. She could not get rid of it.[33]

What shifts in Irene to make her entertain violence against Clare? Threatened by Clare, Irene looses the bonds of race while enlisting the scripts of racism to dream of violence.

Stepping back from *Passing* to consider the story theologically, Irene's disordered desire and racial erasure form a biblical and historical parable. Biblically speaking, Irene's violent ideation highlights James's stark words on idolatry and desire. James 4:1–2 asks incisively, "What causes fights and quarrels among you? Don't they come from your desires that battle within you? You desire but do not have, so you kill" (NIV). Irene desires and possesses, but Clare crouches and threatens, so death is firmly in play, though to be enacted it requires racial reasoning.

Returning to the narrative, Irene's racial reasoning showcases the narrative of racial hierarchy at work through race, class, and gender. Irene resolves to "keep Brian by her side, and in New York," with a series of self-affirmations: "She belonged in this land of rising towers. She was an American. She grew from this soil, and she would not be uprooted. Not even because of Clare Kendry, or a hundred Clare Kendrys."[34]

This creed saves Irene from "the burden of race" by making the first marker of her identity a matter not of race but of class. In her memoir *Negroland*, Margo Jefferson details growing up in 1950s Chicago as part of the Black upper class. Those among this Black elite, Jefferson recounts, believed themselves to be a "Third Race, poised between the masses of Negroes and all classes of Caucasians."[35] Irene does something similar, using class and nation to offset her race. She is a woman of the land of rising towers—industry, capitalism, wealth, and commercial success. Irene is not a Negro American, as the 1920s parlance might say. She is an American with no modifier. Irene eschews race to embrace the identity most conducive to her desire and most likely to endorse Clare's demise. Like a colonizer, Irene sees herself as race-neutral, while Clare is a Black threat, a tragic mulatto; one is entitled, the other expendable. Like a colonizer, Irene lays claim to the soil. No presence of Negro blood or Negro women can stand in her way.

Complicating Notions of Racism

The argument often goes: racism is prejudice plus power; thus by implication Black people are incapable of racism because they are largely systemically and politically powerless. Irene's creed, and the (dis)obedience that her beliefs will produce in the novel's finale, complicates not so much this definition but its implications. Through Irene's evolution and racial reasoning, *Passing* throws a wrench in this line of thought, offering a clearer view of racism's pervasive pull, which makes one internalize racism and enact it upon another.

The "powerless defense," according to Kendi, is the "illusory, concealing, disempowering, and racist idea that Black people can't be racist because Black people don't have power."[36] The primary flaw of this defense is that "like every other racist idea," this belief "underestimates Black people and overestimates White people." Black people "can be racist because Black people do have power, even if limited."[37] Kendi, at least here, is on the right track, not just sociologically but also, inadvertently, theologically. Theologically speaking, a robust grasp of sin democratizes who can be racist while affirming the real and distinct dynamics of power that affect the scale and scope in which different people groups can enforce the ills of racism.

In fact, to think that only those with significant cultural or political power can be complicit in racism is to downplay the performative power of systemic racism and to ignore the atmospheric ways in which racism as sin operates: it pulls a multiplicity of actors and systems into its scripted modes of being and seeing. The sin of racism fuels and sustains a dog-eat-dog world where even those living on the lower sections of the power scales can become incentivized to employ racism and racial difference to secure their desires, to be, for once, those reaping the spoils instead of always being pressed down into the muck.

To be clear, this complication does not validate notions of "reverse racism," the belief that policies and practices that advantage historically marginalized groups like Black people are somehow racist in reverse for not equally advantaging white people. Rather, the complication that emerges from Irene's creedal action demonstrates that we often turn a racialized gaze upon our own—along lines of gender and class—to secure or sustain our social standing. One literary example is how Bigger, early in *Native Son*, robs Black people rather than white people because he knows the cops won't come and won't care. When Kendi writes, "The powerless defense shields its believers from the history . . . of people of color using their limited power to oppress people of color for their own personal gain," do we not find Irene aptly described?[38] As with Irene, our desires battle within us. As we perceive others as a threat, our inherited racial scripts often emerge in our minds, supplying the justification for our cruelty.

As Irene begins to entertain violence against Clare, revelatory light is shed: Irene is also one who passes and, more so, who brings death through violence. Passing as one loyal to her race, Irene in reality dips in and out

105

of racism and classism. The opposite of passing is a healthy embrace of one's ancestry and ethnicity, the sort of concern and identification that is deepened, not erased, by one's allegiance to Jesus, as we'll discuss in our final chapter. But if, like Irene, we allow our disordered desires to rule us, then our fate is sealed. Largely because of Irene's desires and passing, Clare, both by race and by class, is more than expendable.

The Finale

Clare's demise is in effect a lynching. During the last supper before the high-rise party where Clare is betrayed, Brian "spoke bitterly of a lynching that he had been reading about in the evening paper."[39] As Brian explains to his sons the fear and hate that drive whites to lynch "colored" people, Irene halts the conversation: "You're not to talk to them about the race problem."[40] Irene banishes race. The topic threatens her conscience. Moments later, Irene is happy to embrace race, greeting Clare in self-applied racial terms, joking that she "always seem[s] to keep C.P. [colored people's] time, don't I?"[41] Irene presents and passes as Clare's racial ally while contemplating how she can betray her like Judas. The frantic close of *Passing*'s Finale section unfolds under the shadow of lynching, forming the interpretative backdrop against which Clare's death is to be felt and understood.

That Clare's downfall occurs within the thematic frame of lynching illustrates the inability of class status to shield one from the atmospheric assault of racism. As John Bellew crashes the party, searching for Clare and snarling racist slurs, the affluent all-Black space is transformed to operate under the sinister sway of racism. As Clare stands at the full-sized window, "a faint smile on her full, red lips," Irene acts:

> She ran across the room, her terror tinged with ferocity, and laid a hand on Clare's bare arm. One thought possessed her. She couldn't have her free. . . . What happened next, Irene Redfield never afterwards allowed herself to remember. Never clearly. One moment Clare had been there, a vital glowing thing, like a flame of red and gold. The next she was gone.[42]

Despite ascending through passing from familial servitude to wealthy upper-class posh, Clare is killed on account of racism. But the ambiguity of her death—Irene pushes Clare, but Larsen makes it just ambiguous enough—suggests how we obscure our own complicity inside unrighteous systems and scripts. Irene, as we've examined, must sever the bonds of race to push Clare, embracing the superiority of her unmodified American creed. Irene does under the passing guise of race, gender, and friendship what Bellew might have done in his racist rage.

Redeeming and Marking Our Sisters

Passing is a haunting reminder that throughout our national history, Black people, particularly Black women, have especially lived in a space of contradiction, affirming themselves as image bearers while branded anathema by a world awash in racism. In a tragic way, Larsen's own life emphasizes the point. Though it was her husband, a physician, who had an affair with a white woman, it was Larsen who was excoriated in the press. Due to the affair, and a plagiarism scandal, Larsen's social standing was ruined, and she retreated to anonymity as a nurse, never to publish again.[43] Zora Neale Hurston, a fellow member of the Harlem Renaissance, met a similar end, impoverished and forgotten to the point of being buried in a graveyard without the dignity of a tombstone. If this is what happens to our luminaries, what does it say about the way our world views Black women?

The narrative of racial hierarchy, the value gap it births, its atmospheric effects that particularly attack women deemed expendable—the whole matrix of racism must give way to something new. The spirit of the aunts must give way to the Spirit of God, who has been poured out "on all flesh, . . . your sons and your daughters" (Acts 2:17). The Spirit of God comes upon the world to usher in a new order, a new imagination, a new narrative of relating to God and neighbor.

Alice Walker, thirteen years after Zora Neale Hurston's death, marched to her unmarked grave and did something holy: she marked it.[44] This was a sacred act of dignity restored, a resurrection of remembrance: though once forgotten, Hurston would now be commemorated, her existence and legacy as a Black woman certified. Does not Jesus, upon whom the Spirit of God rested, do similar but greater things, both in magnitude and in temporality, for our sisters? This marking Christ performs by his blood, his love, his Spirit. This marking Jesus performs by healing interiors from racism's wounds and strengthening exteriors to be more than conquerors. This marking Jesus enacts by naming the unloved beloved. Jesus blesses by taking those whom racism marks for existential death and resurrecting them to an abundant life of righteous resistance.

Like the Father and the Son, "the Spirit loves women and men, poor and rich, young and old, and every shade of black and white and brown." This trinitarian and "pneumatological love challenges our practices of sexism, racism, and elitism."[45] We remain in need of a renaissance of spirit: we must exhale the spirit of racial hierarchy and inhale the Spirit of God.

Healing and Memory

Toni Morrison's *Beloved*

History, despite its wrenching pain
Cannot be unlived, but if faced
With courage, need not be lived again.

—Maya Angelou, "On the Pulse of Morning"

We are more than what we have suffered, and that is the reason we can do something with our memory of it.

—Miroslav Volf, *The End of Memory*

A peculiar saying is commonplace at one of New York City's thriving churches: "Jesus might live in your heart, but Grandpa lives in your bones."[1] Inside this somewhat cryptic saying is an important insight. The journey to an emotionally healthy life and faith requires honest confrontation with the patterns of the past we carry deep within us. If wholeness is our aim, the past is to be confronted, not denied. Christ may reign in our heart, but his reign must invade the place of our deepest wounds and patterns of being for the purpose of healing.

This question of healing is profoundly crucial for Black people in America. As a communal people, there is baggage in our bones. We carry the stark knowledge of generational suffering. Our social media feeds haunt us with vicarious trauma through dash-cam killings. Our memories house personal wounds that may never be uttered to others. What does healing look like for those who carry Grandpa's default coping mechanism and also a constellation of collective suffering and trauma, both vicarious and personal, from the ravages of racism? In *Healing Racial Trauma*, Sheila Wise Rowe highlights the dire need for reflections that guide us toward healing:

> People of color have endured traumatic histories and almost daily assaults on our dignity, and we are told to get over it. We have prayed about the racism [we have experienced], been in denial or acted out in anger, but we have not known how to individually or collectively pursue healing from the racial trauma.[2]

How might Black Christians specifically process the terror of history in both our personal and ancestral suffering? What does healing look like for those reckoning with unspeakable pain bred in the marrow of memory?

This challenge of healing is the central question of Toni Morrison's acclaimed novel, *Beloved* (1987). Set in 1873, *Beloved* centers on Sethe, a mother and runaway slave now residing in an Ohio farmhouse with her daughter, Denver. Eighteen years escaped from the slavery into which she was born, Sethe is free, but not whole. Part of the horror so intimately depicted in *Beloved* is that the traumas of enslavement do not leave upon reaching freedom but continue to compound and haunt body, mind, and soul. Freedom may be her status, but trauma lives in her bones. For Sethe and the characters still alive after the horror of enslavement at the Sweet Home plantation, *Beloved* asks, Is healing possible, and if so, how can it become actual?

The way *Beloved* guides readers toward healing from racial trauma is through an unrelenting immersion into the dehumanizing horrors of slavery and racial trauma. For this reason, *Beloved* is a painful and demanding text, in subject and form. In Sethe's arduous journey toward healing, we uncover instruction and wisdom for our own.

As with all journeys, certain things are required along the way for us to make it to the destination whole. In *Beloved*, the journey requires searing honesty, redemptive community, and remembering rightly. Following Sethe, we find that our healing is made actual and tangible when we enter honestly into the light and love of community. And community is redemptive only insofar as it risks for the sake of love and teaches us to love our God-givenness. And hope rises only when we reckon with the memories that seek to chain us in despair. The journey to wholeness calls each thread together, weaving a path out of the old and into the new. *Beloved* pushes us into an honest confrontation with pain so that our lives and faith can, through a challenging journey, emerge more whole.

An Honest History

Honesty is where healing begins, and in *Beloved*, historical honesty is hard to bear. Morrison lays out the horrors of enslavement through a mix of the historical and supernatural. The farmhouse in which Sethe resides, at 124 Bluestone Road, is haunted and possessed by the ghost of Beloved, Sethe's dead two-year-old daughter. The challenge of *Beloved* is that Sethe does not simply live with the terrors of racial trauma; she lives inside them.

Beloved's ghost rages against 124's inhabitants, shattering mirrors, making small handprints in food, even permanently driving away Sethe's sons, Howard and Buglar. Sethe is free in one sense but haunted in another, having to "live out her years in a house palsied by the baby's fury at having its throat cut."[3] These revelations, all of which come in the novel's first chapter, are a foretaste of what is foundational to the novel: a blending of genres—the historical (examining slavery), the supernatural (concerned with the spirits), and the gothic grotesque (violence and haunting)—that all coalesce to convey the unrelenting horrors of enslavement.

For readers, especially those coming to the text for the first time, it is easy to miss that none of Morrison's characters are shocked by the presence of Beloved's ghost. Considering the terrors of their suffering, Baby Suggs, Sethe's mother-in-law, proclaims that the haunting that plagues 124 is an unsurprising, national consequence:

> Not a house in the country ain't packed to its rafters with some dead Negro's grief. We lucky this ghost is a baby. My husband's spirit was to come back in here? Or yours? Don't talk to me. You lucky. . . . I had eight [children].

Every one of them gone away from me. Four taken, four chased, and all, I expect, worrying somebody's house into evil.[4]

In Baby Suggs's words, *Beloved* suggests that evil redounds with serious spiritual reverberations. In reading *Beloved*, it is difficult not to consider the shortcomings of secularism. It fails to adequately express and account for the depths of suffering and evil found in this life. Our healing cannot be found in secularism, since it cannot fully account for the world in which we live, love, and suffer.

A Litany of Suffering

"The history of Black people in this country," writes biblical scholar Esau McCaulley, "is a litany of suffering."[5] *Beloved*, as a sort of neo-slave narrative, captures much of this painful litany, plunging readers into the abyss of suffering experienced by Sethe and Paul D. In Morrison's telling, these horrors do not remain in the past but plague every moment of the present. Every day for Sethe and Paul D includes the necessity of work to make ends meet, but even that labor is not primary: "the day's serious work" is the ultimate task "of beating back the past."[6]

The suffering experienced and seen by both characters renders them traumatized and stunted. Without diligently keeping the past at bay, both characters are likely to completely unravel. Sethe's mind is gorged so full of traumatic memories that she laments her "greedy brain," which continues to house horror upon horror.[7] Paul D, subject to slavery and the horrors of a Georgia chain gang, "had to shut down a generous portion of his head, operating on the part that helped him walk, eat, sleep, sing."[8] Doing more than these base functions of survival would require recounting his own suffering and the memory of his friends crushed, lynched, and burned alive.

Morrison captures fragments of narrative and conversation, like slow, unceasing drips of rain, that build a torrent of torment, which steadily drowns readers in the sufferings that accompanied slavery and Reconstruction. In *Beloved*—as in history—Black women, children, and men faced a world where "white people were still on the loose," inflicting suffering; a world consequently where Black pregnant mothers were assaulted and had their milk stolen from their breasts by white boys with "mossy teeth" while their uncle, the slave master, took notes with pencil and paper; a world where "grown men [were] whipped like children," "children [were] whipped like adults," and "whole towns [were] wiped clean of Negroes"; a world where one learned by regular encounter that the stench of human skin stank, "but human blood cooked in a lynch fire was a whole other thing";[9] a world where a Black mother applied a handsaw to the petite neck of her beloved child rather than risk her returning to the plantation to be broken and dirtied worse than the earth's basest animal. The harrowing particulars of the suffering of Sethe and Paul D, of Ella and Baby Suggs, are intimate looks at the evil that happened on an unfathomable scale to women and men whose names history will never utter. *Beloved* bids us sit in the pain of knowing that this story is, as Morrison notes in the novel's dedication, for "sixty million and more."

Suffering and Rage

"To be a Negro in this country and to be relatively conscious," James Baldwin once said, "is to be in a rage almost . . . all of the time."[10] Baldwin's sentiment applies to the experience of reading *Beloved*. To be relatively conscious while reading this text is to feel the tremors of rage, lament, and bewilderment. It is a book that at points must be set down, not because of any shortcomings but because, with intimacy and power, it accomplishes its aim. Stylistically, *Beloved* weaves in and out of its characters' memories of slavery and its brutal assault on the human body and spirit. Morrison fragments the narrative to place readers in Sethe's shoes, demanding that we, like Sethe, reconstruct her suffering with each new piece of her repressed past that she revisits or learns fresh.

As these horrifying fragments of memory emerge, *Beloved* immerses readers in the psychological trauma of enslavement. In taking on Sethe's experience, we find that suffering is not a linear ordeal but a haunting onslaught of trauma, memory, and history that plagues and pounces at any given moment upon the psyche and the soul. Reading *Beloved* means reading gives way to weeping, lamenting, shaking in anger for the sixty million and more for whom these narrative details, and their attendant trauma, were the reality of hell on earth.

In particular, *Beloved* stirs up lament and rage for the devastating anticreational suffering that accompanies the sin of enslavement. In the novel, white people degrade and violate Black people—their fellow image bearers—by tearing their dignity to shreds and dismembering the very good creational design of family at the seams. Sethe, for instance, could not identify her mother by nurture but only at a distance by the shape of her hat. Her mother endured the Middle Passage and the white crew who raped and impregnated her "many times." Sethe's mother tossed overboard all the children she bore from rape by her white captors—"without names she threw them"—but Sethe, born of a Black man and named after him, she kept.[11]

A faith that takes injustice and suffering seriously, both historically and presently, is a faith that makes space for rage in its righteous manifestation. This rage is required, not optional. Without righteous anger, healing is unlikely, for rage is proof that we stared suffering in the eye and saw it for what it is: an affront to the reign of God and the value of his image bearers. A faith that shrugs at suffering is a faith on life support in deep need of revival and reacquaintance with the Scriptures.

The Scriptures speak to the suffering of sixty million and more in part through the ancient suffering of God's people. On Black experience and the question of rage, McCaulley writes, "No one who has read of Black families being ripped apart after having survived the middle passage will fail to see the deep kinship with Israel in our shared stories of trauma."[12] McCaulley points to the imprecatory psalms, specifically Psalm 137, as one of many scriptural texts that resonates with Black Americans—a prayer that calls out with cries of lament and cries for vengeance. Traumatized communities, McCaulley asserts, "must be able to tell God the truth about what we feel . . . and must trust God can handle those emotions."[13] With voices quivering and tears flowing, we must bring our painful memories and traumatic histories to God, who hears our cries.

Healing through Remembering

What is the role of memory when one's history, communal or personal, is marked by intense suffering? Writing about rightly remembering in a world of violence, Miroslav Volf argues that "to remember a wrongdoing is to struggle against it."[14] *Beloved* suggests something similar, demanding that its characters and its readers practice a form of remembering without which healing and recovery are implausible.

By demanding remembrance of the litany and history of suffering, *Beloved* brings readers toward healing. Healing, we learn in *Beloved*, requires honest confrontation with the history and memory of evil. At the same time, *Beloved* reminds us in vivid terms that "a recourse to history will show that as far back into America's story as we want to go we will see the heavy boot of white supremacy stepping on the backs of Black women and men."[15] Just as Sethe's denial of her trauma limits the possibility of her recovery, we cannot expect to journey toward wholeness by denying the sins of our nation or the wounds of our stories or by leaving both on the trash heap of our memory.

Healing in Community

Beloved is emphatic that suffering can find the possibility of healing only in the space of community, where we remember and heal in the light. The prospect of healing comes to Sethe and 124 through the surprising arrival of Paul D, which carries the potential of healing precisely because through his presence Sethe's history must be faced. Through Paul D, Sethe meets and embraces her past. And Paul D, in his coming to 124, must do the same through Sethe. Each must confront the terrors of their plantation past, and each must do this work not alone but *together*. And in the joining together of their wounds, a tiny flicker of hope sparks that may light a path to wholeness. As Paul D and Sethe share details of their attempted escapes and piece together the resultant suffering, both crippling pain and glimmers of hope emerge. Sethe even begins to ponder, "Would it be all right to go ahead and feel?"[16]

Healing as a communal project is evident through all that Paul D brings to 124. It is Paul D who breaks the hold of Beloved's ghost over 124. It is Paul D who brings Sethe and Denver out of the enclosed world of 124 and into the life of their community through a trip to the carnival. These moments—welcoming Paul D and leaving 124 to participate in the community that ostracized her—are risks for Sethe. But these are risks that move her and Denver from isolation into proximity with others and further into a life beyond the literal, spiritual, and figurative confines of 124 and the clutches of Sethe's traumatic past-present.

Our suffering may take place in the shadows, but, as *Beloved* demonstrates, our healing happens in the light of community. Baby Suggs, one of the most vivid of all Morrison's characters, is a conduit for communal healing through the cultivation of a *particular* type of space and community. As we all know well, simply being in relationship with others does not birth a community in which suffering is tended. A particular space must be cultivated for flourishing and recovery. In the years following her freedom, this is precisely the sort of community Baby Suggs builds.

This is why, throughout *Beloved*, Baby Suggs is described as "holy." Baby Suggs transforms spaces into places of holiness, places that are set apart and rare in Black slave life: places where Black people are given voice to rage, places where they can have joy, places where they can lament, and places where they can love themselves.

Under Baby Suggs's watch and before 124 became possessed, even this farmhouse "had been a cheerful and buzzing house" full of meals, messages, shoes, and love for strangers and children. At 124, Baby Suggs established a pit stop for runaways and freed Black folks, a set-apart place where she "loved, cautioned, fed, chastised and soothed."[17] This is the space and work of a shepherdess of the bodies and souls who seek a way to live and thrive against all odds.

Baby Suggs cultivates such a space through the affection and wisdom that emanate from "her great big heart."[18] *Beloved* takes pains to explain that Baby Suggs does her healing work as a consummate wounded healer. She gives "her great big heart"—because "slave life had 'busted her legs, back, head, eyes, hands, kidneys, womb and tongue,' she had nothing left to make a living with but her heart—which she put to work at once."[19] What Baby Suggs offers in her great big heart is an affection, a wisdom, and a love that even slave life cannot degrade. She offers that which, in some miracle of the divine and some testimony to the resilience of the human spirit, has not been extinguished by the trouble she has felt and seen. In offering her heart, she sustains her people by feeding them a sacred truth: what they do to us can never steal our beloved humanity. For this reason, Baby Suggs proclaims, "Love your heart . . . for this is the prize."[20]

However, the magnum opus of Baby Suggs's sacred work is not the transformation of existing spaces, like 124 or AME pulpits, but the creation of the new. The pinnacle of Baby Suggs's work is the fresh space she creates for the freed Black people of her Ohio town, "a wide-open place cut deep in the woods" known as the Clearing.[21] In the Clearing, Baby Suggs operates as more than a preacher. Here she is a spiritual director, a liturgical conductor applying the balm of movements and words to the suffering flock in her charge. In this creation of a new space, Baby Suggs, through her liturgy and proclamation, calls forth a new people:

> When warm weather came, Baby Suggs, holy, followed by every black man, woman and child who could make it through, took her great heart to the Clearing. . . .

After situating herself on a huge flat-sided rock, Baby Suggs bowed her head and prayed silently. The company watched her from the trees. They knew she was ready when she put her stick down. Then she shouted, "Let the children come!" And they ran from the tree toward her.

"Let your mothers hear you laugh," she told them, and the woods rang. The adults looked on and could not help smiling.

Then "let the grown men come," she shouted. They stepped out one by one from among the ringing trees.

"Let your wives and your children see you dance," she told them, and ground life shuddered under their feet.

Finally she called the women to her. "Cry," she told them. "For the living and the dead. Just cry." And without covering their eyes the women let loose.[22]

Baby Suggs, holy, clears and creates a space for her people to heal through the holy movements of humanity: laughing, dancing, crying "let loose" with no covered shame. The sequence of Baby Suggs's repeated "Let" commands and the subsequent results ("*and* the woods rang") evoke the creational pattern of Genesis 1 ("let there be . . . and it was good"), which culminates in the creation of man and woman (Gen. 1:26–28). Here in the Clearing, Baby Suggs restores by directing her people to move and be in the sacred humanity that they are and that has so viciously been attacked by those who enslaved and debased them.

Thus, Baby Suggs, holy, directs her people in a liturgy of healing that runs with the grain of creation and against the horrors of slavery. In this new creational space, the anticreational force of racist violence that bends and breaks persons and communities is for a holy moment cleared away, and her people inch closer to the goodness of God's creational desire:

Children who had picked cotton and plowed fields and cut cane, children who had never *been* children were called *to be* children. She [Baby Suggs] summoned the men to dance and, thus, display their shrouded elegance and beauty to their wives and lovers and children. Men, from whom slavery had usurped the power to love and protect their wives and children, were called to be husbands, lovers, and fathers. She [Baby Suggs] enjoined the women to cry for the living and the dead and, thus, disclose the depth and breadth of their sorrow. Women, who had built walls around their hearts to keep them from exploding at the pain of loss and the anguish of terror, are released to weep, to mourn.[23]

And creation rejoices at this goodness. Baby Suggs's commands of Black people—laugh, dance, cry—are met with nature's amen. Nature offers up an "and it was good" affirmation: woods ring, trees shake, ground shudders.[24] This is good and right creative labor, holy and healing—a labor that seeks to mend and guard the Black humanity that white supremacy has sought to destroy.

A New Commandment

What Baby Suggs directs in the liturgy of movement and expression, she undergirds in her Clearing sermon, in which she gives a new and healing *indicative* and *imperative* to her people. In a world that despises and violates Black flesh, Baby Suggs declares the indicative truth, "In this here place, we flesh." She then gives the imperative command, "Love it. Love it hard," situating both the indicative and the imperative as love's Teflon against the hatred of the world: "Yonder they do not love your flesh."[25] Black life is holy, she proclaims, and her people must not wait for the world to see this truth. Baby Suggs and her proclamation represent a form of "grandmother theology," "rooted in generational wisdom, in the way that time and age and maturity provide an alternative lens through which to know and understand God" and life.[26] Out of this wisdom, Baby Suggs commands her people not to wait for others to do this spiritually pivotal work, which recognizes that we are more than the sum of our sufferings.

Baby Suggs fuses the indicative and the imperative into a new commandment, what M. Shawn Copeland calls a "decolonial episteme."[27] Baby Suggs's commands enact a new knowledge and action, free from the debased cognitive confines that say Black is animalistic, evil, cursed of Ham, of lesser value than white. This imperative call to love Black flesh, Copeland writes, is also a calling out of a people. It is an exodus out of the logic of white supremacist knowledge and a crossing over for "black children, women, and men to new life *as a people*, to new identity-in-community" in which we love our "own and others' black flesh, black bodies, black selves."[28] For "in calling the people to love their black flesh, Baby Suggs conjures children, men, and women *anew*—makes them *whole* again." Through the embrace and praxis of this command to love Black flesh, we overturn "the equation of whiteness with goodness and dominance, of blackness with evil and subservience."[29] Loving the God-givenness and goodness of our flesh together is how healing happens.

Though not explicitly so, Baby Suggs's exhortation to move away from false definition and self-debasement to a self-identity of belovedness is deeply Christian. In urging her people to not permit slavery, white people, or suffering to define them or pull them into self-hatred, Baby Suggs helps her people see and savor their humanity. This is profoundly holy work, work that, in effect, calls her people to not let their suffering shape their identity. Volf writes wisely about memory and suffering in a way that illumines Baby Suggs's Clearing ministry:

> Christians believe, however, that neither what we do nor what we suffer defines us at the deepest level. . . . We are defined by God, not by wrongdoers' evil deeds and their echo in our memory. . . . They may live in us, but they no longer occupy us; they may cause pain, but they no longer exhaustively define us. We are more than what we have suffered, and that is the reason we can do something with our memory of it.[30]

Interestingly, what Baby Suggs does not preach at the Clearing is as significant as what she does proclaim. Baby Suggs's message is foregrounded by its decisive break with the slave-master-sanctioned preaching presented to Black slaves, selective messages of docility, purity, and eternity. This is precisely what Baby Suggs does *not* offer for the healing and survival of her people: "She did not tell them they were the blessed of the earth, its inheriting meek or its glorybound pure. She told them that the only grace they could have was the grace they could imagine. That if they could not see it they would not have it."[31] In these words, we find a repudiation of a docile Christianity—the domesticated strand as seen in James Baldwin's Gabriel—and an imaginative gesture toward a better and, incidentally, more authentically Christian message for the enslaved. For a suffering people, the religion used to keep them docile must necessarily be imagined again— imagined and seen aright—or else there will be no "grace" to be had. The slave master's Christianity has no tenderness, love, or dignity for the enslaved; thus something else has to be imagined if grace is to redemptively intersect and transform Black pain.

Baby Suggs shows that the survival *and* healing of her people requires the rejection of a warped Christianity that endorses earthly subjection because of a heavenly hope. As examined in the chapter on Zora Neale Hurston's *Moses, Man of the Mountain*, the recovering and reimagining done by the earliest African American Christians saved American Christianity from being wholly consumed by racism, greed, and power by promoting a "glory-bound" future and freedom in the present. When the faith is bastardized from the actual compassion and concern of God and Scripture, the most

Christian thing to do is to practice a religious imagination that draws us back to the wholeness of the faith by dismantling its distortion. This too is how we heal: by rejecting unbiblical notions that deny human concerns in the name of unbiblical distortions.

The New Commandment and the Quiet Exodus

The litany of Black suffering must be attended to through a liturgy of healing—that is, a shared work of the people to love, cry, laugh, and dance together in the affirmation and belief that we are not cursed as the world says but loved and blessed. Through the spiritual direction of Baby Suggs, *Beloved* teaches us that healing from racial trauma, slavery or otherwise, is tied to the recovery of the freedom to be human in a collective space where the mask, under which pain and trauma are hidden for survival's sake, can finally be lifted, cast aside, and hopefully one day destroyed. Healing comes as Black children see their grown Black men—their uncles, cousins, daddies, neighbors—waltz with safety in the joyful, vulnerable movements of childlike dance. Healing comes as strong Black woman can voluntarily opt out of that modifier—strong—and be so deeply affirmed and supported that their requirement is to be no longer superhuman but simply human.

The question for healing is, Where is this space? Where is our Clearing? The freedom and order of the Clearing no doubt captures the invisible institution of secret slave-church meetings, where life and worship existed beyond the white master's watchful eye. But even today, we must ask: Do we have communities where the mask is not an entrance requirement and where the freedom to be, heal, lament, praise, cry is welcomed and celebrated?

When the *New York Times* catches wind of the quiet exodus of Black Christians from white evangelical churches, one wonders how few Black believers have felt the freedom of the Clearing in their church experiences.[32] In the world of therapy, two types of pain are often discussed when it comes to processing wounds and trauma: clean pain and dirty pain. Clean pain is the inescapable part of a difficult or challenging experience, but dirty pain is avoidable—it's all the pain we experience as a way to avoid clean pain. Dirty pain "prolongs the discomfort" and compounds our suffering and trauma through "avoidance, blame, and denial."[33] This is why Rowe argues rightly that "the stories of racial trauma and oppression of African Americans and other people of color must be shared."[34] The paralyzing irony is that when Christian racial minorities do the very thing needed for our healing—honest conversation about race and racial trauma—this step toward clean pain in the name of healing can produce the dirty charge of "divisive." Too often the pain of the suffering is taken and made dirty. Vulnerable honesty is met with loud backlash or silent hostility. The attempt to process racial trauma can at times end up compounding it. Without an honest and patient community, our attempts to walk toward healing become a tumble into deeper heartache.

The Backlash

In *Beloved*, healing always faces backlash. As readers, we learn the starkest backlash occurred eighteen years before the novel's present timeline, shortly after Sethe's escape from slavery and reunion with Baby Suggs at 124. The subsequent hope and healing that bloom in the Clearing is destroyed days later with the arrival of schoolteacher, the vile master of the Sweet Home plantation who comes to 124 to capture and re-enslave Sethe and her children. The Black community, which will play a pivotal part in Sethe's redemption, first plays a fatal part in her tragedy through the sin of omission. Resentful at the excessive feasting at 124, the community does not alert Sethe and 124 to the arrival of the four horsemen. Once the armed captors approach, Sethe kills her oldest daughter rather than have her return to the plantation to be perpetually raped and beaten. The evil of white supremacy and enslavement and, in a much smaller but not insignificant way, the failure of her community break both Sethe and Baby Suggs, whose great big heart is no more.

As readers, we learn of the Clearing's disintegration in fragmented retrospect, but the erosion of Paul D and Sethe's relationship occurs in the novel's present timeline with a backlash that is decidedly supernatural.[35] In their reentry into social life, Sethe and Denver begin to flourish through the healing power of relationship that has come from Paul D. Sethe is no longer ostracized from the community, and Denver moves from resentment to "swaying with delight." Together with Paul D, they begin to look like a new family—"And on the way home . . . the shadows of three people still held hands"—on the path to a new life.[36]

Any hope of a new future as a new family is quickly shattered when "a fully dressed woman walked out of the water."[37] When Sethe's bladder fills to capacity upon seeing the woman's face, it is clear, at least to Denver, that this woman who has come to 124 is the incarnate ghost of Beloved.

121

Exorcised from 124, the ghost it seems has incarnated as a woman come to haunt Sethe and disrupt Paul D and Sethe's bond, the very relationship that holds the possibility of Sethe's healing and new life. The redemptive promise of their threefold family and the healing community of the Clearing are both disrupted, first by the act of white supremacist evil (enslavement and re-enslavement of image bearers) and second by the legacy and trauma of that suffering (the ghost of Beloved).

Memory and Possession

As one might expect, there is a wide range of readings on the incarnate Beloved. Because Beloved is a catalyst for Sethe's eventual healing from her guilt and despair, some readings prioritize Beloved as akin to a Christlike figure, whose arrival in incarnate flesh leads, through trial and near death, to Sethe's redemption. Yet it is the arrival of the enfleshed Beloved *and* the eventual quasi-exorcism of Beloved that bring healing. It seems more appropriate to see Beloved as something seeking to control Sethe, not for the purpose of redemption but for the sake of possession. In the middle section of the novel, Beloved speaks in disorienting, fragmented sentences that possess no immediately discernible coherence except the expression of pain and the desire for possession, calling out "mine" over Sethe and beckoning her with the declaration and invitation, "I am the join."[38]

Admittedly, these are difficult sections to interpret. For some, this language of "the join" and the emphasis on "mine" suggest Beloved's diabolical intent to imprison her mother in the perpetual loop of guilt and memory, never to heal, never to move forward in time. But when we consider Morrison's emphasis that this story is for "sixty million and more" and the theft of the mother-child connection that plagues Beloved, Sethe, and Denver in this section, it is difficult not to settle on a both/and reading. Beloved seeks to possess Sethe as the grown ghost child and also as a manifestation of the generational trauma resulting from chattel slavery's dispossession of mothers and children and the oppressive loop of this cumulative traumatic memory.[39] What Beloved longs for—union and oneness with her mother—is good and creational, but the traumatic memory of the loss of this bond haunts and overwhelms Sethe. Thus, Beloved traps Sethe inside 124, haunting her with the guilt of her murder while feeding Sethe memories and locking her in a paralyzing cycle of despair that threatens to swallow her whole.

In *Confessions*, Augustine marvels at the wonder of memory, exclaiming, "The power of memory . . . is tremendous . . . intimidatingly great: an extensive, a boundless innermost recess."[40] Through memory, we possess our identity, retelling and remembering the stories that shape our lives and supply us meaning. Through memory, we remember the God who made us and redeems us. Yet memory, like every other human faculty, is tainted under the sway of sin. We forget that which we wish to remember and remember that which we pray we could forget. Dealing with our wounds and suffering means having to deal with the fallen side of memory, in which memory becomes tyrannical, trapping us, like Sethe, inside its ceaseless spiral of despair.

Sethe's descent to the brink of death suggests that there is grave danger from two distinct directions when dealing with the trauma of memory: the denial of the past and imprisonment in the past. Denying the past is false freedom, and obsessing over it is false reckoning. The past is to be remembered in order to progress toward healing, which is impossible apart from memory. Beloved's desire to possess Sethe in an endless loop of "rememory," never forgetting but never healing, always remembering but never recovering, is death by memory. "Rememory" without movement toward a redemption is not restorative or healing. It is hellish.

From this we learn that memory or "rememory" is muscle that must be exercised in a particular way, transparently, communally, and redemptively. Memory is to be practiced in the light, with others, and aimed toward a holy telos—life and truth. Under Beloved's possession, Sethe's rememory is weaponized as a living purgatory with no satisfaction in sight. Beloved would have Sethe become a prisoner of her own memory, forever trapped. This weaponization of memory tells the lie that Sethe is irredeemable, that the evil done to her that gave rise to her impossible choice is *the* definer of her life. This is memory at work in the dark. The purpose is not freedom but a fresh form of re-enslavement.

Remembering and Redemptive Community

Redemption always includes risk. Only through the power of the village of freed Black people does Sethe break free from Beloved's possession, the tyranny of memory, and her subsequent descent into despair. It is yet again the healing power of community that draws one of its members toward wholeness. Notably, it is Denver who plays a pivotal role in her mother's liberation by moving away from 124 and toward community, knowing she "would have to leave the yard; step off the edge of the world . . . and go ask somebody for help." Afraid of the racial violence of the world beyond 124 and her mother's shameful public reputation, Denver is unable to leave 124's porch until "her heart kicked." Denver then hears Baby Suggs as "clear as anything," and her words urge Denver to live despite the suffering that may come.[41] It is Baby Suggs's great big heart that proves redemptive, empowering Denver to risk and set off a sequence of communal rescue.

Denver has not transcended the grief in 124, but she has, through the movement into the light, transformed a source of shame into an opportunity for redemption. Denver's risk into community is met with mercy and action from the very people who after the feast of 124 refused to alert its inhabitants to the deadly approach of the four horsemen. Through Denver's risk into the world, into the light, and into community, there will be redemption for the community and rescue for Sethe. The thirty women of the town, upon discovering Beloved's identity and her violence against Sethe, prepare to act, convinced that a "rescue was in order."[42]

Ella, a former slave and leader of the thirty, is moved to act despite her misgivings about Sethe and her past. What compels Ella to organize a rescue is that Beloved's enfleshed domination of Sethe represents something Ella cannot stomach: the audacity of past sin controlling and imprisoning the hope of the present. "Whatever Sethe has done, Ella didn't like the idea of past error taking possession of the present. Sethe's crime was staggering and her pride outstripped even that; but she could not countenance the possibility of sin moving on the house, unleashed and sassy."[43] Memory and sin cannot imprison the future.

When evil and suffering are unmasked, as in the case of Beloved's all-consuming desire for possession, the community acts because what is at stake is clear. Through a mixture of prayer, charms, and magic, Ella and the women march to 124 to confront Beloved and rescue Sethe. In their voices they follow the liturgy of healing laid out by Baby Suggs, who taught them to "cry for the living and the dead."[44]

> The voices of the women searched for the right combination, the key, the code, the sound that broke the back of words. Building voice upon voice until they found it, and when they did it was a wave of sound wide enough to sound deep water. . . . It broke over Sethe and she trembled like the baptized in its wash.[45]

Through the communal chorus of voices lifted to contend and battle for her life—a true sign of her belovedness—Sethe senses that "the Clearing had come to her"[46] and is cleansed and freed.

Remembrance in the Light and through the Feast

The novel's grim violence, the ghostly haunting of 124, and Beloved's spiritual possession—what Christina Bieber Lake classifies as "the grotesque"—all serve a specific purpose: honest confrontation with the trauma and truth of memory. Through these elements, Morrison desires "her readers to enter the pain of Sethe's past experiences as much as she wants Sethe to do so."[47] Like Sethe, we cannot exercise memory, whether national or personal, in the name of denial or in the name of imprisonment or in the name of vindictiveness and expect our lives to be whole.

Just as Sethe must encounter the trauma of memory to heal, our holy work of healing involves both remembering and relinquishing in the space of communal care, prayer, and belonging. The need to remember and relinquish is captured in the novel's closing phrase, "This is not a story to pass on."[48] The ambiguity is purposeful: memory is not to be passed to others or overlooked by others.

Healing, then, can become actual only when the dangerous thing is done: the trauma of memory is brought to the light and remembered right. No wonder our country fails to heal from racial sins. There is contested debate about the history of our nation and the haunting legacy of that history upon the present. *Beloved* can help us—if we risk the retraumatization that comes with memory. Morrison's novel serves as "a shock to anyone's efforts to deny the impact of America's slaveholding past as much as it is to Sethe's denial of her own past."[49] For both Sethe and our nation, this past holds almost unspeakable terrors, but the remembrance of this past shines light not only on Black suffering but also on Black survival, emphatically proving "that these past sins will ultimately fail to destroy Sethe and the African American community."[50] In other words, we are still here.

Remembering rightly means that we love our God-givenness by remembering that you and I are not the sum of our suffering. Our remembering draws us toward a theological remembrance: before we are those who have suffered, we are those who in God's eternal mercy are ourselves beloved. In the end, part of our healing work is the remembrance that deals honestly with our wounds but is never consumed by them, for when in the pit of despair or when sin gets sassy and wants to derail us, there is someone to love us, risk for us, or sing over us that we are beloved. Healing is found in the constant individual and communal turn toward the tender mercies of God, who calls us to a theological remembrance: to locate our history in his, to make sense of our memory in his memory, to process our wounds in his wounds.

In *Beloved*, Sethe is still here because she is not left to self-definition or to her self at all; she is still here because somebody prayed for her, because somebody risked for her. Thus, we reciprocate this risk of love with those like us and unlike us, in love of neighbor and of enemy (Matt. 5:43–44; Mark 12:31). Sethe endures because her village of Black women, who abandoned her once, did not abandon her twice. They lifted their prayers, charms, and voices to set her free. The embrace of a community that calls on the transcendent name, practices forgiveness, and enacts a rescue when sin and evil get "unleashed and sassy" is how we have come this far. We are still here.

Because we are still here, there is still healing and wholeness to be had. We heal in the light. We heal in redemptive community. We heal through the truth. We heal by loving our God-given flesh. And we heal in the theological remembrance that we can see and taste: the feast that leads not to betrayal, as in the case of Baby Suggs, but to the joy of our rescue and salvation. It may seem like trite preacher-talk to say that Holy Communion is healing work. It is nonetheless true. There is a reason Jesus told us to "do this in remembrance of me" (Luke 22:19). It is in this holy meal of remembrance that Christ meets us, greets us, and situates our wounds and memories inside his very own with a grace we can taste and touch.

In this meal of remembrance, we taste and see that we are—no matter our past—marked and possessed by a love the world cannot take. In this meal that demonstrates Christ as the fulfillment of the Passover and God's deliverance from Egyptian slavery, we remember that God delivered his people then and will deliver us again. In this meal of remembrance, those who feast by faith remember that no matter our history, the Lord has cleared a sacred place for us at his table. He has taken those who were said to not be his people, those whose flesh was despised—just like his Son's—and has called us beloved.

Lament

W. E. B. Du Bois's "The Litany of Atlanta"

African-American prayers as a literary genre, and a religious social practice, assume that God is just and loving, and that the human dilemma is that we cannot always experience and see God's justice and love. We pray for faith to trust God's ultimate disclosure.

—James Melvin Washington, *Conversations with God*

My soul is in deep anguish.
How long, Lord, how long?
—Psalm 6:3 (NIV)

In September 1906, a mob of white men brutalized the Black community in Atlanta in a three-day riot of racial terror. Hundreds of Black people were maimed. Many more fled the city with their homes and businesses destroyed. And at least twenty-five Black people lay dead. Local newspapers catalyzed the violence by publishing the alleged assaults of white women by Black men. In reality, the causes were legion: the boom of the Black population in the city caused fear among white elites; the rise of Black politicians, a Black elite, and a Black middle class threatened to undo segregation; and recent white gubernatorial candidates catered to and fomented racial fears.[1]

The Atlanta Race Riot of 1906 was therefore not simply a singular tragedy and injustice but yet another vicious backlash against the slow, generational gains Black America had made in the march toward recognized dignity and full citizenship. When attempts to build a life of dignity, equity, and unity are met with vicious violence at nearly every turn, where else can one turn but prayer?

W. E. B. Du Bois wrote "The Litany of Atlanta" (1906) on the train back home to the city, fearful for his family's safety and distraught at such a devastating display of racial hatred.[2] The hatred that decimated Black businesses and homes and left upward of twenty-five Black families to bury their loved ones is what historian Carol Anderson calls "white rage." Anderson writes, "The trigger for white rage, inevitably, is black advancement. It is not the mere presence of black people that is the problem; rather, it is blackness with ambition, with drive, with purpose, with aspirations, and with demands for full and equal citizenship."[3] Du Bois's prose poem wails and wrestles with God over the trauma of white rage that has historically confronted Black advance in a sickening cycle of progress, resistance, and violence.

Though Du Bois's religious views are complex and debated, he writes not only as one of America's finest intellectuals but as a man deeply acquainted with Christianity and faith. Thus "The Litany of Atlanta" instructs about the nature of prayer in Black experience, a lesson that draws us closer to an authentic spiritual life that is honest before God, and therefore a faith that finds a way toward resilience in a world of rage, terror, and pain.

The Nature of Lament: Prayer to a Silent God

How do we pray when we know God's will is for us to survive but suffering is all we find? We lament in tears and groans. Lament is prayer that engages God from within the vortex of suffering and pain. Whether a bewildered cry, a frenzy of heated words fired to the heavens, or an anguished sob too deep for words, lament is a guttural groan of the soul offered up in pain with the hope that the heavens will reply with something resembling relief.

Put more succinctly, lament is "a prayer in pain that leads to trust."[4] For David in Psalm 13, lament takes various forms, including the cry, "How long, O LORD? Will you forget me forever?" (v. 1). The book of Lamentations contains five poems, voiced by the prophet Jeremiah, lamenting over the destruction of the Israelites' lives and their holy city. The spirituals voiced lament in profound ways, crying out, "Lord, sometimes I feel like a motherless child" and lifting pain to God in the tearful cadence of prayer and song.

"The Litany of Atlanta" stands with its feet firmly planted in both the scriptural and the Black tradition of lament. Thus Du Bois begins his litany in the place of sorrowful questioning, as indicated in the opening words and first reference to the divine: "O Silent God." God is the addressee and the subject under questioning, as it were. Du Bois's opening invocation reverses the liturgical pattern of beginning with a comforting attribute of God by beginning with the distance of God:

O SILENT GOD, Thou whose voice afar in mist and mystery hath left our ears an-hungered in these fearful days—
Hear us, good Lord!

Listen to us, Thy children: our faces dark with doubt are made a mockery in Thy sanctuary. With uplifted hands we front Thy heaven, O God, crying:
We beseech Thee to hear us, good Lord!

Where is God in "these fearful days"? Du Bois asks on behalf of his people. Where is God in the backlash of death as his people seek dignity and deliverance? He is silent—his "voice afar in mist and mystery"—which leaves Black people marked by doubt and appearing foolish for trusting he would do otherwise. Such words are grim and honest, the required material of true lament.

Lament is not sanitized prayer. Lament interrogates God on the terms of his character, with questions based on our pain. Lament arises from the incongruence between God's justice and goodness and our experience of evil and suffering. Instead of throwing off faith because of this disorienting discrepancy, lament questions and cries out. To lament is to get raw and real with God in a way we refuse to do with others. Lament is therefore the movement of relationship, trusting that God can in fact stomach our bracing honesty. Lament does not run from God but runs to him by vocalizing the pain that disorients.

In all this, lament does not presume upon God. Lament does not ask God for extra. It asks for the justice and provision God has previously promised. For this reason Du Bois's invocation of silence yields to humble acknowledgment: "We are not better than our fellows, Lord, we are but weak and human men." Du Bois is not presuming upon God. He is searching for God in the storm of particular and historical Black suffering. Lament seeks God in the silence by asking, Where are you? Why? How long?

Du Bois's questions instruct readers in the survivalist practice of lament. Upon considering the violent whites as "our devils [who] do deviltry," Du Bois questions why they do evil to "innocence and weakness, to womanhood and home." This anguished lament pushes the litany from invocation to substance, presenting the specifics of Du Bois's pain before God ("Who made these devils? Who nursed them in crime and fed them on injustice?"). Du Bois's words are echoed by Stamp Paid's lament in *Beloved*—"What *are* these people? You tell me, Jesus. What *are* they?"— when he sees the carnage of a Black child killed by white folks.[5] What is behind such evil? Du Bois, like Stamp Paid, wonders. And where is God to "curse . . . the doer and the deed"? These charges culminate in the burning question at the heart of the Atlanta riots and Black suffering more broadly:

> Is this Thy justice, O Father, that guile be easier than innocence, and the innocent crucified for the guilt of the untouched guilty?
> *Justice, O Judge of men!*

The substance of Du Bois's lament is not only the suffering that has struck his people—one rock of a mountain of evil that has befallen them in our nation—but also the nature of this suffering. It is from the hands of hypocrites who seem to be blessed in the acts of injustice rather than being judged. Note the tenor of Du Bois's lament as the litany moves toward its center:

> A city lay in travail, God our Lord, and from her loins sprang twin Murder and Black Hate. . . .
> In the pale, still morning we looked upon the deed. We stopped our ears and held our leaping hands, but they—did they not wag their heads and leer and cry with bloody jaws: *Cease from Crime!* The word was mockery, for thus they train a hundred crimes while we do cure one.
> *Turn again our captivity, O Lord!*

This is not the suffering of a natural disaster, devastating and lamentable as such tragedies are. This suffering is born of white rage; it is the purposeful, hypocritical work of vile adversaries who seek the blood of Black people even as Black people seek the path of uplift and righteousness. For this reason, Du Bois aligns the evildoers of the riots with the evil persecutors of the Lord's anointed in the Psalms who wag their heads and jeer (Pss. 22:7; 109:25). These are people who are opposed to God. So Du Bois, like the psalmists, wonders: Why does God not rise up and oppose them?

Lament as Interpretation

Lament searches to make sense of the most destabilizing human experience under the sun: profound, unexplainable suffering. Observe Du Bois's search for understanding:

> Bewildered we are, and passion-tost, mad with the madness of a mobbed and mocked and murdered people; straining at the armpits of Thy Throne, we raise our shackled hands and charge Thee, God, by the bones of our stolen fathers, by the tears of our dead mothers, by the very blood of Thy Crucified Christ: *What meaneth this?* Tell us the Plan; give us the Sign!
> *Keep not thou silence, O God!*

Throughout the poem, Du Bois searches to grasp the plan or sign that can interpret the "maimed and murdered" and a "city lay[ing] in travail." The interpretive options in the face of suffering are not endless. In terms of negative conclusions, they can be boiled down to two, which Du Bois examines: God's nonexistence or God's disinterest. "The Litany of Atlanta" attends to the former almost immediately, questioning, "Wherefore do we pray? Is not the God of the fathers dead?" This interpretative road is quickly closed off: "Thou are not dead." Instead, Du Bois concludes in the direction of deism. God is "flown afar," concerned with other worlds and other suns. God's existence is not questioned. It is God's interest and concern that come under interrogation.

In this sense, "The Litany of Atlanta" reflects the liturgical lament of the Psalms. While the poem carries the general pattern and language of psalmic lament, Du Bois is particularly attentive to and influenced by the movement of Psalm 44, written by the Sons of Korah. As Derek Kidner notes, Psalm 44 voices the national devastation of the people of God in their suffering as those slaughtered and scattered among the nations while retaining innocence before God.[6] Verses 11 and 17 of Psalm 44 lament:

> You have made us like sheep for slaughter
> and have scattered us among the nations. . . .

> All this has come upon us,
> though we have not forgotten you,
> and we have not been false to your covenant.

In other words, the suffering the people of God face is what they would expect and embrace *if* they had transgressed the covenant (Deut. 4:23–27). Instead, they are undone by the suffering that is unforeseen and humanly inexplicable. It is no surprise that Du Bois draws from this text. Du Bois highlights the moral innocence of his people, like that of Israel, in contrast to the deep injustice permitted to come upon them.

Psalm 44 contains typological connection with the movements of Black American history. Although any comparison between the story of Israel and African Americans needs to be mindful of the distinctions of each respective group, there are some outlines of commonality. In moving through Israel's glorious past (vv. 1–8), its disastrous present (vv. 9–16), and its lament and call for God to arise (vv. 17–26), the psalm connects with the painful patterns of Black experiences. A people seeks righteousness and experiences historic deliverance, yet is seemingly and perpetually overcome by trials, which lead to songs of lament endlessly spewed from the people's lips.

In Du Bois's context, Reconstruction would have been a glorious light shining in the night of white supremacy, but it became a short-lived light extinguished by Jim Crow and the disastrous presence of backlash, as manifested in the race riots. Now quoting Psalm 44:23, Du Bois speaks for his people, issuing the same plea that first lived on the tear-soaked lips of Israel: "*Awake, Thou that sleepest!*" "The Litany of Atlanta" suggests that the same movements God's people experienced in Psalm 44, Black people experienced in Atlanta and America.

Lamenting Together unto God

This connective tissue means that just as we look to psalms of lament to give shape to how we process suffering, we can also look to them to gain a sense of lament's restorative power. Though many psalms of lament are individual in nature, which is itself instructive and encouraging, Psalm 44 teaches us that lament is honest prayer in pain performed individually and communally. The superscription of Psalm 44—"To the choirmaster. A Maskil of the Sons of Korah"—strongly suggests that this lament was to be made up of voices from Israel's communal worship. "The Litany of Atlanta" resembles Psalm 44's language, historical-communal connection, and also performative nature: it gives communal voice to communal pain.

The very nature and structure of Du Bois's poem as a litany demonstrates that lament is most redemptive when it is communal. The structure of "The Litany of Atlanta" embodies the congregational pattern suggested by Psalm 44's superscription and its call-and-response pattern. Thus Du Bois's words cast him in the place of the minister, and the words of the Black community (italicized as the response) put them in the place of the responsive congregation. The poem demonstrates the importance of lament performed communally.

Devastating as it is, "The Litany of Atlanta" carries something redemptive in its vocalized suffering: we do not lament and suffer alone. When God is silent, we need to hear the voices of the weary faithful, even as they too raise their lament. Their lament in faith can revive our hearts as we bring our pain before the Lord in the light of community. If lament "uses the language of pain, anger, and confusion and moves toward God," then lamenting together means journeying in the shadow of profound suffering toward God in unison and unity.[7]

What, then, might happen if non-Black persons took up lament over the loss of Black life in the mold of Psalm 13, Psalm 44, or "The Litany of Atlanta"? Might lament be the secret, vulnerable path to the promised land of a united church? In *Weep with Me: How Lament Opens a Door for Racial Reconciliation*, Pastor Mark Vroegop offers a compelling case and testimony for how lament binds and builds reconciliation, solidarity, and Christian love across racialized lines.[8] This reconciling and unifying power of lament among divided and distinct Christians is missing from the American church's bumbling quest to experience the oneness for which Jesus prayed (John 17).

Pastor Mika Edmondson captures the power of empathy and lament by decrying its absence: "If Christians would simply listen to the cries of their own brothers and sisters in Christ, the Church would be ahead of the national conversation about racial justice instead of behind it."[9] The wisdom of this insight is profound and wide, supplying a pattern for healing across lines of race, gender, and background through communal lament. As we step into this wisdom, we must also extend it. To reach its full healing potential, lament must reach its full communal expression. Even if the privileged have pain and wounds that are not comparable to those of the disadvantaged, love means practicing communal lament. Listening and then lamenting together—itself a biblical command (Rom. 12:15)—can help repair the torn fabric of the divided church.

The Loss of Lament

Is lament a language we speak or a tongue we have been taught to suppress? Each of us has tasted or will taste the suffering endemic to a world under the shadow of sin and death. Lament is not simply an elective for the faithful; it is required for spiritual and existential survival.

The loss of lament, as alluded to above, can unravel persons and communities. Because we do not lament together, as Du Bois and the Psalms model, because our churches, broadly speaking, do not call us into this vulnerable spiritual work, we struggle to empathize with sufferers. We stifle our own pain. We disciple ourselves and others to run from God in pain rather than to him through the discipline of lament. Our lack of communal lament produces disciples unable to process brokenness in a spiritually coherent and emotionally honest way. Without lament, by default we produce disciples who are pathologically happy, and find this a badge of true spirituality.

The faulty presuppositions that undergird the loss of lament are captured well by author and counselor Dan Allender:

> Christians seldom sing in the minor key. We fear the somber; we seem to hold sorrow in low esteem. We seem predisposed to fear lament as a quick slide into doubt and despair, failing to see that doubt and despair are the dark soil that is necessary to grow confidence and joy.[10]

In reality, lament before God builds the faith of individuals and communities, leading both into the healing path of yielding to a hard-earned trust in God in the context of pain. As Allender observes, "To lament—that is to cry out to God with our doubts, our incriminations of him and others, to bring a complaint against him—is the context for surrender." Allender continues, focusing on the church gathered together:

To sing a lament against God in worship reveals far, far greater trust than to sing a jingle about how happy we are and how much we trust him. . . . Lament cuts through insincerity, strips pretense, and reveals the raw nerve of trust that angrily approaches the throne of grace and then kneels in awed, robust wonder.[11]

Whether sung or prayed or practiced in honest conversation, lament is a faith language we avoid at the risk of our own spiritual disintegration. Of course, not all Christians avoid singing in the minor key, literally or figuratively. The Negro spiritual tradition is Christian lament par excellence, second only to Scripture itself. And even Du Bois as an agnostic proves that Black religious experience can instruct us to return to the scriptural practice of lament.

The power of communal lament is that our suffering is not in isolation, which means that our interpretation of that suffering is not isolated either. James Baldwin, whose complex relationship with the Christian church we examined earlier, had this to say about the power of the church together voicing its joys and pains:

There is no music like that music, no drama like the drama of the saints rejoicing, the sinners moaning, the tambourines racing, and all those voices coming together and crying holy unto the Lord. . . . Nothing that has happened to me since equals the power and the glory that I sometimes felt . . . when the church and I were one. Their pain and their joy were mine, and mine was theirs—they surrendered their pain and their joy to me, I surrendered mine to them.[12]

Together, in lament, we traverse the challenge of faith, pain, and surrender.

Lament as Confrontation

Lament is a longing for God's justice, personally and societally. Our voices cry out "How long?" because we do not yet experience God righting wrongs, or protecting the weak, or restraining evildoers. Lament confronts God on the basis of his goodness and righteousness. In one of the poem's most heartrending stanzas, the litany confronts God not because it denies God's justice but because it believes it. Thus the litany places an intimate suffering before the eyes of God, imploring God to "behold this maimed and broken thing"—a "humble black man who toiled and sweat to save a bit from the pittance paid him." Told to "Work and Rise," this man did. And for what? This Black man "lieth maimed and murdered" because of the crime and false testimony of white society: "Did this man sin? Nay, but some one told how some one said another did—one whom he had never seen nor known." In light of this, Du Bois confronts God: "Doth not this justice of hell stink in Thy nostrils, O God?"

Communal lament unleashes a movement of confrontation—we confront God with our pain, asking God to confront evil, which forms and teaches us to confront evil in his name. Lament confronts God, saying, "Behold this broken thing." In that first movement, lament inherently asks God to confront the status quo and upend it with his restorative justice, to behold what is broken and to replace it with restoration. It may be helpful to think of lament as an anguished sibling of that revolutionary request in the Lord's Prayer: "Your kingdom come, your will be done, on earth as it is in heaven" (Matt. 6:10). Lament inflects that petition with "Why?" and "How long?" and refracts the prayer through tears and the longing for personal and societal restoration.

At its core, the cry of lament is concerned with a political order: that God would unsettle the status quo of evil in personal and societal forms, unleashing his rectifying justice to mend and end that which is bent toward evil, and in that redemptive reconstruction establish a new status quo that resembles both his character and his kingdom. The touchstone of Black Christianity, the exodus, was a redemptive act of God that liberated his people unto himself by upending evil and idolatry through atonement and salvation, and this redemptive act was launched by lament (Exod. 2:23–24). Lament is a cry of pain and a cry for confrontation, a cry for God to act and a hope that our groans will not go unanswered.

The Formative Power of Lament

When the litany decries the death of Black image bearers as "this justice of hell," it demonstrates how prayer generally and lament specifically become a pronounced act and utterance of counterformation. This counterformation resists and confronts the lies of white rage, which rails against Black persons' given and asserted dignity and against the false ideologies that say the wounded deserve their suffering. Prayer and lament become "a primal way of justice education," a practice that recalibrates the soul even in suffering by rehearsing that evil is a parasitic violation of creation. There is therefore power in lament that names injustice for what it is. By naming it as such and placing it before God as counter to his moral will, lament teaches us to make no peace with injustice or oppression. On the other hand, the loss of lament strips us of emotional and spiritual honesty and political urgency. We either ignore or suppress the cries of the suffering and then resign ourselves to the fact that things will never change.

Lament's movement of confrontation contains a formative thread of paradox. In contending with God by lamenting the evil we experience, we affirm the revolutionary truth God has taught us: we are worthy of dignity and justice, and suffering is not the way the world was made to be. This is a paradox sustained by faith—though we don't see God's goodness in an instant, we trust it over the full course of time.

Lament forms us in another way: restraint. After confronting God's tolerance of "this justice of hell," the litany calls for God to "pile the pale frenzy of blood-crazed brutes . . . high on Thine altar." To which the congregation responds, *"Forgive us, good Lord; we know not what we say!"* As in the imprecatory psalms, honesty is voiced, but vengeance is restrained by an ethic of forgiveness. The litany holds out hope through raw lament that there is a better way than a cycle of retributive violence. It is better to carry violence on our lips before God in lament than to enact it upon the image of God, even if that image is an enemy.

Returning to Lament

The problem for many Christians is not that we lack things to lament; it's our inability or refusal to slow down and cry out. Without lament, we live with hearts buried in what Claude McKay calls "sweet deceit."[13] We act as if life is all good and dandy when it is most decidedly not. Sweet deceit is a realm Christians are not permitted to enter, a mood in which we cannot dabble. Sweet deceit spoils the soul, lies about reality, and tarnishes our witness.

How, then, do we learn to lament again, or maybe for the first time? To ask this is to ask how to be better at being human before God and grounded in the pain of reality. In other words, how do we process our emotions and suffering before God rather than living in sweet deceit, settling for the numbing elixir of emotional suppression, media gorging, and simple avoidance?

As "The Litany of Atlanta" demonstrates, the answer, in part, includes a return to the Psalms. At a basic level, individuals and churches can return to praying and singing the Psalms, if this is not already part of their devotion and worship. Life is full of suffering, and what we sing shapes us. Many churches seem to have not yet connected the dots. With more than a third of the Psalms containing lament, attending individually and communally to the Psalms will teach us this forgotten dialect and the broader language of an emotionally whole spirituality. Imagine debates about race, justice, and the disinherited if congregations were accustomed to singing and praying psalms like this: "Can wicked rulers be allied with you, those who frame injustice by statute?" (Ps. 94:20).

"By praying the Psalms year after year for millennia in nearly every language and place on earth," Anglican priest Tish Harrison Warren writes, "the church learns to remain alive to every uncomfortable and complex human emotion." "We learn to celebrate and we learn to lament."[14] Enrolled in the school of the Psalms, our humanity breaks out of the confines of neutered emotions and tepid spirituality, a release that is a gift to us and a token of intrigue to the world.

Learning the church's mother tongue of lament makes the gospel more plausible to the world around us. In an age that prizes authenticity, the church will become a more compelling and peculiar people who, because of our trust in the triune God, speak about and deal honestly with pain, injustice, and suffering. We will share more so in the strange and peculiar power of our forebears in the Black church who believed in the goodness of God despite the evil of the world. Indeed, the broader church has much that it can learn from the Black church about inhabiting "a faith that celebrates God's goodness in equal measure with lament over humanity's sinfulness."[15] As we do so, lament becomes both a balm to the soul and a witness to the world.

The Problem of Evil and Silence

There is still the burning question at the aching heart of Du Bois's litany: "*What meaneth this*? Tell us the Plan; give us the Sign!" As mentioned above, in response to bewildering suffering and inexplicable evil, one stands before a limited set of interpretive paths. One can conclude God's nonexistence or his disinterest. One can pass through—not pass over—acute spiritual, physical, and existential pain via lament and trust God's mysterious goodness, even if it is not situationally present or comprehended. Again,

"The Litany of Atlanta," by demanding a definitive divine plan, is firmly intent to walk the harsh and holy road of unrestrained lament.

It is important to note that the poem does not seek to search the unsearchable or to peer into the eternal wisdom of God to understand all things. What is sought is not an answer to the question of theodicy for the sake of pontification. Du Bois, like countless suffering people before and after him, seeks a responsive word from God for the sake of survival. For this reason, after refusing to believe that the Lord is "white" and "heartless," the litany is pleased to possess even a "whisper" from God. This suggests, as I have experienced anecdotally in life and ministry, that the suffering often do not require a full-throated answer to the question of theodicy, if the human mind could even comprehend such a thing. Like Du Bois, the suffering seek at bottom the knowledge that God is not "dumb to our suffering." We seek, in a word, a "whisper." We seek anything but silence and rejection.

This is a posture not simply of exasperated humility but of philosophical wisdom. Drawing poignantly from Augustine, James K. A. Smith shows the nature of the problem: explaining evil paradoxically normalizes it. For "to have an explanation for [evil] . . . would mean that it has a place in the world." But evil "is what ought not to be, the *dis*order of creation, the violation we protest." Lament bears true witness against evil not by explaining it but by protesting it. Smith goes on:

> If you could discern a cause and hence provided an explanation [for evil], then evil makes sense. You might even say evil is "natural." But if you say evil is natural, then it's no longer evil. It's the way things are, the way things are supposed to be. You can't protest what is natural; you can't lament what is meant to be. The price to pay for explaining evil is to give up naming and opposing it.[16]

Despite all this, despite seeking a whisper that God is for and with the suffering, the litany ends in the very state it prays to avoid: silence.

Our voices sink in silence and in night.
  Hear us, good Lord!

In night, O God of a godless land!
  Amen!

In silence, O Silent God.
  Selah!

Here again it is worthwhile to return to Psalm 44. No doubt the people of God sought some communicative act from God that would make sense, even obliquely, of their suffering. Instead, on account of God, they cried out, "Yet for your sake we are killed all the day long; we are regarded as sheep to be slaughtered. Awake! Why are you sleeping, O Lord? Rouse yourself! Do not reject us forever!" (vv. 22–23). The question of divine silence in the face of human suffering is part of the lament of the litany. Both the litany and Psalm 44 call out for God to awake, rise, and act—to whisper even—to assure the bloodied and suffering of his concern and presence, to give something to make sense of one's pain in light of the plan.

Interpreting Pain through the Cross

There are numerous robust intellectual responses to the problem of evil. But since suffering is not so much an intellectual problem as an experiential one, the ultimate answer is not a theory or a syllogism but the entrance of God into human suffering in Jesus crucified. The litany does not seek a comprehensive answer but simply a "whisper"—looking for disclosure, the very basis of African American faith and prayer:

> African-American prayers as a literary genre, and a religious social practice, assume that God is just and loving, and that the human dilemma is that we cannot always experience and see God's justice and love. We pray for faith to trust God's ultimate disclosure.[17]

The ultimate disclosure, the whisper that the litany seeks, finds its response in Jesus's cry of lament quoted from Psalm 22: "My God, my God, why have you forsaken me?" (Matt. 27:46). To our lament, God in Christ offers his own, demonstrating his identification with the suffering and the forsaken. The cross proves God's care for the suffering and demonstrates his plan to overcome injustice, evil, and sin by absorbing their vicious blows himself for the life of the world. Humanity's "cry of lament," Allender writes "is never answered." Instead "it is confounded" at the cross and the wonder of the crucified God.[18] The whisper is a salvation and an identification that produces rectification—through Christ's death and resurrection, a new world will rise and every wrong will be set right.

Careful readers will observe that the litany is attentive to the crucifixion but seems to bypass its significance for the question of Black suffering: "By the very blood of Thy Crucified Christ: What meaneth this?" As explored in the Jesus chapter, Christ's solidarity and identification with the suffering through his cross have historically been the sign, the whisper, the shout that sustains us in our suffering. Attending to the cross of Jesus does not halt our anguished tears, but it does reinterpret them. His lament becomes the interpretive frame for our own, our cries become situated in the tears of the victim of all victims, who nonetheless trusted the goodness of God despite the profound suffering he bore. Our laments, in which we seek to interpret our pain before God, must undergo a cruciform reinterpretation that comes when we attend to our raw pain and stifled groans in light of what we know to be true of the God who gave himself for us.

One can only speculate as to whether, for Du Bois, the cross as God's response to Black pain rang emotionally and experientially satisfying. The wonder of lament is that God does not rush the suffering to push through the trauma of pain. We are invited—as the Scriptures and the litany demonstrate—to sit in our lament and to bring our confrontation and pain into his presence. This invitation to lament is why so many psalms of lament often progress from raw confusion and pain to quiet trust. The Lord meets us in our tears.

To ask "What is the plan?" is to believe even faintly that there is one. The question of evil and suffering is not one that Christians can hide from, nor should we feel the need to. Instead, like the litany—and the apostle Paul before it—we shoot straight about the problem of evil, for this is reality as it is. When Paul quotes Psalm 44:22 in Romans 8:36, he is unafraid to underscore the profound suffering that comes our way—a suffering that can find its answer only in the victory of Jesus through his own suffering (Rom. 8:37–39). This is the pattern for hope in our pain. But sometimes, like the litany, and like Holy Saturday, it is all right to end in silence.

Justice

Richard Wright's *The Man Who Lived Underground*

He has shown you, O mortal, what is good.
And what does the LORD require of you?
To act justly and to love mercy
and to walk humbly with your God.

—Micah 6:8 (NIV)

Eighty years after it was rejected by publishers, Richard Wright's *The Man Who Lived Underground*, in full novelistic form, has come to see the light of day. Its release date solidified its timelessness: Wright's novel about a Black man brutalized by the police entered the world on the day the officer who killed George Floyd was sentenced. Even with all our collective racial progress, the American society Wright captures is far from unfamiliar. The novel's release renders a sentencing upon us all: How has a more just society been so long delayed?

The jarring continuation of injustice that Wright's novel represents for contemporary readers reaches beyond the crucial subject of police brutality. For as much attention as Wright's novel might receive for its prescience about police violence, the novel's power is rooted less in a subject and more in a question: Through what frame or personal action can one survive in an unjust world? And what does this look like today in a country that seems, in terms of justice, to both progress and remain timelessly the same?

The way *The Man Who Lived Underground* answers questions and instructs about justice is through a stark confrontation with the cold Jim Crow world of the 1930s. The novel demonstrates "the illusions and idolatries" by which life is "destroyed"—and justice perverted.[1] In its bleak wake, the novel leaves it to contemporary readers to contemplate *if* and *how* society today might be reconfigured so that the vulnerable are not forced underground or abused aboveground but instead dignified and lifted up to flourish. Though the book is ostensibly about police brutality, the deeper meditative riches are the novel's portrayal of a cold, senseless world and the explicit challenge that portrayal places upon a theological reading: How might we make our lives and communities more just?

Justice Briefly Defined

These days justice is on everyone's lips, whether disparagingly or excitedly. There are bestsellers by Christians against it and bestsellers advocating for it, while most congregants wonder about and hear competing answers to the question, What is it? Justice, biblically speaking, in basic terms, is giving people their due as image bearers of God in terms of dignity. Justice also carries a strong restorative emphasis on caring for the vulnerable with protection, mercy, and generosity. Of course, justice also includes God's retribution—judgment and accountability for evil committed (Acts 17:30–31).

In a broader sense, doing justice is seeking the reign of righteousness manifest in real time. It is a gracious and Christ-driven labor to make society more whole. Biblical justice is born of God's longing for his own righteousness to be reflected in places and among people—something that is thus inescapably social—for our flourishing and his honor.

Doing justice, specifically in the restorative sense, is not a Christian elective. It is a living testimony and familial trait, a reflection of God himself (Ps. 89:14). It is a discipleship requirement, a fulfillment of the call to love

God and love neighbor as oneself. Biblical justice is what happens when the two greatest commandments go public through our lives and communities in ways that go beyond individual piety.

God's desire for his holiness, grace, and righteousness to go public is why the Bible is emphatic about justice in more ways than we have space to list: "Defend the rights of the poor and needy," says Proverbs 31:9. "Render true judgments, show kindness and mercy to one another, do not oppress the widow, the fatherless, the sojourner, or the poor, and let none of you devise evil against another in your heart," the Lord commands in Zechariah 7:9–10. Do not neglect the weightier matters of the law, justice and faithfulness, Jesus warns in Matthew 23:23.

Justice matters so much to God that he marks himself as the glad defender of the ancient world's lowly and vulnerable. The triune God is so deeply protective and compassionate—in a word, *just*—that he brands himself "Father of the fatherless and protector of widows" (Ps. 68:5). God seeks identification not with the powerful rulers but with the lowest on the social ladder and "takes up their cause."[2] He is just, and his people are to do justice in his name (Mic. 6:8).

Confrontation, Justice, and Sight

"Honest stories," writes Eugene Peterson, "respect our freedom: they don't manipulate us, don't force us, don't distract from life."[3] Wright's novel is the opposite of distraction—it is honest confrontation about injustice. This is freeing and necessary, for to imagine a more just world, one must reckon with the world as it is. *The Man Who Lived Underground* provides such a reckoning, peering at the world from the land of the rejected, the underground. This visceral experience of injustice drives Wright's novel as we experience Fred Daniels's transformation from a man in society to a personality below it.

Wright uses a straightforward plot to carry the weighty theme of his story. Fred Daniels is a commendable, if unremarkable, man. He is an expectant father, a man of faith, and an employee of a respected white family. He is in almost every way the opposite of *Native Son*'s Bigger. Of course, none of Daniels's respectability matters when he finds himself confronted by three white police officers as he walks home from work:

> Before him was the white face of a policeman peering over the steering wheel of a car; two more white faces watched him from the rear seat. For

145

a seemingly endless moment, in the balmy air of an early summer night, he stood immobile . . . staring straight into the blurred face of a policeman who was pointing a blinding spotlight full into his eyes. He waited for them to question him so that he could give a satisfactory account of himself. After all he was a member of the White Rock Baptist Church; he was employed by Mr. and Mrs. Wooten, two of the best-known people in all the city.[4]

This police confrontation occurs hardly a page into the novel. Our first impression of Daniels is that the man smacks of naivete, likely because of his religion. Somehow blind to the threat of unjust authority, Daniels cannot sense the stark danger before him. Daniels is snatched by white officers, pinned as the perpetrator of a gruesome double homicide, and brutalized until he signs a confession for a crime he did not commit.

The way Daniels seeks to fight this miscarriage of justice—"through a satisfactory account of himself"—tells us something of the nature of injustice.[5] Injustice renders persons invisible, human dignity and respectable accoutrements be damned. Throughout his torturous ordeal, Daniels pleads his innocence by imploring the police to call his reverend or his white employers, all to no avail. The officers refuse to reckon with Daniels as a human, respectable accoutrements or not. Eventually, bloodied and delirious, Daniels "grew hysterical as he felt that he did not exist for them."[6] Daniels is confronted with the injustice of the world he inhabits.

Justice requires right sight. Here we return to the *imago Dei* and our earlier treatment of Ralph Ellison's *Invisible Man*. This is fitting, for in a sense, Daniels is Wright's version of Invisible. Daniels is not seen as a man, and because of this injustice, he will flee underground, just as Ellison's Invisible does at the end of his novel. The thread of justice and sight between Ellison and Wright further affirms what we looked at in chapter 1: justice requires the recognition of every person's dignity, and action that accords with the truth of that recognition. Indeed, "if justice is making right, then seeing people rightly is a form of justice."[7]

Injustice, then, is false sight, both of persons and of God. It is false sight in that it attacks the image and concern of God—the human person. It is thus an attempted assault on God himself, his law, and the shalom— the deep fullness and flourishing peace—for which God made the world. In a real sense, "all injustice is a violation of the first commandment," for injustice is always "a refusal to give the Creator the worship only the

Creator is due" by disrespecting his person through the refusal to be just to all his created people.[8] Just acts emerge from just sight, and idolatry denies both.

Notes from the Underground

The Man Who Lived Underground questions if and how the downtrodden can survive in a senseless, unjust society. This question is why Daniels's experience of police brutality happens briskly, almost as a preface to the fundamental journey of the novel: Daniels's dislocation and pilgrimage to a new domain, the underground. In the move to the underground, Daniels enters the earth, eventually to question the foundation of the world.

It is in the underground that the absurdity and injustice of the world above are exposed. When Daniels escapes from custody, in a dreamlike sequence, he enters the sewer system. Daniels experiences a violent death to one world and a violent baptism into another: "He dropped into water that was surprisingly warm and was washed violently forward into a vast ocean." The waters assault his body, as did the systems of injustice in the aboveground world: "His body was whirled round and round; while spinning in the water, he gave up. His head struck the concrete wall of the sewer and he wondered if he would be battered to death." When Daniels survives and stands, he is a new man, alive in "the whispering rush of the water," which "creat[ed] an illusion of another world with other values and other laws."[9] Away from the world, Daniels is effectively baptized into new knowledge as the waters strike his head and body, a foreshadowing of the cognitive reset of the world, physically and metaphorically, that he will experience in the underground. His naivete will be replaced by reality.

In this way, Wright presents an inversion of Plato's cave. Daniels does not leave an enclosed setting to gain a glimpse of reality as it is; he goes into a modern cave—the underground—to gaze upon the truth at "the heart of the earth."[10] Daniels experiences an unfurling of reality in the cave-like sewer. He burrows and peers into churches and businesses. He interrogates society and its symbols at its foundational structure, literally and metaphorically. What he finds is not a moral arc that bends toward justice but a clash of symbols, first incomprehensible, then clarified: the world is senseless and unjust, something for which, it seems, White Rock Baptist Church left him unprepared.

Religion in a Senseless World

The first layer of defense that Daniels sought to protect him from the world's senselessness—his church membership and thus his religion—is the first falsehood confronted and exposed in the "terrifying knowledge" of the underground.[11] Daniels, wandering through the sewers, hears through the walls the familiar sound of a church singing and cuts a hole, eager to "observe the church service without being seen, without being a part of it."[12] Here is the critical distance emerging from Daniels's dissipating naivete. The underground has conferred upon him a new knowledge, making the faith he once knew the object of his derision:

> He . . . saw a narrow segment of black men and women, dressed in black robes, singing, holding tattered song books in their black palms. His first impulse was to give vent to a loud laugh, but the laugh choked in his throat. Then he wanted to leap through the quarter-inch of crack, straight into the midst of those foolish people and gather all of them, about him, telling them: "Don't *do* this to yourselves!"[13]

Daniels is haunted and conflicted by what he sees and how he responds:

> His emotions subsided and he came to himself. What was he saying? A sense of the life he had left aboveground crushed him with a sense of guilt. Would not God strike him dead for having such thoughts? As he lay upon the bed of pipes, he knew this: His life had somehow snapped in two. But how? When he had sung and prayed with his brothers and sisters in church, he had always felt what they felt; but here in the underground, distantly sundered from them, he saw a defenseless nakedness in their lives that made him disown them. A physical distance had come between them and had conferred upon him a terrifying knowledge.[14]

What are we to make of Daniels's dueling religious consciousness? Of interpretive importance is the song the congregants sing, which is both familiar and repulsive to Daniels:

> *Jesus, take me to your blessed home above*
> *And wrap me in the bosom of thy love*[15]

Daniels himself has just tasted the destructive blows of injustice, and barely survived. Under this hellish assault, religion proved a blindfold of naivete:

Daniels was not prepared for the threats of racism. Once he was under assault, religion proved a paper-thin shield: he thought his religious references could grant him safety. And now, "here in the underground," Daniels sees his people clinging to the same thin defense that has proven to be no defense at all.[16] No doubt Daniels sees in the congregants' "defenseless nakedness" a projection of his hours-earlier self.[17]

Daniels's religious rejection is understandable in the context of torture and injustice. If our faith's *only* resistance to injustice is to ache for escape to the "blessed home above," to cry out for a beeline to heaven, then it is only a matter of time before that faith withers. This is the docile Christianity whose sermons Baby Suggs refuses to preach. This defenselessness that Daniels sees in the church, and in himself, pains his body and spirit. It is "a pain induced by the naked sight of the groveling spectacle of those black people whose hearts hunger for tenderness" and "whose lives were full of fear and loneliness" and "whose hands were reaching outward into a cold, vast darkness for something that was not there."[18]

A faith that fails to gird the weak for survival in a societal war zone is a faith that offers little coherence or protection to those who live with their backs against the wall. Might this be why Wright immediately introduces Daniels to readers as "a member of the White Rock Baptist Church"?[19] The foundation of the religion Daniels has known is clearly inept for the daily survival of Black persons.

In the explanatory essay that accompanies the novel, titled "Memories of My Grandmother," Wright explains the religious import of the novel's physical divide between life aboveground and life underground. The divide supplied for Wright's mind the form to freely explore the rigid, otherworldly Seventh-day Adventist faith of his grandmother, for whom "eternity was so real . . . that human life had an air of unreality."[20] She was in the world but detached from it, adversarial to it, and not in conversation with it. Her faith offered no word to life but heaven.

Despite distortions, Christianity is uniquely fit for this survivalist task. Did Daniels know, as Howard Thurman claims the disinherited must, the "new courage, fearlessness, and power" that come from the "awareness of being a child of God"?[21] The lesson from the underground is that a faith needs to say something to the downtrodden, a word of good news for the life to come that simultaneously gives them power to survive in the life that is. Faith also needs to say something to the powerful, shaping persons and systems for relations of concern and righteousness.

The Whole Configuration of the Senseless World

There is little righteousness in society, but there is little more than death in the world according to Wright's rendering. Once Daniels is underground, the injustice of the world is laid bare as a domain of death that the downtrodden cannot overcome. After peering in on Black worshipers, Daniels spots the floating corpse of a mother and child. "He flushed with a nameless shame . . . and his lips moved in an effort to utter angry words against the whole configuration of the senseless world."[22]

The injustice of the world is illustrated in the logic of its structures and symbols, specifically the triad of religion, money, and narrative. Quite naturally, then, Daniels's crucial underground experience is a confrontation with these three symbols and others. At the "heart of the earth," Daniels encounters society's fundamental meaning-making realities.[23] Daniels digs into basements and peers into banks and steals tools, diamonds, money, a radio, and a typewriter. These "were the toys of men who lived in the dead world of sunshine and rain he had left, the world that had condemned them."[24] And as toys of these men, they were used to build a world to condemn some and protect others. Daniels plasters money to his cave wall and scatters diamonds on the sewer floor, with the full glee and partial understanding of a mischievous child who is free to roam the house when the parents are gone. The tools the masters used to condemn are now in the servant's underground hands.

The novel puts these "toys of men," in Daniels's possession, out of context for the sake of exposure and deconstruction. When the society-building toys of men are decontextualized from their normative function and place in aboveground society, when their meaning and use are no longer an unquestioned given, the injustice performed through and for these items—particularly the money (greed) and the typewriter (narrative)—is made plain.

For believers, this exposure is a challenge and an opportunity. In hands controlled by God's heart for justice, these toys can be rewired to yield life and flourishing rather than death and exploitation. Find injustice in a societal setting, and you will often find Wright's trio of symbols used not in creative stewardship but in and for idolatrous gain. For this reason, the novel pays particular attention to religion, as mentioned above, and also to greed and narrative. The latter two toys of men are prominent through descriptive length and a dual pairing in which Daniels twice investigates the cash and then pecks away at the typewriter. This attention suggests that greed and narrative, like docile religion, are vitally connected to matters of injustice.

The stronghold of greed is part of the lifeblood of injustice. The novel makes this point when Daniels finds his way into the basement vault of a real estate and insurance firm, which "collected hundreds of thousands of dollars in rent from poor colored folks." Daniels takes money from their vault, "not to spend, but just to keep around and look at it." He rubs the money "as though expecting it suddenly to reveal secret qualities," after which he smiles and observes, "It's just like any other kind of paper."[25] The bills that Daniels examines are neither holy nor evil but a means and a motive for goodness or greed, justice or injustice.

It is the *love* of money that produces all manner of evil and injustice (1 Tim. 6:10). Wealth and economics are, Marva Dawn writes, "perhaps the dimension[s] in which Western Christianity is most often subverted by the powers." Dawn asks the sort of arresting questions that a just faith requires: "If so much of the Bible deals with wealth and the problems of mammon and with such strong invitations to give, then why are our churches so rich? . . . Why have we made mammon such a god in our personal and corporate lives?"[26] Will we let such questions interrogate us or will we erect defenses that keep these questions out of mind?

The use of narrative, like that of greed, is a matter of justice. Words conjure worlds and who is worthy to inhabit them fully. Words conjure histories and the power of memory and belonging. Narrative control determines who is cursed of Ham and who bears the image of God. Thus narrative and greed often collaborate in a terrifying tandem: the stories we tell are the stories that sell. If spinning a story, or rationalizing an inequity, or papering over serious iniquity will protect or profit, then greed and self-preservation will shape and birth the necessary narrative.

All of which makes Daniels's theft and use of the typewriter—a toy and tool of narrative conjuring and creation—poignant, if tragic, acts of just deconstruction:

> He walked to a desk upon which sat a typewriter. He was fascinated with the machine; never in his life had he used one of them. It was a queer instrument, something beyond the rim of his life. . . . As he had seen others do, he inserted a sheet of paper into the machine. It went in lopsided but he did not know how to straighten it. Spelling in a soft, diffident voice, he pecked his name on the keys: *freddaniels*. He looked at it and laughed.[27]

Underground, Daniels subverts the narratival tool to affirm his own personhood and mischievously mock the world and its toys, which have conspired to condemn him. Aboveground, this same tool, through newspaper head-lines, proclaims his guilt and empowers society to hunt him: "HUNT BLACK MAN WHO COMMITTED DOUBLE MURDER." Even Dan-iels's self-affirmation is dwarfed by the world above. Hope is fleeting in a senseless world.

Reconfiguring a Senseless World

If not already apparent, *The Man Who Lived Underground* is not con-cerned with presenting hopeful hints that the world reconfigured can em-body something more whole and just. If you are looking for something like Ellison's hopeful closing I/you dynamic, Wright is not your man. Nor will we find Baldwin's nuanced and complex treatment of hard figures and harder issues. Wright's prophetic gift is showing that reality is grim, and for this, many have critiqued him, Baldwin and Ellison included. The critique says that in presenting the suffering and stark pain of his Black characters so pessimistically, Wright failed to do justice to our hopefulness and our humanity.[28] But Imani Perry contends that the release of this novel stands as new evidence in Wright's defense, as does the long march of history:

> Now the tragic absurdity of Fred's life seems all too familiar. We see it on our screens regularly: the snuff films of white supremacy. Perhaps we have too readily judged Wright's bearing of witness to be reductively stark and fatalistic. What he observed is still happening, despite all those generations of unyielding hope.[29]

Perry makes a strong point. Though at times overly fatalistic and ideologi-cal, Wright's bleak honesty is necessary, and Christian readers must engage it, even if the worldview is not something to embrace. Christians are people of hope, so it is no strange thing to carry hope to bleak texts, just like we bring God's hope to a chaotic world. This means that even the violence and bleak cosmology that Wright presents are constructive insofar as we do not dismiss them but address them with Spirit-enflamed hope and action.

How do we do God's just work—the work of word and deed for the good of the world—when our own hearts are prone to idolatries and the world feels awash in injustices? To do this work means, first, to think carefully, critically, and Christianly about the structures and symbols and actions that breed death and oppression, and then to creatively imagine and redemptively build something different. If Daniels is trapped in the "whole configuration of the senseless world," then Christians are those under deep and unalterable orders to see this senseless world reconfigured into wholeness and justice, trusting in the eschatological hope that will come on that last day but implementing it now as best we can as a life-giving witness to the gospel.[30]

Doing justice is reconfiguring the senseless world according to the life and logic of the kingdom—and doing so joyfully and relentlessly—even as some stand opposed to our good news and our good works. For "to try to improve society is not worldliness but love. To wash your hands of society is not love but worldliness."[31] Christian commitment to the world and age to come means tangible and countercultural engagement with the world that is.

Practically speaking, this just reconfiguring happens, in part, as we lay holy hands on the primary trio of symbols Daniels encounters—religion, greed, and narrative. In the grip of idolatry, Christian faith, greed, and narrative become tools to construct and sustain a world in which Daniels and those like him are invisible and rejected. This is at root idolatry that violates the order of the cosmos and the good rule of the Creator. There is an alternative: through the hands of a new counter-community, faith, material means, and story can be the tools used to work toward a justice that reflects God and orients people to his kingdom. Such action bears interpretive witness that though the powers stalk the land, God's redeeming power is upending sin and evil. Wright's exploration of this trio—religion, greed, narrative—serves indirectly as a challenge to Christians to reconstruct or retrieve the vision of each that is whole and just and that demonstrates the in-breaking kingdom.

The Costs of Doing Justice

The Scriptures speak at length about each of the three primary realities that Daniels confronts and ponders in the underground, describing and prescribing the people of God as a just people in communion with the God of all righteousness. The issue is not whether God is concerned with justice but whether—or to what degree—his people will take up the concern in the sort of way that makes justice more tangible, our witness more credible, the downtrodden less vulnerable. This means caring for the unarmed, the unborn, the unmarried, the immigrant, the elderly, and the impoverished and forgotten in our cities.

Often the cost is prohibitive, since doing justice, biblically understood, always includes a hefty charge on our time, talent, and treasure. More than that, our reputations and comforts will be gloriously upended when we pursue justice that embodies *all* of Christ's concerns, not simply a pet ideological narrative. This disruptive plunge into the just way of Jesus often feels like a loss for disciples who have equated comfortableness with blessedness.

Part of the barrier to doing justice is that often we use a one-sided measure. We do this in order to maintain the comfort of mind—we think we are just—and the comforts of life—we don't disrupt our status quo. It's easy to let ourselves off the hook by considering one side of the justice coin. Biblical justice, however, asks not simply "Have I done anything wrong?" but "Have I done anything right?"[32]

Biblical justice uses the scales of omission and commission. Money in unholy hands, animated by a prone-to-wander idolatrous heart, can be used to further accelerate the spiraling forces of injustice. Or it simply languishes: used to not do wrong but also to not do right. Lord, have mercy on us. In Jesus, there is indeed mercy, but that mercy is not only forgiveness. Wrapped inside his grace is a merciful alternative. There is another way, a just way in which, under Jesus's Spirit, means and money are not tools for destruction but things stewarded to create belonging.

In Acts 4:32–35, Luke highlights this reconfiguring of the world as captured in the early church through means stewarded under the Spirit's wondrous sway:

> Now the full number of those who believed were of one heart and soul, and no one said that any of the things that belonged to him was his own, but they had everything in common. And with great power the apostles were giving their testimony to the resurrection of the Lord Jesus, and great grace was upon them all. There was not a needy person among them, for as many as were owners of lands or houses sold them and brought the proceeds of what was sold and laid it at the apostles' feet, and it was distributed to each as any had need.

Here money disrupts division and binds transnational persons together in the story of Jesus. This is one snapshot of biblical justice and jubilee (Deut. 15:4), where means are used to defend the needy, give life to those with their backs against the wall, and embody the gospel of Jesus, who, Luke declared, came "to proclaim good news to the poor" (Luke 4:18).

Through the just and generous use of means, believers together can express the life-giving power of Jesus as a people of light and justice in a world of greed and self.

Justice and Narrative

The stories we embrace become the tracks on which our lives run. Just as justice demands attention to sight, it demands attention to narrative, the stories we tell and believe of others in long form. It is instructive that as Daniels rubs the money between his fingers, "he was intrigued with the manifold reaction and attitudes he knew that men and women held toward it."[33] These reactions come from narrative—the stories we shape and believe—and the disordered desires of the heart that function as author. The power and idolatry of narrative is what allows Daniels to be arrested and branded as an object to be hunted.

In terms of narratival power, what Wright knew and described in 1941 remains in our world today. Wright's twentieth-century fiction resembles twenty-first-century fact: being Black in the vicinity of a crime is itself a crime that threatens to disrupt and alter one's existence and psyche permanently. The narrative of Black criminality, like racism in America, is both anti-Christian and historically sourced by Christians. As discussed in relation to *Passing*, Christianity is one national cause and the global cure for racial-narrative lies that denigrate image bearers. The narrative power of the Christian faith, rightly embraced, is not only true but also uniquely good and just.

Even the enormous injustices done under the banner of Christianity fail to overcome the fact that our essential and baseline beliefs about human dignity and equality emerge from Christianity. In *Dominion*, historian Tom Holland makes the point that what we take for granted as secular values—human dignity, equality, concern for the oppressed and marginalized—are indeed Christian in origin and nature.[34] Christians seeking to do justice do not need a new narrative but need to return to the ancient story and to do—and in many cases continue—the fresh and deep work of living it out.

This is where things seem to fall apart. Some American evangelical Christian quarters seem absorbed not with the task of doing justice but of debating it. Though it has not been the focus here, the distinction between a biblical conception of justice and the broader American society's definition *needs* to be distinguished and defined, as would be the case in any

155

cultural time and place. The issue is not debating complexities but that the debating has displaced the very clear and simplest commands of doing justice in our towns and cities.

Though Wright would have never guessed it, the very mediums in which this discourse is debated are themselves testament to the absurdity and bleakness of the world. Consider this: the democratization of platforms where anyone can launch an opinion into the far reaches of the internet has duped too many into fashioning themselves as active in fighting injustice by posting an image of a black square. Wright's critical portrait of the church in 1941 hits different nearly eight decades later. For contemporary believers, Wright's challenge is not that churches are useless through spiritualizing but that they are useless through fruitless debate, distraction, and eventually resignation.

Two Ways, One Demise

There are two ways to consider Daniels's demise at the novel's end. These two ways come from two different directions but reach this same bleak destination: the injustice of the world cannot be overcome. The two interpretive ways to understand Daniels's final acts—resignation to guilt or heroic assertion—become clear after we first look at the end, which will then help us consider the better way of God's just and hopeful kingdom.

First, a sense of Daniels's finale. In the underground, Daniels repeatedly hears the songs of the church. And when he resists the "old conviction" of religion rising in him, the novel seemingly rewards him with a new knowledge: "he was all people" and "banishing all fear and doubt and loss: he now knew the inexpressible value and importance of himself." By rejecting the religion that branded him with guilt first and dignity never, Daniels is now presented as metamorphosed. Or at least partly so: "Before he could live again, hope, or plan again, a regrouping of his faculties into a new personality structure would be necessary." This new transformation—the powerful cumulation of all the sewer symbols—drives Daniels to "assert himself . . . to devise a means of action by and through which he could convince those who lived aboveground of the death-like quality of their lives."[35] Daniels renounces the guilt of docile religion and becomes heroic: in the face of a fatalistic world, he has found something worth dying for.

That something is perplexing and the source of the novel's haunting close: Daniels dies because he chooses to return to the police who tortured him. This fateful return happens after Daniels peers through a basement wall and witnesses a young Black man being accused of stealing the radio—which Daniels took—and protesting his innocence while being beaten by the cops who earlier tortured Daniels. He goes aboveground to seek "expiation" and to confess his guilt—he took the radio—and then hopefully to show them the underground, that they might "be governed by the same impulse of pity."[36] In the end, they shoot Daniels dead.

The return of religious guilt—Daniels sings the repeated church song in the presence of the police just before his death—signifies that he throws his life away in simplistic naivete as "some deed of expiation."[37] He is guilty of theft and guilty of existence, and he embraces both. In this case, Daniels reflects some of Baldwin's critique of Bigger. He believed a theology of himself and his worthlessness that led him to death. For Wright, Daniels's embrace of moral and existential guilt by returning to the police is as natural as gravity: "Where else is there for him to go? The police have given him his meaningful life, such as it is, filled with horror." For Wright, Daniels's return to the police is more than "an overt act"—it is the completion of "a logical circle of feeling," over which, "within the limits in which he lives," he has "no control." Indeed, as Daniels runs to return to the police, his mind says no, but his body will not relent. Ultimately, Wright identifies Daniels's religious formation as the fatal cause: "I might add that had Fred Daniels been lucky enough to have had a different past, dream, and tradition, he would have acted differently."[38] Perry clearly sums up the view that guilt held sway over Daniels, from beginning to end: Wright has Daniels "careen from rage at the pervasive burden of guilt to an embrace of it."[39]

Though textually coherent, this reading of Daniels's resigned return to guilt and his naivete can equally be read as forced determinist logic that almost overthrows the credulity of the story. But maybe that is the point. Based on the deep racial trouble Wright knew in the early twentieth-century Jim Crow South and racialized North, showcasing a novelistic world "in which race is supremely deterministic, eclipsing notions of Truth and Justice," is more than understandable; it is historically and, in some ways, presently honest.[40]

At the same time that Wright paints Daniels as resigned to guilt, Wright suggests that Daniels is heroic, for he finds a cause worth dying for and he asserts himself. He finds something to live for in a world that has marked him out for death. He constructs personal purpose out of cosmic senselessness. In a strong nod to existentialism, Daniels "throws his life away" only to the outside perspective. From Daniels's internal view, "he emerges from the underground to communicate what he has seen, and to give testimony to what one feels is a right worth dying for."[41]

Both readings lead to the same conclusion: for the downtrodden, the world is cold and senseless, and it deals out death and exploitation. That Wright planned to follow up *Native Son* with Daniels's story proves the point: though Bigger is aimless and averse to religion and Daniels is employed and devout, the differences do not matter. Neither survive in a Jim Crow world or, Wright would suggest, in a world that deeply carries its origins and residue.

The fairest reading, textually speaking, of Daniels's end is likely an intersection of the two interpretive roads. It seems in Wright's view that Daniels cannot escape a death-giving inner logic, even as he attempts to heroically and existentially war against it. Even if he wars against it successfully, his best life is one outside of society, lived in the underground. Though docile religion via paralyzing guilt is clearly Wright's target, the same death-dealing outcomes emerge from heroic assertion, which Daniels attempts, and the assertive nihilism that Bigger, Daniels's predecessor, performs. Death abounds. If we singularly read Daniels's fate as driven by guilt and docile religion, then Daniels—like Bigger—has suffered a patterned hopelessness upon the soul, and as with a knife wound, one can choose to pull the blade out or plunge it deeper. Both men, according to their respective novels, struggle to locate the source of their wound.

For Wright, the moral arc of the universe is so deeply bent toward injustice that neither Bigger nor Daniels has much ability to resist a predetermined fate. Wright alerts us to the powers that plague systems and structures in which image bearers are crushed. This is stark and true—but it is not the whole story. The world is not senseless; it is contested. The world is not usually a just place, but neither is it fixed and static and bent irreparably toward futility. The kingdom of God is at hand. The reality of injustice is not a reason to abandon hope but a reason to vigorously fan it into flame and reconfigure the world. Heroic assertion is striving for justice and goodness, knowing that even in the dark, the light might shine. The best theological interpretation of *The Man Who Lived Underground* is an interpretation that is lived, lamenting injustice and laboring in faith for righteousness. This work of hopeful action is what we will turn to next.

Hope

Margaret Walker's "For My People"

It enriches the Christian life to see the future from a life lived in the power of God's Spirit in the present, and then see the present, from the vantage point of the kingdom that is to come.

—J. Deotis Roberts, *Liberation and Reconciliation*

I am neither an optimist nor a pessimist. Jesus Christ is risen from the dead.

—Lesslie Newbigin

There's something deeply stirring about Margaret Walker's "For My People" (1942). It is a poem that soars off the page and bounds across the imagination, evoking, with a marching drumlike cadence, both the plight and the resilience of Black American experience. Read aloud, it sings the harmonies of hope against the downbeat of pain. What Walker wrote for her people has been loved and seized by her people. It has become, as one critic expresses, a poem of communal property:

159

We knew the poem. It was ours. . . . And as [it] moved on, rhythmically piling image after image of our lives, making us know again the music wrenched from our slave agony, the religious faith, the toil and confusion and hope-lessness, the strength to endure in spite of it all, [it] went on mirroring our collective selves, [and] we cried out in deep response.[1]

The poem is ours, property of the Black existential public domain. It tells our story, and it teaches us—and any teachable, eavesdropping reader—what it means to keep hope alive. For this reason, there's no better final text to explore. Because Walker's poem recounts multiple images of Black experience, the poem gathers many of the themes we've examined in Wright, Baldwin, Ellison, and others. In a way, each stanza assembles the-matic pieces of previous texts and constructs a mosaic of Black pain, Black trouble, and Black hope.

In other words, "For My People" is a living history, an ode, an exhor-tation, a lament, a prayer. And through the fusion of those genres and the cumulative power of its imagery, it is a sermonic, poetic meditation on hope offered up to our people. Walker, like Countee Cullen, was the child of a Black minister. Undoubtedly, the sermonic influences from her father's ministry in the Methodist Episcopal Church shaped the homileti-cal cadence and biblical imagery of Walker's poetry, this poem especially. The influence of this poem on readers is of a biblical sort as well. From a theological perspective, Walker's words teach us that our sufferings and hardships need not put us to shame if we as a people partake in the faith and activity that belong to a true and thick hope.

A Recapitulation of Trials and Triumphs

Each of the first nine stanzas captures a panoramic slice of Black America—our hardships, failings, and triumphs. Themes found in other texts we have examined are present here, piled on each other in the retelling of our story: there is the disregard of dignity and image, as explored in *Invisible Man* (stanza 4); the threat of sin, systems, and powers, as seen in Wright (stanza 7); and the conundrum of religious hypocrisy depicted by Baldwin (stanza 8). This experiential panorama produces a profoundly visual qual-ity, additionally fueled by the poem's structure: the alternating length of the first seven stanzas and Walker's graceful and layered use of *-ing* verbs. The result is a poem that sounds and feels and portrays like Spike Lee's famous dolly-camera shots in *Malcolm X*: Walker's movements swivel and swoop to capture every angle and era of Black pain and hope in this land.

Walker does not simply capture images of Black life; she exhorts, dreams, and commands her people to imagine and build something new. Each of the poem's first nine stanzas is both a dedication to and a call to action for Black people universally ("for my people everywhere") and particularly ("for my playmates in the clay and dust and sand of Alabama").[2] Walker calls to her people in each stanza with affection that demands action, history that speaks honestly, and love that exhorts an active, participatory hope.

In terms of history, the poem begins with the fact that the challenge of surviving and thriving for our people is not first an internal problem but an external force of hatred, greed, and racism. The first stanza situates Black life in America as still ensconced in the legacy of slavery ("for my people everywhere singing their slave songs repeatedly"). This leads to the never-ending struggle of daily life found in the second stanza ("for my people . . . washing ironing cooking . . . never gaining never reaping"). Even so, there is a sense in which Walker calls her people up from despair and nihilism into joy, perseverance, and righteousness. Instead of wandering like a proverbial Israel through the wilderness of our cities as "lost disinherited dispossessed and happy people" who fill "cabarets and taverns and other people's pockets," we need "milk and land and money and something—something all our own." The allusions to Israel and the promised land serve to call Black people to do what we can "to fashion a better way," the very work she urges her people to do and commends them for doing in the penultimate stanza.

Thus, the vision of hope so visually contained in "For My People" is not a naive or contentless hope but a hope that knows its history, believes in participation, and urges us toward something that is in every way better. The hope that the poem portrays is communal, a truth that is both reminiscent of Christian faith and a corrective vision to Christian shortcomings. In other words, "For My People" teaches us something of what it means to hope for our people and all people in a spirit that is honest (historical) and God-centered (theological) and that imagines a better future to be sought in the present (eschatological).

Faith and Hope

Hope is one of the pillars of African American religious life. Black Christians have come this far by faith, which is another way of saying we have come this far by hope. The two are ultimately inseparable. As John Calvin famously noted in his *Institutes*, "Faith is the foundation on which hope rests; hope nourishes and sustains faith." What faith believes, hope expects: "Faith believes that God is true; hope expects that in due season he will manifest his truth. Faith believes that he is our Father; hope expects that he will always act the part of a Father towards us."[3] J. Deotis Roberts, one of the central voices of Black theology, speaks centuries later of the same interplay between faith and hope but with attention to Black Christian experience, in which faith and hope rest on the belief that God, not our suffering, has the last word:

> Black hope is rooted in the faith that the God of "the end time" is also the God of the "present time." God is our present Redeemer as well as our future Judge. This faith has kept hope alive when there was no tangible basis for hope. . . . Our faith in God has kept hope alive.[4]

This symbiotic relationship between faith and hope gives us a hope distinct from wishful thinking or human optimism. Such would be thin hope, not bad but simply insufficient for the rigors of suffering that Walker depicts and that Black folks have lived.

Strands of Hope: Experiential, Theological, Eschatological

Contrary to a thin hope, thick hope, even if fanned into flame by the faintest flickers of faith, is still an unmatched power through which one is sustained to keep fighting, to keep trusting, to keep living. Thick hope is like a sturdy rope, multiple strands merging together, which we use to rise from the pit of dejection and despair to stand, endure, and overcome. The analogy of a rope implies rescue and surrender. Someone else is letting hope down and guiding us up. Thick hope is not a wholly self-generated good. This hope consists of three strands or aspects. First, hope exists almost only in the context of experiential pain or dejection. Second, hope is decidedly theological, believing something about God and the world, as Calvin, pillar of the Reformed tradition, notes. Third, as Roberts, stalwart of the Black theology tradition, suggests, hope is eschatological, believing something about God, the present, and the future. Hope is then three-dimensional, featuring the experiential, the theological, and the eschatological.

Hope is not naivete; hope recognizes reality. One prerequisite for hope is the sober assessment of reality that comes from experiencing life as the bleak domain of sin and death. If life were not hard and harsh, hope of any sort would be unnecessary. Thick hope, real hope in this sense, is the opposite of naivete. The possibility of hope can emerge only when the world is viewed for what it is: a place where we sing our dirges, blues, and slave songs repeatedly.

In this historical and experiential realism, born of pain and suffering, hope finds its other defining feature: the theological. Thick hope is a theological hope, turning from the pain of this life to the goodness that is God. This hope pledges an allegiance of trust to God's goodness and faithfulness. This hope believes the world to be the domain in which his presence and compassion now reside, even in the face of overwhelming catastrophe. This hope goes further, affirming the future as the coming day in which measures of his goodness will more prominently take center stage while longing for the new age in which his perfect reign will not take center stage but will upstage and remake this broken world.

Walker's final stanza shows the future orientation or eschatological dynamic of hope, when she seeks to call forth a "new earth." The desire for the *new* to intersect with and consume the *now* is a sign of eschatological yearning, a long-standing element of Black religious and Christian hope. In this tradition, eschatology concerns "the consummation and rectification of history and the persistence of hope." A prime example is how "the vision of a new order was indispensable to Africans languishing in the foul embrace of slavery because it kept the fires of freedom burning in their hearts."[5] Future hope is not an opiate but a steroid that enhances endurance, resistance, and participation for change.

Eschatology permits us to fight against sin and injustice with the resolve that comes from knowing that in the end victory is guaranteed. The power of this hope is difficult to overstate; it is one of the few realities that truly transforms everything. To catch even the briefest glimpse of the finish line, of the promised land, is to receive from the Spirit a second wind. Backlash, barriers, and even our own feet may trip us up on the way toward personal and social righteousness, but the knowledge of the end reveals that what might look like "permanent defeats" are, in the shadow of the eschaton, "momentary failures." In this way, eschatology—the reality of God's coming full reign over all things—"provides a vision of hope that saves the oppressed from being overwhelmed by historical disillusionment."[6] Hope is eschatological because all history will be redeemed. All wrongs will be set right, and the world of sin and death will give way to the new heaven and new earth, where Christ will reign and righteousness, beauty, and goodness will never fade (Rev. 21). For the brokenhearted and suffering, the promise of the new heaven and new earth is essential to endure in suffering and to contend against evil.

If Not Hope, Then What?

In his incisive 2016 book *Between the World and Me*, Ta-Nehisi Coates speaks unflinchingly about the permanence of racism and its relentless assault on Black life.[7] Many Christians took note of his truth-telling. But what stood out most to many readers of faith was Coates's hopelessness that society would ever change. Again, if hope is a happy naivete, then it should and must be banished and replaced with something of real substance. But to reject a thin or trite hope and to replace it with nothing is like dancing with despair. If not hope, then what?

Walker's poem rejuvenates hope through the rejection of despair. The poem gives the sense that Walker registers all that is at stake: she writes, waging war for the life and soul of the Black community. The threat of death and despair is a matter of the exterior and the interior. Death already rages against us bodily through the forces of sin and injustice. To give way to hopelessness is to lose ground in the sacred territory of our hearts, our souls, for if hope has been evicted in the interior, despair will move in and set up shop for an internal decay. Death and despair will then claim victory from within (the soul) and without (society). When Walker writes of her people as "lost disinherited dispossessed" and "drinking when hopeless," we encounter her voiced concern that despair has indeed trespassed upon her people.

In the poem's cosmology, these vices of despair are the choice of our people in league with the machinations of malevolent powers. Despair and nihilism are human actions driven by hostile forces: "drinking when hopeless, tied, and shackled and tangled among ourselves by the unseen creatures who tower over us omnisciently and laugh." In Psalm 2, the Lord laughs at the nations who plot against his purposes, but here malevolent powers plot against Black image bearers and laugh at our vices of despair. Theologically speaking, the warning is clear: to give in to despair is to yield ground to the powers against us. The immediate thought might be to steel one's spine with the resolution to be full of hope. That sort of rugged individualism will not save us in this fight. It is not what Walker—or Scripture—prescribes. And really, what is one woman—or man—standing against the forces of sin and death, in the modern guise of racism, despair, nihilism, addiction, self-hatred? To stand, we must stand in the name of the suffering and conquering one and in the locked-arm power of community, recognizing that both God and others see us and say, "This one, yes, even the one who has baptized themselves into despair, this one belongs to my people."

It is difficult to remain in the pit of despair and shackled by hopelessness when we remember and know that we are part of a people. Remembering that we belong to a collective, a people, a body, is a ladder out of the pit, a lifeline in the valley of death, the breaking of dawn in the hour of utter darkness. Walker's poem stirs up communal hope by way of helping Black folks remember that we belong to the "countless generations" of Africans and all humanity. Specifically, Walker's panoramic journey through the travails and triumphs of Black experience intensifies hope through remembrance of whom we belong to: a people who have endured by power, hope, grace, guile, and faith. As a people, we have been afflicted in every way but not crushed; perplexed but not driven to despair; lynched but not forsaken; enslaved but not destroyed; assaulted but not vanquished; accused but not guilty; rejected by all manner of people but embraced by the God who stands over all. Thus, despair, as tempting as it is, is actually experientially lacking, for we as a communal people are still here. More than that, despair is a theological falsehood, for Christ, who suffered for us, like us, and with us, is risen.

Communal Hope

All of this means that at its best and brightest, hope is decidedly communal. Too often the boundaries of hope and its concomitant concern are drawn to encompass only the individual: hope terminates on me, never touching we. But God is rectifying the world not simply for me but for us. Even the rejuvenating results of hope bend toward community. Faith and hope lift you from the pit of despair so that you might turn, reach down, and lift up your brother, your sister, even your enemy.

Churches regularly and rightly speak about the need for community. And for those inside or outside the church, there's likely not a person who hasn't heard a diatribe against American individualism. Widespread research reports that American adolescents and adults are isolated and lonely, and they struggle outside of the prime years of college to make friends and maintain friendships.[8]

The communal nature of Walker's poem is therefore seriously compelling: it embodies and highlights something American society lacks. But the communal nature of Walker's poem is different from the important but general emphasis of churches to share life together or researchers' exhortation that Americans get more social. The communal hope at work in "For My People" emerges from a communal identity that senses and finds that one's own fate and well-being are tied up in that of another. It is a belief that includes and transcends an individual and is practiced by the individual for the whole. On a metalevel, this communal hope is the distilled essence of the poem. The title says it all: "For My People." It's a hope for those even beyond the writer's scope of personal relation, a hope that reaches out in the world, longing, praying, pleading, exhorting, and acting that others would experience with us that which is true and good.

Identity, Hope, Unity

"For My People" embodies the fiery passion of a communal hope, a bond of persons and destiny that flies in the face of American individualism. More than that, I hear in Walker's "for my people" refrain a reverberation of the apostle Paul's anguished cry for his "kinsmen according to the flesh" (Rom. 9:3). In Walker's case, she hopes and longs for Black Americans—her people—to rise in a new world of power, love, beauty, and freedom. In the apostle's case, he desires that Israel—his ethnic people—to whom "belong the adoption, the glory, the covenants, the giving of the law, the worship, and the promises" (v. 4), would receive the salvation promised in the Christ. He wants them to experience the fullness of God's saving power—holiness, freedom, beauty, and the salvation that comes from God's Messiah.

The connection is noteworthy because African Americans over the centuries have perceived and related to the apostle Paul in ways that are varied and complex. One scholar traces this historical reception of Paul using a few broad categories: radical rejection, reverential appropriation, typological correlation.[9] Because select Pauline texts were construed to sanction slavery, the apostle to the Gentiles became the favored minister of the slave master. As a result, many Black folks proceeded to joyfully embrace Jesus and radically reject Paul. Howard Thurman's grandmother, Nancy

Ambrose, is a well-cited example. Born a slave, she used to have him read the Bible aloud to her. He regularly read her the Gospels, Isaiah, and some psalms, but never anything from Paul besides 1 Corinthians 13. Years after, Thurman asked about the exclusion of Paul. Because her slave masters always preached slavery as God's will from Pauline texts, Ambrose made a vow to God: "I promised my Maker that if I ever learned to read and if freedom ever came, I would not read that part of the Bible."[10]

Though there is a complexity to the few texts regarding Greco-Roman slavery, the weight of Paul's writing and the Scriptures as a whole clearly affirm God's concern for Blacks' deliverance and our sense of identity, hope, and unity.[11] Rather than rejecting the apostle for perversions of the text used against us, we should see this thread of connection between Walker and the apostle's communal impulse as one small encouragement among many more substantive ones to reconsider how his world and words declare something hopeful and good that applies to Black experience and our physical and spiritual strivings.

What is instructive between both texts—Walker's and the apostle's text of longing—is the union of communal identity and communal hope. Belonging to a people means a passionate, unyielding hope for those very people to whom we are intimately tethered. Christianity sanctifies the ethnic bond without severing it. The revelation of Jesus as Lord and Christ has not for Paul led to the repudiation of what we would call his ethnic identity but rather to its holy intensification. He has become more zealous for the well-being of his people in light of his understanding that the God of Israel has been revealed in Jesus Christ.

Our own reading of Scripture and participation in the Christian life must lean in this way as we look for threads of scriptural connection that tighten and sanctify our bond to our people rather than rend it asunder. Jupiter Hammond, a preacher and the first published Black poet in America, often found a typological correlation between Paul and Black hope and longing. Explicitly using Romans 9:2–3, Hammond, despite the abuses of Pauline texts for enslavement, "perceives in Paul's writings a way to express his own care for his fellow enslaved Africans."[12] In a sense, Walker's poem could be seen as a contemporary riff on Paul's aching longing in Romans 9:2–3. It is a desire for one's people to thrive and flourish into the fullness of life and light.

The denial of ethnic bonds, identity, and solidarity in the name of Jesus is therefore a strange and concerning phenomena. Progressing as a Christian—that is, becoming more sanctified, more in step with the

Spirit—does not mean becoming less Nigerian, Korean, Irish, Puerto Rican, or otherwise. Sin is put off, the flesh is to be starved, Jesus is to be put on, but our ethnic identity and solidarity is not erased. It is enhanced by the Spirit, who purifies and intensifies. Because of Jesus, a holy Black Christian loves and embraces their identity and community more than they did the hours before they first believed. In so many ways, this is the applicational logic of Paul in Galatians. Christian unity makes senses only when ethnic difference is not erased by the gospel. Otherwise unity would be the default because conversion would produce uniformity through an ethnically neutered church. When in Galatians Paul denies that Gentile believers need to be circumcised to truly belong to the family of God through Jesus the Messiah, Paul affirms that Gentiles can be saved without becoming ethnic and cultural Jews. Galatians 3:28–29 states, "There is neither Jew nor Greek, there is neither slave nor free, there is no male and female, for you are all one in Christ Jesus. And if you are Christ's, then you are Abraham's offspring, heirs according to promise." The apostle cites three entrenched lines of human division and domination—ethnic, class, gender—all of which do not divide the oneness of the church nor preclude one from full status as an heir of God's promise. Paul's point is not the "obliteration of difference" but rather the "obliteration of dominance." This means that "quests for unity that presuppose or even demand sameness misconstrue Paul's dynamic, expansive notion of Christian unity."[13]

If Christian unity means the obliteration of dominance and the Spirit's purifying and intensifying zeal for Christ and our kinfolk according to the flesh, then the life of the Christian is an enfleshed memoir of love lived for one's people in the name of Jesus. The spiritual and material uplift of one's people is not compartmentalized from one's allegiance to Jesus. Christian hope touches our ethnic hope in an embrace that is altogether holy.

You Who Were Not My People

The ninth and penultimate stanza of Walker's poem places readers in the dialectic dance between the particular and the universal, between the hope for my people and the hope for all people. Similar to Ralph Ellison's I/you dynamic in *Invisible Man*, this ninth stanza reveals that there are two planes of beautiful obligation in human relation, and one need not trample the other. Walker shifts from the particular call to her Black kin to call out to all kin—"all the adams and eves." In our polarized age, full of fractured identities, we need this word that we remain bound to one another on ethnic, national, and local levels. But for those who follow the risen Lord, there is a deeper sense of didactic wonder. Walker's expansion of "my people" reminds us of the expansive, boundary-shifting love of God, who comes to "those who once . . . were not a people, but now . . . are God's people" (1 Pet. 2:10).

Walker's poem reflects some of the New Testament ethic of hope in another significant way, giving us a poetic lens through which to contemplate and savor a scriptural truth: who we call "my people" broadens without sacrificing the God-givenness of our ethnic and cultural origins. Put another way, the bonds of communal identity and hope expand, with new borders drawn by the very body of Christ. Those who were not our people become our people through spiritual union, by being bound up together in Jesus. And in the very same moment that "my people" undergoes a threefold transformation—expanding our identity, longing, and hope based on the new communal borders of Christ's body—the love for our first people does not die. It is resurrected to be a hope shaped by the self-giving, cruciform mind of Jesus. Paul again becomes an example when we recall that the kinsmen longing of Romans 9 does not negate the Gentile inclusion of Galatians 3:28. As the apostle to the Gentiles, he longed for *his people* (Israel) and welcomed *those people* (Gentiles) in a way that melded them into one new longing patterned after God's expansive love in Jesus. The more we remember our origin story in the people of God as one of inclusion—as *those people* grafted in by the crucified Christ—the more our perception of "my people" is aligned with God's divine prerogative and then performed in Christian embrace of each other and the other, for that too was once our name. This means that, in Jesus, we gain a new diverse people without the obliteration of our ethnic identity, which is now purified and intensified by the love and Spirit of Christ.

Let the New Creation Arise

In the summer of 2020, Ta-Nehisi Coates's tune on hope changed. In the wake of national protests over the police killings of George Floyd and Breonna Taylor and the vigilante killing of Ahmaud Arbery, a racial awakening dawned in our national consciousness. Asked by *Vox*'s Ezra Klein to describe what he saw in witnessing American cities filled with protests and American lives filled with conversations about racism and injustice, Coates replied, "I can't believe I'm gonna say this, but I see hope. I see progress right now."[14] But what happens if the progress stops or proves to be a false start, a flash lit in the cultural pan because it is now in vogue to speak and march and read and protest? If the progress halts, then what? Can we have hope without that hope needing to rest, in a way, on white people finally getting it? Surely there is something better, something more sturdy.

My hope is not wrapped up in the enlightening of people, white or otherwise, as much as that is to be pursued. My hope is not tied to social progress, as much as that is to be desired. These are secondary causes for hope. My hope is wrapped up in nothing less than the one whose death conquered death and in whose life I find my own and through whose resurrection the new creation has launched and landed on this old broken world. The foundation of hope is the empty tomb.

A new world has indeed arisen. It rose when Jesus's dead body was filled with resurrection life and his feet marched out of the grave, each step confirming his victory and authority. If the new creation is among us, why then such suffering and devastation? Christians are well familiar with the dual reality of our eschatology. We reside in the in-between times. Our address is solidly fixed at the intersection of the already and the not yet. Sin and death have been defeated but not yet destroyed (1 Cor. 15:26). This tension between this present evil age and the new creation on the way finds its microcosm in the war that rages inside each Christian. Just as we work in our lives for the Spirit to reign over the flesh, communally we fight for righteousness to reign over injustice.

This theological lens illumines the visceral and militant terms Walker uses to summon a new world of goodness and freedom. "Let a bloody peace be written in the sky," Walker writes when she calls out for a "new earth [to] rise," one that "will hold all the people." To secure this new world of unity, justice, and freedom, Walker declares the marching orders: "Let the martial songs be written, let the dirges disappear." Songs of war paradoxically lead to a world of healing. The suggestion is that hope is active, taxing work. It is decidedly a battle against the aforementioned "unseen creatures who tower over us," a fight against the temptation to nihilism (stanza 6) and racism's deep presence and long shadow (stanza 1). Hope is not passive work. It is love dressed in battle armor, a war waged with weapons of righteousness—faith, love, resistance, peace, protest, proclamation, prayer.

Walker's sermonic poem culminates in the connection between eschatology and activity, or said differently, eschatology and ethics. Theological hope, which is by nature eschatological, means we do different and we do

170

right in the moments known as now because we long and ache for what is to come. Faith in the resurrection births active faith in the world. In *Liberation and Reconciliation: A Black Theology*, J. Deotis Roberts unpacks this crucial connection:

> Ethics and eschatology are related in Black Theology. This is the basis of the black hope. This is the bridge between the now and the not yet, the promised and the fulfilled. . . . Things hoped for and reached after always elude complete fulfillment, but the promises and ideals of the Christian faith inspire us to keep "reaching." Indeed, a Christian dies reaching.[15]

This reaching is a form of "martial song," a type of active skirmish against sin and unrighteousness, a means of active participation so the kingdom might come on earth as it is in heaven. "The eschatological life" is therefore "the active life . . . lived in mission and service, in love and in worship."[16] We must then ask ourselves, "Are we active? Are we fighting? Are we loving? Are we reaching?"

Most days it does not feel like the new world is rising. It does not feel like Christians are reaching. It does not feel like we are living and loving in step with the new definition of "my people." It feels like death is gaining steam. It feels like injustice is taking fresh ground. It feels like instead of doing justice, many churches are policing how to talk about injustice. Hope is not irrational, though these factors make it seem so. Hope is, however, paradoxical. Walker's most vivid image of hope for all people—"a bloody peace written in the sky"—is powerful precisely because of its paradox. The paradox of hope is the paradox of the new creation, which comes through death giving way to life and through light that shines in the darkness.

The new creation is rising because Christ has died, Christ is risen, and Christ will come again. Walker calls her people up to labor and love to attain a new world, but Christ is calling the new world down to be received as a gift from his crucified hands and life-giving Spirit. This new world is inaugurated paradoxically by a bloody peace:

> For God was pleased to have all his fullness dwell in him, and through him to reconcile to himself all things, whether things on earth or things in heaven, by making peace through his blood, shed on the cross. (Col. 1:19–20 NIV)

Let us fix our eyes on that bloody cross that hung against the backdrop of the arid Palestinian sky, for the hope Walker expresses for her people is fully realized in the risen and present Christ, who has made Black people—and all people—his people through the offer of the gospel and the gift of the Holy Spirit. New life in the Spirit means new hope in the flesh, for the new creation is not only on the way but also underway, personally and cosmically (2 Cor. 5:17–19). It is then time for the martial songs of holiness and love. In the place of passivity and despair, let us march and live according to the pattern of the resurrection and the world to come. Let us love our people and all people through the Spirit, who gives us the mind of Christ. Let us put on hope as a posture, a practice, a patience, a participation. Let us meet despair with hope and hate with love because Christ is risen. Let us labor today in the Spirit's power for the reign of righteousness and peace that will come in fullness on that day. Into the hope of this new creation, let all people come.

Acknowledgments

If these acknowledgments read like the words of someone who didn't think this would happen, it's because that's exactly how I feel. I am profoundly grateful for the grace and opportunity to write this book and for the many people who helped make it a reality.

Thank you to Bob Hosack and the entire amazing team at Brazos Press. It has been a joy to work with you all, and I'm grateful for your belief in me and this project.

Thank you to every teacher, classmate, and librarian who throughout my life placed in me and cultivated a love of reading, writing, and the wonder of words. Thanks to every pastor, church, and friend who helped cultivate in me a love for Christ and his kingdom. And thanks to the many examples who showed me how to put these two loves together.

Thank you to all my English professors at Western Washington University for their investment and instruction, especially Lysa Rivera, Bill Smith, Donna Qualley, and the late Kathy Lundeen.

Endless thanks to Tiffany Kriner. You have been a champion of this book since day one. Your encouragement and feedback have truly made this book better. I'm grateful for your brilliance and generosity.

Thank you to Karen Swallow Prior, Erin Straza, Esau McCaulley, Rebecca McLaughlin, and others who helped this unknown writer get his foot in the door of the publishing world. Thank you for your generosity, wisdom, and advocacy. Thank you, Karen, for helping to spark this book idea in my mind through your wonderful work.

Thank you to Rob and Kati Berreth, Rechab Gray, Josh Kluth, Cynthia Wallace, CJ Quartlbaum, Jason Cook, Matt Wilcoxen, Keidrick Roy, Cole Brown, and any others I may have forgotten for offering thoughtful and helpful feedback on early (and last-minute!) drafts.

Grace and peace to the people of Fellowship Memphis. Thank you for praying for me and being a wonderful church. Thanks and love to the FM staff for being amazing and also celebrating me with a cereal party. Thanks to the McCurry crew for letting me stay and write in your pool house.

To my mom, I cannot thank you enough for loving me and doing everything to provide for me. I hope you are proud. We made it. I love you.

To my wife, Kelsey, thank you for choosing me. This is your book too. Thanks for being my best friend, my first reader, and my beloved. You mean everything to me.

To my kids, Julian, Adrian, and Tatum, thank you for sacrificing time with me so I could write this book. I hope you'll be proud when you read it. Now that it's done, I'll get back to writing Aldimer Cat stories for your eyes only.

Discussion Questions

Chapter 1—Image of God: Ralph Ellison's *Invisible Man*

1. How have you generally understood what it means to be made in the image of God?
2. How does the novel's emphasis on bodies and physicality contribute to its theme of invisibility?
3. In what ways are dignity and imaging dependent on mutual recognition? What might this mean for establishing meaningful communities and life together?
4. What do you make of Ellison's I/you dynamic in the epilogue?
5. Who are the "invisible" in your community? What would it take for them to be seen?

Chapter 2—Sin: Richard Wright's *Native Son*

1. How does Bigger's journey illumine or complicate notions of personal and systematic sin?
2. James Baldwin critiqued Wright's portrayal of Bigger. Does Bigger feel like a fully realized person or a character flattened to achieve Wright's protest against social conditions?

3. What is the role of fear and fate in *Native Son*?

4. Do you think Sin produces a "feedback loop"? Why or why not?

5. Does *Native Son* suggest any ways for contending against Sin as both a noun and a verb?

Chapter 3—God: James Baldwin's *Go Tell It on the Mountain*

1. In what ways do Gabriel's actions provide an important cautionary tale?

2. In what ways do you see people try to domesticate God? In what ways are you prone to this same impulse?

3. How does time function in support of the novel's thematic concerns?

4. What can Christians learn from the theme of witness in the novel?

5. Prior to the release of Baldwin's *The Fire Next Time*, *Go Tell It on the Mountain* was not roundly read as a critique of Christianity. Do you see the novel as more a critique, a condemnation, or a vindication of the faith?

Chapter 4—Jesus: Countee Cullen's "Christ Recrucified" and "The Black Christ"

1. Which of Cullen's poems resonates most with you? Discuss Cullen's use of imagery and perspective in each and its impact.

2. What does it mean to consider Jesus as one who suffers for, like, and with us?

3. In what ways are the cross and lynching connected? Are there any dangers in pressing this connection too far?

4. In what ways were Cullen's poems a corrective to the christological and ethical failures of his day? What correctives—or retrievals—are needed today in the American church's vision of Jesus?

5. How do we avoid Jesus becoming in our minds and practice a contentless banner for our pet causes?

Chapter 5—Salvation: Zora Neale Hurston's *Moses, Man of the Mountain*

1. How should Christians approach novelistic works that engage in alternative renderings of biblical narratives?
2. Discuss Hurston's alterations to the biblical exodus narrative and your response to such changes. How do these changes support or limit Hurston's reflections on liberation?
3. Discuss the relationship between liberation and salvation in *Moses, Man of the Mountain* and in the Christian life.
4. Did *Moses, Man of the Mountain* defamiliarize the biblical narrative for you? Did you find this constructive or unhelpful?
5. In what ways can Christians today learn from African Americans' attention to the exodus narrative?

Chapter 6—Racism: Nella Larsen's *Passing*

1. How do race and class collide in the motives and actions of Clare? Irene?
2. In what ways does *Passing* complicate present-day conversations on race and racism?
3. What role does Christianity play in the novel? In what ways is this important for us to consider today?
4. Have you seen or experienced a "dueling racial consciousness" or the "narrative of racial hierarchy"? How have you dealt with either?
5. Discuss the novel's ending in light of the novel's epigraph, particularly the last line, "What is Africa to me?" How does this shape your view of Irene in the finale?

Chapter 7—Healing and Memory: Toni Morrison's *Beloved*

1. How do the novel's form and structure support its content and themes?
2. Discuss and hold space for your personal responses to the horrors of American slavery as depicted in *Beloved*.

3. In what ways do community and memory contribute to both tragedy and healing in *Beloved*? What lessons can Christians glean from this?

4. Discuss your understanding of Beloved and the grown woman who visits 124.

5. How might Sethe's journey to hope and healing instruct your own?

Chapter 8—Lament: W. E. B. Du Bois's "The Litany of Atlanta"

1. What distinguishes lament, biblically understood, from venting or complaining?

2. What traces of biblical lament are present in "The Litany of Atlanta"?

3. Discuss the thematic and rhetorical impact of the congregational responses in "The Litany of Atlanta."

4. What might be behind the general lack of lament in many American churches?

5. In what ways can lament form us in authentic spiritual maturity?

Chapter 9—Justice: Richard Wright's *The Man Who Lived Underground*

1. Discuss the importance and symbolism of the underground.

2. Discuss the similarities and differences between Wright's Fred Daniels and Ellison's Invisible in *Invisible Man*.

3. What's the relationship between religion and justice in the novel? Is this similar to or different from the scriptural vision?

4. What does it mean to do justice according to the Bible? How might individuals or communities do justice using the symbols and tools Daniels explores in the underground?

5. Do you read the novel's end as guilty resignation, heroic assertion, or something else? Why?

Chapter 10—Hope: Margaret Walker's "For My People"

1. Discuss the poetic devices Walker uses to portray a panoramic view of Black experience.

2. Discuss the differences between thin and thick hope.

3. What is the relationship between hope and faith?

4. In what ways does the gospel produce in Christians a particular and a universal understanding of "my people"?

5. What does Walker's poem suggest about the place of realism and eschatology in one's conception of hope? What can we learn from this?

Notes

Introduction

1. Roger Ebert, "Ebert's Walk of Fame Remarks," RogerEbert.com, June 24, 2005, https://www.rogerebert.com/roger-ebert/eberts-walk-of-fame-remarks.

2. Martha C. Nussbaum, *Poetic Justice: The Literary Imagination and Public Life* (Boston: Beacon, 1997), 5.

3. Frederick Douglass, *Narrative of the Life of Frederick Douglass, An American Slave* (New York: Signet Classics, 1997), 120.

Chapter 1 Image of God

1. DeNeen L. Brown, "'I Am a Man': The Ugly Memphis Sanitation Workers' Strike That Led to MLK's Assassination," *Washington Post*, February 12, 2018, https://www.washingtonpost.com/news/retropolis/wp/2018/02/12/i-am-a-man-the-1968-memphis-sanitation-workers-strike-that-led-to-mlks-assassination.

2. Brown, "'I Am a Man.'" See also Taylor Branch, *At Canaan's Edge: America in the King Years, 1965–1968* (New York: Simon & Schuster, 2006), 684–85.

3. For a helpful introductory overview on the *imago Dei*, see Beth Felker Jones, *Practicing Christian Doctrine: An Introduction to Thinking and Living Theologically* (Grand Rapids: Baker Academic, 2014), 97–116.

4. Gerald Bray, "The Image of God," in *Lexham Survey of Theology*, ed. Brannon Ellis and Mark Ward (Bellingham, WA: Lexham, 2018).

5. Anthony A. Hoekema, *Created in God's Image* (Grand Rapids: Eerdmans, 1986), 73.

6. Marc Cortez, *Theological Anthropology: A Guide for the Perplexed* (New York: T&T Clark, 2010), 21.

7. Cortez, *Theological Anthropology*, 9.

8. Herman Bavinck, *Reformed Dogmatics*, vol. 2, *God and Creation*, ed. John Bolt (Grand Rapids: Baker Academic, 2004), 55.

9. Ralph Ellison, *Invisible Man* (New York: Random House, 1994), 3.

10. Hoekema, *Created in God's Image*, 73.

11. Ellison, *Invisible Man*, 3.

12. Ellison, *Invisible Man*, 3.

13. Ellison, *Invisible Man*, 18.

14. Ellison, *Invisible Man*, 32.

15. Ellison, *Invisible Man*, 31–32.

16. Ellison, *Invisible Man*, 31.

17. Bruce L. Fields, *Introducing Black Theology* (Grand Rapids: Baker Academic, 2001), 67.

18. Ta-Nehisi Coates, *Between the World and Me* (New York: Random House, 2015), 10.

19. Sojourner Truth, *Ain't I a Woman?* (United Kingdom: Penguin, 2020).

20. Ellison, *Invisible Man*, 253.

21. Invisible's early perspectives on personal responsibility and education are clear allusions to the philosophies of Booker T. Washington, as are the Negro college, its statue and rhetoric, and the references to the Founder in the novel's first two chapters.

22. Ellison, *Invisible Man*, 138.

23. Ellison, *Invisible Man*, 147.

24. Ellison, *Invisible Man*, 159–60.

25. Ellison, *Invisible Man*, 15.

26. Fields, *Introducing Black Theology*, 67.

27. Howard Thurman, *Jesus and the Disinherited* (Boston: Beacon, 1996), 39.

28. Ellison, *Invisible Man*, 298.

29. Ellison, *Invisible Man*, 465–66.

30. Ellison, *Invisible Man*, 499.

31. Ellison, *Invisible Man*, 500.

32. Michael Eric Dyson, "We draw breath. They draw conclusions. Our lives draw to an end.," Twitter, May 27, 2020, 11:43 a.m., https://twitter.com/michaeledyson/status/1265670025152794629.

33. Kevin DeYoung, "Thinking Theologically about Racial Tensions: The Image of God," The Gospel Coalition, July 15, 2020, https://www.thegospelcoalition.org/blogs/kevin-deyoung/thinking-theologically-about-racial-tensions-the-image-of-god.

34. Ellison, *Invisible Man*, 500.

35. See Ralph Ellison, "The Novel as a Function of American Democracy," in *The Collected Essays of Ralph Ellison*, ed. John F. Callahan (New York: Random House, 2003), 759–70.

36. Karl Barth, *Church Dogmatics*, vol. III/2, *The Doctrine of Creation*, trans. G. W. Bromiley and T. F. Torrance (New York: T&T Clark, 2004), 250.

37. M. Cooper Harriss, *Ralph Ellison's Invisible Theology* (New York: New York University Press, 2017), 27.

38. Barth, *Church Dogmatics* III/2, 251–52.

Chapter 2 Sin

1. Richard Wright, *Native Son* (New York: Harper Perennial, 2005), 3.

2. Howard Thurman, *Jesus and the Disinherited* (Boston: Beacon, 1996), 26.

3. Wright, *Native Son*, 6.

4. Beverly Roberts Gaventa, "The Cosmic Power of Sin in Paul's Letter to the Romans: Toward a Widescreen Edition," *Interpretation* 58, no. 3 (July 2004): 232.

5. Fleming Rutledge, *The Crucifixion: Understanding the Death of Jesus Christ* (Grand Rapids: Eerdmans, 2015), 189.

6. James K. A. Smith, *Desiring the Kingdom: Worship, Worldview, and Cultural Formation* (Grand Rapids: Baker Academic, 2009), 92.

7. Richard Wright, quoted in Louis Menand, "The Hammer and the Nail," *New Yorker*, July, 20, 1992, https://www.newyorker.com/magazine/1992/07/20/the-hammer-and-the-nail.

8. Wright, *Native Son*, 20.

9. Wright, *Native Son*, 295.

10. Matthew Croasmun, *The Emergence of Sin: The Cosmic Tyrant in Romans* (New York: Oxford University Press, 2017), 36.

11. Croasmun, *Emergence of Sin*, 36.

12. Scot McKnight, "Rethinking Systemic Sin," *Jesus Creed*, February 6, 2020, https://www.christianitytoday.com/scot-mcknight/2020/february/rethinking-systemic-sin.html.

13. Millard J. Erickson, *Christian Theology*, 3rd ed. (Grand Rapids: Baker Academic, 2013), 584.

14. Martin Luther King Jr., *Where Do We Go from Here: Chaos or Community?* (Boston: Beacon, 2010), 37.

15. Wright, *Native Son*, 10.

16. Martha C. Nussbaum, *Poetic Justice: The Literary Imagination and Public Life* (Boston: Beacon, 1997), 11.

17. Thabiti Anyabwile, *The Faithful Preacher: Recapturing the Vision of Three Pioneering African-American Pastors* (Wheaton: Crossway, 2007), 123.

18. Wright, *Native Son*, 20.

19. Thurman, *Jesus and the Disinherited*, 29.

20. Thurman, *Jesus and the Disinherited*, 71.

21. Wright, *Native Son*, 354.

22. King, *Where Do We Go from Here?*, 64.

23. Reinhold Niebuhr, *Man's Nature and His Communities* (Eugene, OR: Wipf & Stock, 2012), 24.

24. Wright, *Native Son*, 419.

25. From the hymn "Joy to the World" by Isaac Watts (1719).

Chapter 3 God

1. Though Gabriel is in fact John's stepfather, he is called his father throughout the novel.

2. Clarence Hardy observes, "In much of his early work, Baldwin describes a Christianity that equates the black with the ugly and the damned, even as it paradoxically provides the rhetorical and institutional space for black resistance and black humanity." Hardy, "James Baldwin as Religious Writer: The Gifts and Burdens of Black Evangelicalism," in *A Historical Guide to James Baldwin*, ed. Douglass Fields (New York: Oxford University Press, 2009), 65.

3. Sondra O'Neale observes that such a reading of the novel did not emerge until after the publication of *The Fire Next Time*, in which Baldwin sharply continues his critiques of the Christian church. O'Neale, "Fathers, Gods, and Religion: Perceptions of Christianity and Ethnic Faith in James Baldwin," in *Critical Essays on James Baldwin*, ed. F. Stanley and N. V. Burt (Boston: G. K. Hall, 1988), 140. Michael F. Lynch notes, "Whatever his feelings about the Christian Church and religion, Baldwin clearly must be considered a theological writer, one who continually wrestles with the identity and meaning of God and whose debt to Christian ideals informs his own evolving vision." Lynch, "Just above My Head: James Baldwin's Quest for Belief," *Literature and Theology* 11, no. 3 (September 1997): 290.

4. James Baldwin, *Go Tell It on the Mountain* (New York: Random House, 1995), 110.

5. See James K. A. Smith, *You Are What You Love* (Grand Rapids: Brazos, 2016); and *Desiring the Kingdom: Worship, Worldview, and Cultural Formation* (Grand Rapids: Baker Academic, 2009), for some of the flaws in this dictum, which views human action as overly driven by explicitly rational motivations, overlooking the place of the heart and desire.

6. This hiddenness of the divine fits with Clarence E. Hardy's observation about Baldwin's general approach to God-talk: Baldwin seldom specified "how Christian beliefs might have shaped institutional and individual religious practice" but would often "instead describe and criticize general tendencies within Christian institutions." Attached as it were to the

underside of these descriptions and critiques of Christian practice are questions about God hiding in plain sight. Hardy, *James Baldwin's God: Sex, Hope, and Crisis in Black Holiness Culture* (Knoxville: University of Tennessee Press, 2003), 11.

7. Douglass Decelle, "How Christianity Lost James Baldwin," First Light, January 14, 2018, http://www.douglasdecelle.net/how-christianity-lost-james-baldwin.

8. Baldwin, *Go Tell It on the Mountain*, 15–16.

9. Baldwin, *Go Tell It on the Mountain*, 15–16.

10. Baldwin, *Go Tell It on the Mountain*, 25–26.

11. John turns to self-love as self-salvation. This theme of a sort of self-salvation found outside the church is forcefully depicted in Baldwin's play *The Amen Corner*.

12. Baldwin, *Go Tell It on the Mountain*, 75.

13. Baldwin, *Go Tell It on the Mountain*, 111.

14. Baldwin, *Go Tell It on the Mountain*, 113.

15. Notice the prominence of power in Gabriel's sexual pursuit of a woman that leads, the next morning, to his conversion moment: "And he drank again, allowing, unconsciously, or nearly, his face to fall into the lines of innocence and power which his experience with women had told him made their love come down." Baldwin, *Go Tell It on the Mountain*, 116. Gabriel puts on a performance to seduce, a mixture of innocence and power. These two attributes, though deployed in a different way, are the heart of his terrorizing religious hypocrisy: he lusts for power as a religious figure, and at every turn he claims innocence of his clear faults and sins. As Florence asks, Can someone really change, or is Gabriel the same man he's always been, just now in religious garb?

16. Andy Crouch's paradigm that flourishing comes from authority and vulnerability is illuminating here and provides another way to understand and learn from the tragedy of Gabriel. See Andy Crouch, *Strong and Weak: Embracing a Life of Love, Risk, and True Flourishing* (Downers Grove, IL: InterVarsity, 2016).

17. Though this phrase has become conflated with Reformed or Calvinistic theology, the term does not necessarily possess the same connotation for African American Christians, for whom the term "Big God" does not lead them to think the way white evangelical believers may think of Reformed doctrine.

18. Baldwin writes, "He imagined her, because of the sermon he would preach, on her knees before the altar." Baldwin, *Go Tell It on the Mountain*, 147. As with Gabriel's conversion, there is a connection between the spiritual and the sensual.

19. Baldwin, *Go Tell It on the Mountain*, 126.

20. Baldwin, *Go Tell It on the Mountain*, 190.

21. Dietrich Bonhoeffer, *The Cost of Discipleship*, First Touchstone ed. (New York: Simon & Schuster, 1995), 44.

22. Timothy Keller, pastor and author, has said this throughout the years in sermons and interviews. See, e.g., Timothy Keller, "If your god never disagrees with you, you might just be worshiping an idealized version of yourself," Twitter, September 12, 2014, 12:00 p.m., https://twitter.com/timkellernyc/status/510458013606739968.

23. Hardy, "James Baldwin as Religious Writer," 73.

24. The link between Gabriel and a slaveholding religion is also quietly suggested through the mediatory role played in his conversion by his mother, a former slave who even when freed "had no wish to go North," where "wickedness dwelt," but was "content to stay in this cabin and do washing for the white folks." Baldwin, *Go Tell It on the Mountain*, 84–85.

25. James Baldwin and Margaret Mead, *A Rap on Race* (New York: Random House, 1992), 83.

26. Quoted in Lynch, "Just above My Head," 289.

184

27. James Baldwin, "In Search of a Majority," in *Collected Essays* (New York: Library of America, 1998), 221.

28. For the historical basis of such claims, see works such as Jemar Tisby, *The Color of Compromise: The Truth about the American Church's Complicity in Racism* (Grand Rapids: Zondervan, 2019); and Robert P. Jones, *White Too Long: The Legacy of White Supremacy in American Christianity* (New York: Simon & Schuster, 2020).

29. Baldwin, "In Search of a Majority," 220.

30. Lynch, "Just above My Head," 288.

31. James Baldwin, *The Fire Next Time* (New York: Vintage International, 1993), 31.

32. Michael Ramsey, *The Christian Priest Today*, rev. ed. (Eugene, OR: Wipf & Stock, 2012), 25.

33. Baldwin, "In Search of a Majority," 220.

34. In our attempts to know God, we come to face the fact that God is incomprehensible but has in his accommodating kindness revealed himself to us (Ps. 139:17–18).

35. Martin Luther King Jr., "Letter from Birmingham City Jail," in *A Testament of Hope: The Essential Writings and Speeches of Martin Luther King, Jr.*, ed. James Melvin Washington (New York: HarperCollins, 1991), 298.

36. O'Neale, "Fathers, Gods, and Religion," 132–33.

37. O'Neale, "Fathers, Gods, and Religion," 133.

38. Frederick Douglass, *Narrative of the Life of Frederick Douglass, An American Slave* (New York: Signet Classics, 1997), 120.

39. O'Neale, "Fathers, Gods, and Religion," 140–41.

40. Baldwin, *Go Tell It on the Mountain*, 17, 76.

41. Baldwin, *Go Tell It on the Mountain*, 23.

42. Clarence E. Hardy, *James Baldwin's God: Sex, Hope, and Crisis in Black Holiness Culture* (Knoxville: University of Tennessee Press, 2003), 10.

43. Baldwin, *Go Tell It on the Mountain*, 266.

44. Baldwin, *Go Tell It on the Mountain*, 279.

45. Baldwin, *Go Tell It on the Mountain*, 281.

46. Baldwin, *Go Tell It on the Mountain*, 279–80.

Chapter 4 Jesus

1. Edward J. Blum and Paul Harvey, *The Color of Christ: The Son of God and the Saga of Race in America* (Chapel Hill: University of North Carolina Press, 2014), 8.

2. Campbell Robertson, "A Lynching Memorial Is Opening. The Country Has Never Seen Anything Like It," *New York Times*, April 25, 2018, https://www.nytimes.com/2018/04/25/us/lynching-memorial-alabama.html.

3. James Cone, *The Cross and the Lynching Tree* (Maryknoll, NY: Orbis Books, 2011), xiv.

4. Cone, *The Cross and the Lynching Tree*, xiii, xiv.

5. Quoted in Lisa M. Bowens, *African American Readings of Paul: Reception, Resistance, and Transformation* (Grand Rapids: Eerdmans, 2020), 197.

6. Countee Cullen, "The Black Christ," in *The Black Christ and Other Poems* (New York: Harper & Brothers, 1929), 96.

7. Cullen, "The Black Christ," 96.

8. Cone, *The Cross and the Lynching Tree*, 95.

9. John Stott, *The Cross of Christ*, 20th anniversary ed. (Downers Grove, IL: InterVarsity, 2006), 211.

10. For more on atonement views, see James Beilby and Paul R. Eddy, eds., *The Nature of the Atonement: Four Views* (Downers Grove, IL: IVP Academic, 2006).

11. Joshua M. McNall, *Mosaic of Atonement: An Integrated Approach to Christ's Work* (Grand Rapids: Zondervan Academic, 2019), 21.

12. Simon Gathercole, quoted in McNall, *Mosaic of Atonement*, 23.

13. Though penal-substitutionary atonement is biblically, theologically, and ethically coherent, the doctrine is often preached in ways that are anything but. Stott notes that substitution demands we speak in a manner that reflects the unity of the Father and the Son in the work of atonement. We "have no liberty . . . to imply either that God compelled Jesus to do what he was unwilling to do himself, or that Jesus was an unwilling victim of God's harsh justice. Jesus Christ did indeed bear the penalty of our sins, but God was active in and through Christ doing it, and Christ was freely playing his part. . . . We must not, then, speak of God punishing Jesus or of Jesus persuading God, for to do so is to set them over against each other as if they acted independently of each other or were even in conflict with each other. . . . Both God and Christ were subjects not objects, taking the initiative together to save sinners." Stott, *Cross of Christ*, 150–51.

14. Karl Barth, *Church Dogmatics*, vol. IV/1, *The Doctrine of Reconciliation*, trans. G. W. Bromiley and T. F. Torrance (New York: T&T Clark, 2004), 75.

15. This line comes from the hymn "When I Survey the Wondrous Cross" by Isaac Watts (1707).

16. Fleming Rutledge, *The Crucifixion: Understanding the Death of Jesus Christ* (Grand Rapids: Eerdmans, 2015), 5.

17. 1981 PBS series *The Christians*, quoted in Rutledge, *Crucifixion*, 75.

18. Cone, *The Cross and the Lynching Tree*, 21–22. Cone seems to acknowledge the limits of his theological project: "I realize that my theological limitations and my close identity with the social conditions of black people could blind me to the truth of the gospel. And maybe our white theologians are right when they insist that I have overlooked the *universal* significance of Jesus' message." James H. Cone, *God of the Oppressed* (Maryknoll, NY: Orbis Books, 1997), 126.

19. Joshua M. McNall argues that Abelard's view was not the total rejection of satisfaction often ascribed to him. See McNall, *Mosaic of Atonement*, chap. 11 ("Beckoning Love: Rethinking Abelard and Moral Influence").

20. This concept of unearned suffering as redemptive is central to the life and work of Martin Luther King Jr. For more, see Mika Edmondson, *The Power of Unearned Suffering: The Roots and Implications of Martin Luther King Jr.'s Theodicy* (Lanham, MD: Lexington Books, 2017).

21. Kelly Brown Douglass, *The Black Christ* (Maryknoll, NY: Orbis Books, 1993), 12.

22. This is why, despite the bankruptcy of the term in American circles due to political idolatry and malpractice, the majority of African American Christians are the best of the evangelical tradition in that we believe in the personal, attractive, victorious reality of Jesus in our daily lives.

23. Thabiti M. Anyabwile, *The Decline of African American Theology: From Biblical Faith to Cultural Captivity* (Downers Grove, IL: InterVarsity, 2007), 146.

24. Willie James Jennings, *The Christian Imagination: Theology and the Origins of Race* (New Haven: Yale University Press, 2010), 277.

25. Tony Evans, *Oneness Embraced: Through the Eyes of Tony Evans* (Chicago: Moody, 2011), 153–54.

26. Quoted in Stephen Wellum, *Christ Alone: The Uniqueness of Jesus as Savior: What the Reformers Taught . . . and Why It Still Matters* (Grand Rapids: Zondervan, 2017), 35.

27. H. Richard Niebuhr's original wording was this: "A God without wrath brought men without sin into a Kingdom without judgment through the ministrations of a Christ

without a Cross." Niebuhr, *The Kingdom of God in America* (Middletown, CT: Wesleyan University Press, 1988), 193.

28. Tony Evans, "Guest Commentary: Jesus Didn't Come to Take Sides; He Came to Take Over," Religious News Service, September 15, 2008, https://religionnews.com/2008/09/15/guest-commentary-jesus-didnt-come-to-take-sides-he-came-to-take-over1.

29. James Baldwin, "In Search of a Majority," in *Collected Essays* (New York: Library of America, 1998), 220.

30. Cullen, "Heritage," in *Norton Anthology of African American Literature*, 3rd ed., ed. Henry Louis Gates Jr. and Valerie A. Smith (New York: Norton, 2014), 1:1354–56.

31. J. Deotis Roberts, *Liberation and Reconciliation: A Black Theology*, 2nd ed. (Louisville: Westminster John Knox, 2005), 130, cited in James H. Evans Jr., *We Have Been Believers: An African American Systematic Theology*, 2nd ed. (Minneapolis: Fortress, 2012), 102–3.

32. Hannah King, "Body Broken," The Living Church, May 25, 2021, https://livingchurch.org/covenant/2021/05/25/body-broken.

Chapter 5 Salvation

1. Violet J. Harris, "In Praise of a Scholarly Force: Rudine Sims Bishop," *Language Arts* 85, no. 2 (November 2007): 153.

2. Eddie S. Glaude Jr., *Exodus! Religion, Race, and Nation in Early Nineteenth-Century Black America* (Chicago: University of Chicago Press, 2000), 3.

3. Maryemma Graham and Amritjit Singh, eds., *Conversations with Ralph Ellison* (Jackson: University Press of Mississippi, 1995), 115.

4. Zora Neale Hurston, *Moses, Man of the Mountain* (New York: HarperCollins, 2009), viii.

5. Hurston, *Moses, Man of the Mountain*, 180.

6. Hurston, *Moses, Man of the Mountain*, 57.

7. Eugene Peterson, *Eat This Book: A Conversation in the Art of Spiritual Reading* (Grand Rapids: Eerdmans, 2006), 34.

8. Howard Thurman, *Deep River and the Negro Spiritual Speaks of Life and Death* (Richmond, IN: Friends United Press, 1975), 34.

9. Raphael G. Warnock, *The Divided Mind of the Black Church: Theology, Piety, and Public Witness* (New York: New York University Press, 2014), 25.

10. Kevin Vanhoozer, *The Drama of Doctrine: A Canonical Linguistic Approach to Christian Doctrine* (Louisville: Westminster John Knox, 2005), 10.

11. Vanhoozer, *Drama of Doctrine*, 102.

12. Hurston, *Moses, Man of the Mountain*, vii.

13. Albert J. Raboteau, *A Fire in the Bones: Reflections on African-American Religious History* (Boston: Beacon, 1995), 28.

14. See Willie James Jennings, *The Christian Imagination: Theology and the Origins of Race* (New Haven: Yale University Press, 2010), 24–38.

15. For a detailed introduction to biblical interpretation, see Craig L. Blomberg, Robert L. Hubbard Jr., and William W. Klein, *Introduction to Biblical Interpretation* (Grand Rapids: Zondervan, 2017); and Grant R. Osborne, *The Hermeneutical Spiral: A Comprehensive Introduction to Biblical Interpretation* (Downers Grove, IL: IVP Academic, 2006). For a shorter introduction, see Richard Alan Fuhr Jr. and Andreas J. Köstenberger, *Inductive Bible Study: Observation, Interpretation, and Application through the Lenses of History, Literature, and Theology* (Nashville: B&H Academic, 2016).

16. Esau McCaulley both describes and employs such a hermeneutic, which he calls "Black Ecclesial Interpretation." According to McCaulley, this interpretive impulse prompted early African Americans to read Scripture as *socially located* (seeking to understand what it means to be both Black and Christian), *theological* (using categories like the character of

God or the *imago Dei* to refute "biblical" cases for slavery and discrimination), *canonical* (examining difficult texts in light of the whole Bible), and *patient* ("trusting that a careful and sympathetic reading of the text brings a blessing"). McCaulley, *Reading While Black: African American Biblical Interpretation as an Exercise in Hope* (Downers Grove, IL: Inter-Varsity, 2020), 21, 184.

17. Hurston, *Moses, Man of the Mountain*, 121.

18. Hurston, *Moses, Man of the Mountain*, 123.

19. Hurston, *Moses, Man of the Mountain*, 121.

20. T. Desmond Alexander, "How to Read Exodus Theologically," *Credo Magazine*, March 2, 2020, https://credomag.com/2020/03/how-to-read-exodus-theologically/.

21. Alexander, "How to Read Exodus Theologically."

22. Warnock, *Divided Mind of the Black Church*, 25.

23. For an important historical overview of American Christianity's participation in racism, see Jemar Tisby, *The Color of Compromise: The Truth about the American Church's Complicity in Racism* (Grand Rapids: Zondervan, 2019).

24. McCaulley, *Reading While Black*, 133.

25. James H. Evans Jr., *We Have Been Believers: An African-American Systematic Theology*, 2nd ed. (Minneapolis: Fortress, 2012), 19.

26. Hurston, *Moses, Man of the Mountain*, 141.

27. Raboteau, *Fire in the Bones*, 32.

28. Raboteau, *Fire in the Bones*, 33.

29. Hurston, *Moses, Man of the Mountain*, 188–89.

30. Zora Neale Hurston, "Folklore and Music," *Frontiers: A Journal of Women Studies* 12, no. 1 (1991), 183.

31. Raboteau, *Fire in the Bones*, 33–34. This is Raboteau's summary of African Methodist Episcopal pastor William Paul Quinn's ministry testimonies and writings about the liturgical power of worship for Blacks.

32. Langston Hughes, "Mother to Son," in *The Collected Poems of Langston Hughes*, ed. Arnold Rampersad (New York: Knopf, 1994), 30.

33. Martin Luther King Jr., "I've Been to the Mountaintop," sermon delivered at Bishop Charles Mason Temple, Memphis, Tennessee, April 3, 1968, in *A Call to Conscience: The Landmark Speeches of Dr. Martin Luther King, Jr.* (New York: Hachette, 2001), 223.

34. Hurston, *Moses, Man of the Mountain*, 282.

Chapter 6 Racism

1. Rogert Ebert, "Freeway," RogerEbert.com, January 27, 1999, https://www.rogerebert.com/reviews/freeway-1997.

2. Henry Louis Gates Jr. and Valerie A. Smith, eds., *Norton Anthology of African American Literature*, 3rd ed. (New York: Norton, 2014), 1:1079.

3. Nella Larsen, *Passing* (Mineola, NY: Dover, 2004), 30.

4. Larsen, *Passing*, 41.

5. Larsen, *Passing*, 16.

6. Larsen, *Passing*, 16–17.

7. Larsen, *Passing*, 17.

8. Larsen, *Passing*, 17.

9. Ibram X. Kendi, *How to Be an Antiracist* (New York: One World, 2019), 49.

10. Eddie S. Glaude Jr., *Democracy in Black: How Race Still Enslaves the American Soul* (New York: Crown, 2016), 31–34.

11. Karen E. Fields and Barbara J. Fields, *Racecraft: The Soul of Inequality in American Life* (Brooklyn, NY: Verso, 2014), 51.

12. George Kelsey, *Racism and the Christian Understanding of Man* (New York: Scribner's Sons, 1965), quoted in James H. Evans Jr., *We Have Been Believers: An African American Systematic Theology*, 2nd ed. (Minneapolis: Fortress, 2012), 121–22.

13. Fields and Fields, *Racecraft*, 18–19. Karen E. Fields and Barbara J. Fields use the term *racecraft* in part to build on the illogic of believing in witchcraft. Racist beliefs and actions exist, in their view, not because people are irrational. They use *racecraft* to link to witchcraft in part due to their interest "in the process of reasoning that manages to make both plausible." Fields and Fields, *Racecraft*, 19.

14. Jemar Tisby, *How to Fight Racism: Courageous Christianity and the Journey toward Racial Justice* (Grand Rapids: Zondervan, 2021), 21.

15. Kendi, *How to Be an Antiracist*, 49.

16. Larsen, *Passing*, 21.

17. Larsen, *Passing*, 24.

18. Larsen, *Passing*, 25.

19. Larsen, *Passing*, 26.

20. Zora Neale Hurston, *Their Eyes Were Watching God* (Urbana: University of Illinois Press, 1991), 20.

21. I use *Blackness* as a term that encompasses African American skin color, ancestry, and ethnicity.

22. Alice Walker, *In Search of Our Mothers' Gardens* (New York: Harcourt Brace, 1983), 290.

23. Larsen, *Passing*, 26.

24. I am indebted to Dr. Tiffany Kriner for bringing this insight to my attention.

25. Delores S. Williams states, "Many black Americans have internalized this negative disposition toward black." She then recounts a variation of this same rhyme: "If you white, you all right. If you yellow, you mellow. If you brown, you can stick around. But if you black, get way back." Williams, *Sisters in the Wilderness: The Challenge of Womanist God-Talk* (Maryknoll, NY: Orbis Books, 1993), 86–87.

26. Kendi, *How to Be an Antiracist*, 119.

27. Lori L. Tharps, "The Difference between Racism and Colorism," *Time*, October 6, 2016, https://time.com/4512430/colorism-in-america.

28. Dream McClinton, "Why Dark-Skinned Black Girls Like Me Aren't Getting Married," *The Guardian*, April 8, 2019, https://www.theguardian.com/lifeandstyle/2019/apr/08/dark-skinned-black-girls-dont-get-married.

29. M. Shawn Copeland, *Enfleshing Freedom: Body, Race, and Being* (Minneapolis: Fortress, 2010), 24.

30. Larsen, *Passing*, 65.

31. Larsen, *Passing*, 78.

32. Larsen, *Passing*, 78.

33. Larsen, *Passing*, 81.

34. Larsen, *Passing*, 87.

35. Margo Jefferson, *Negroland: A Memoir* (New York: Pantheon, 2015), 51.

36. Kendi, *How to Be an Antiracist*, 136.

37. Kendi, *How to Be an Antiracist*, 142.

38. Kendi, *How to Be an Antiracist*, 142.

39. Larsen, *Passing*, 82.

40. Larsen, *Passing*, 83.

41. Larsen, *Passing*, 84.

42. Larsen, *Passing*, 90–91.

43. Cheryl A. Wall, *Women of the Harlem Renaissance* (Bloomington: Indiana University Press, 1995), 118.

44. Valerie Boyd, *Wrapped in Rainbows: The Life of Zora Neale Hurston*, 2nd ed. (New York: Scribner, 2004), 437–38.

45. Beth Felker Jones, *Practicing Christian Doctrine: An Introduction to Thinking and Living Theologically* (Grand Rapids: Baker Academic, 2014), 186.

Chapter 7 Healing and Memory

1. Jessica Hanewinckel, "Peter Scazzero: Digging Deeper into Discipleship—Part 1," *Outreach*, May 7, 2018, https://outreachmagazine.com/interviews/29100-pete-scazzero-digging -deeper-discipleship-part-1.html.

2. Sheila Wise Rowe, *Healing Racial Trauma: The Road to Resilience* (Downers Grove, IL: InterVarsity, 2020), 15.

3. Toni Morrison, *Beloved* (New York: Vintage International, 2004), 6.

4. Morrison, *Beloved*, 6.

5. Esau McCaulley, *Reading While Black: African American Biblical Interpretation as an Exercise in Hope* (Downers Grove, IL: InterVarsity, 2020), 121.

6. Morrison, *Beloved*, 86.

7. Morrison, *Beloved*, 83.

8. Morrison, *Beloved*, 49.

9. Morrison, *Beloved*, 78, 83, 212, 213.

10. This quote from Baldwin occurs during a conversation between Baldwin, Langston Hughes, Lorraine Hansberry, Emile Capouya, and Alfred Kazin, Los Angeles, Pacifica Radio Archive, January 10, 1961, available at "'The Negro in American Culture' a group discussion (Baldwin, Hughes, Hansberry, Capouya, Kazin)," YouTube video, 1:37:02, posted by thepostarchive on January 17, 2016, https://youtu.be/jNpitdJSXWY.

11. Morrison, *Beloved*, 74.

12. McCaulley, *Reading While Black*, 124.

13. McCaulley, *Reading While Black*, 126. McCaulley rightly notes that in keeping record of Israel's pain and rage "in Israel's sacred texts, God made their problems our problems" (126).

14. Miroslav Volf, *The End of Memory: Remembering Rightly in a Violent World* (Grand Rapids: Eerdmans, 2006), 11.

15. McCaulley, *Reading While Black*, 120–21. Note that alongside this history of suffering, McCaulley notes the story of redemptive history, in which "the Bible shows that as far back as we can go in the biblical story we will find African brothers and sisters participating in God's great redemptive work" (120).

16. Morrison, *Beloved*, 46.

17. Morrison, *Beloved*, 102.

18. Morrison, *Beloved*, 103.

19. Morrison, *Beloved*, 102.

20. Morrison, *Beloved*, 104.

21. Morrison, *Beloved*, 102.

22. Morrison, *Beloved*, 103.

23. M. Shawn Copeland, "Enfleshing Love: A Decolonial Theological Reading of *Beloved*," in *Beyond the Doctrine of Man: Decolonial Visions of the Human*, ed. Joseph Drexler-Dreis and Kristien Justaert (New York: Fordham University Press, 2019), 98.

24. Morrison, *Beloved*, 104.

25. Morrison, *Beloved*, 103–4.

26. Yolanda Pierce, *My Grandmother's House: Black Women, Faith, and the Stories We Inherit* (Minneapolis: Broadleaf, 2021), xvii.

27. Copeland, "Enfleshing Love," 92.

28. Copeland, "Enfleshing Love," 100–101.

29. Copeland, "Enfleshing Love," 100–101.

30. Volf, *End of Memory*, 80.

31. Morrison, *Beloved*, 103.

32. Campbell Robertson, "A Quiet Exodus: Why Black Worshipers Are Leaving White Evangelical Churches," *New York Times*, March 9, 2018, https://www.nytimes.com/2018/03/09/us/blacks-evangelical-churches.html.

33. Resmaa Menakem, *In My Grandmother's Hands: Racialized Trauma and the Pathway to Mending Our Hearts and Bodies* (Las Vegas: Central Recovery Press, 2017), 76.

34. Rowe, *Healing Racial Trauma*, 47.

35. It is worth noting that there is another communal aspect to the disruption of Paul D and Sethe's relationship. Stamp Paid, an elderly community leader, tells Paul D that Sethe killed Beloved. This plays a significant part in Paul D's departure from 124.

36. Morrison, *Beloved*, 58–59.

37. Morrison, *Beloved*, 60.

38. Morrison, *Beloved*, 251.

39. I am indebted to Dr. Cynthia Wallace for her insights and comments on this reading of *Beloved* and "the join."

40. Augustine, *Confessions*, trans. Sarah Ruden (New York: Random House, 2017), 290.

41. Morrison, *Beloved*, 286.

42. Morrison, *Beloved*, 301.

43. Morrison, *Beloved*, 302.

44. Morrison, *Beloved*, 103.

45. Morrison, *Beloved*, 308.

46. Morrison, *Beloved*, 308.

47. Christina Bieber Lake, "Toni Morrison's Theological Grotesque," *Church Life Journal*, August 8, 2019, https://churchlifejournal.nd.edu/articles/the-theological-grotesque-of-toni-morrisons-beloved.

48. Morrison, *Beloved*, 324.

49. Lake, "Toni Morrison's Theological Grotesque."

50. Lake, "Toni Morrison's Theological Grotesque."

Chapter 8 Lament

1. Gregory Mixon and Clifford Kuhn, "Atlanta Race Riot of 1906," *New Georgia Encyclopedia*, August 27, 2020, https://www.georgiaencyclopedia.org/articles/history-archaeology/atlanta-race-riot-1906.

2. W. E. B. Du Bois, "The Litany of Atlanta." All quotations of this source in this chapter come from Henry Louis Gates Jr. and Valerie A. Smith, eds., *Norton Anthology of African American Literature*, 3rd ed. (New York: Norton, 2014), 1:684–86.

3. Carol Anderson, *White Rage: The Unspoken Truth of Our Racial Divide* (New York: Bloomsbury, 2016), 3.

4. Mark Vroegop, *Weep with Me: How Lament Opens a Door for Racial Reconciliation* (Wheaton: Crossway, 2020), 37.

5. Toni Morrison, *Beloved* (New York: Vintage International, 2004), 213.

6. Derek Kidner, *Psalms 1–72: An Introduction and Commentary*, Tyndale Old Testament Commentaries 15 (Downers Grove, IL: InterVarsity, 1973), 185–86.

7. Dan Allender, "The Hidden Hope in Lament," Allender Center, June 2, 2016, https://theallendercenter.org/2016/06/hidden-hope-lament.

8. Vroegop, *Weep with Me*, 79–95.

9. Mika Edmondson, "If Christians would simply listen to the cries of their own brothers and sisters in Christ," Twitter, September 9, 2020, 8:35 p.m., https://twitter.com/mika_edmondson/status/1303854688522178562.

10. Allender, "Hidden Hope in Lament."

11. Allender, "Hidden Hope in Lament."

12. James Baldwin, *The Fire Next Time* (New York: Vintage International, 1993), 33.

13. Claude McKay, "A Negro Writer to His Critics," in *The New Negro: Readings on Race, Representation, and African American Culture, 1892–1938*, ed. Henry Louis Gates Jr. and Gene Andrew Jarrett (New York: Princeton University Press, 1969), 391.

14. Tish Harrison Warren, *Prayer in the Night: For Those Who Work or Watch or Weep* (Downers Grove, IL: InterVarsity, 2021), 47.

15. Jemar Tisby, *The Color of Compromise: The Truth about the American Church's Complicity in Racism* (Grand Rapids: Zondervan, 2019), 203.

16. James K. A. Smith, *On the Road with Saint Augustine: A Real-World Spirituality for Restless Hearts* (Grand Rapids: Brazos, 2019), 183.

17. James Melvin Washington, ed., *Conversations with God: Two Centuries of Prayers by African Americans* (New York: HarperCollins, 1994), xlvi.

18. Allender, "Hidden Hope in Lament."

Chapter 9 Justice

1. Imani Perry, "The Bleak Prescience of Richard Wright," *Atlantic*, June 2021, https://www.theatlantic.com/magazine/archive/2021/06/richard-wright-man-who-lived-underground/618705.

2. Timothy Keller, *Generous Justice: How God's Grace Makes Us Just* (New York: Penguin, 2012), 6.

3. Eugene Peterson, *Eat This Book: A Conversation in the Art of Spiritual Reading* (Grand Rapids: Eerdmans, 2006), 41.

4. Richard Wright, *The Man Who Lived Underground* (New York: Library of America, 2021), 6.

5. Wright, *The Man Who Lived Underground*, 6.

6. Wright, *The Man Who Lived Underground*, 23.

7. Karen Swallow Prior, *On Reading Well: Finding the Good Life through Great Books* (Grand Rapids: Brazos, 2018), 81.

8. Thaddeus J. Williams, *Confronting Injustice without Compromising Truth: 12 Questions Christians Should Ask about Social Justice* (Grand Rapids: Zondervan Academic, 2020), 18.

9. Wright, *The Man Who Lived Underground*, 53.

10. Wright, *The Man Who Lived Underground*, 159.

11. Wright, *The Man Who Lived Underground*, 63.

12. Wright, *The Man Who Lived Underground*, 62.

13. Wright, *The Man Who Lived Underground*, 63.

14. Wright, *The Man Who Lived Underground*, 63.

15. Wright, *The Man Who Lived Underground*, 62.

16. Wright, *The Man Who Lived Underground*, 63.

17. Wright, *The Man Who Lived Underground*, 62.

18. Wright, *The Man Who Lived Underground*, 63.

19. Wright, *The Man Who Lived Underground*, 6.

20. Wright, "Memories of My Grandmother," in *The Man Who Lived Underground*, 169.

21. Howard Thurman, *Jesus and the Disinherited* (Boston: Beacon, 1996), 39.

22. Wright, *The Man Who Lived Underground*, 66.

23. Wright, *The Man Who Lived Underground*, 159.

24. Wright, *The Man Who Lived Underground*, 91.

25. Wright, *The Man Who Lived Underground*, 90.

26. Marva J. Dawn, *Powers, Weakness, and the Tabernacling of God* (Grand Rapids: Eerdmans, 2001), 109.

27. Wright, *The Man Who Lived Underground*, 91.

28. See James Baldwin, "Everybody's Protest Novel" and "Alas, Poor Richard," in *Collected Essays* (New York: Library of America, 1998), 11–19, 251.

29. Perry, "Bleak Prescience of Richard Wright."

30. Wright, *The Man Who Lived Underground*, 66.

31. Sir Frederick Catherwood, quoted in J. I. Packer, "J. I. Packer: The Bible's Guide for Christian Activism," *Christianity Today*, August 17, 2020, https://www.christianitytoday.com/ct/2020/september/j-i-packer-activism-politics-christian-citizenship.html.

32. Tony Evans, *Oneness Embraced: Through the Eyes of Tony Evans* (Chicago: Moody, 2011), 217.

33. Wright, *The Man Who Lived Underground*, 91.

34. Tom Holland, *Dominion: How the Christian Revolution Remade the World* (New York: Basic Books, 2019), 521.

35. Wright, *The Man Who Lived Underground*, 106–7.

36. Wright, *The Man Who Lived Underground*, 155.

37. Wright, *The Man Who Lived Underground*, 125.

38. Wright, *The Man Who Lived Underground*, 194.

39. Perry, "Bleak Prescience of Richard Wright."

40. Malcolm Wright, afterword to *The Man Who Lived Underground*, by Richard Wright, 218.

41. Wright, *The Man Who Lived Underground*, 200.

Chapter 10 Hope

1. Eugenia Collier, cited in Henry Louis Gates Jr. and Valerie A. Smith, eds., *Norton Anthology of African American Literature*, 3rd ed. (New York: Norton, 2014), 2:319.

2. Margaret Walker, "For My People." All quotations of this source in this chapter come from Gates and Smith, *Norton Anthology of African American Literature*, 2:319–20.

3. John Calvin, *Institutes of the Christian Religion*, vol. 1., ed. John T. McNeill, trans. Ford Lewis Battles (Louisville: Westminster John Knox, 2011), 590.

4. J. Deotis Roberts, *Liberation and Reconciliation: A Black Theology*, 2nd ed. (Louisville: Westminster John Knox, 2005), 92.

5. James H. Evans Jr., *We Have Been Believers: An African American Systematic Theology*, 2nd ed. (Minneapolis: Fortress, 2012), 178.

6. Evans, *We Have Been Believers*, 179.

7. Ta-Nehisi Coates, *Between the World and Me* (New York: Random House, 2015).

8. Roge Karma, "Former Surgeon General Vivek Murthy on America's Loneliness Epidemic," *Vox*, May 11, 2020, https://www.vox.com/2020/5/11/21245087/america-loneliness-epidemic-coronavirus-pandemic-together.

9. See Abraham Smith, "Paul and African American Biblical Interpretation," in *True to Our Native Land: An African American New Testament Commentary*, ed. Brian K. Blount (Minneapolis: Fortress, 2007), 35–37. See also Lisa M. Bowens, *African American Readings of Paul: Reception, Resistance, and Transformation* (Grand Rapids: Eerdmans, 2020).

10. Howard Thurman, *Jesus and the Disinherited* (Boston: Beacon, 1996), 19–20.

11. For a theological and accessible case on why Scripture and Paul stand against American chattel slavery, see Esau McCaulley, "The Freedom of the Slaves," in *Reading While Black: African American Biblical Interpretation as an Exercise in Hope* (Downers Grove, IL: InterVarsity, 2020), 137–63.

12. Bowens, *African American Readings of Paul*, 42.

13. Brad R. Braxton, *No Longer Slaves: Galatians and African American Experience* (Collegeville, MN: Liturgical Press, 2002), 94–95.

14. Ezra Klein, "Why Ta-Nehisi Coates Is Hopeful," *Vox*, June 6, 2020, https://www .vox.com/2020/6/5/21279530/ta-nehisi-coates-ezra-klein-show-george-floyd-police-brutality -trump-biden.

15. Roberts, *Liberation and Reconciliation*, 90.

16. Beth Felker Jones, *Practicing Christian Doctrine: An Introduction to Thinking and Living Theologically* (Grand Rapids: Baker Academic, 2014), 225.